Creating Dynamic Web Sites

A Webmaster's Guide
to Interactive Multimedia

Scott Fisher

ADDISON-WESLEY DEVELOPERS PRESS

An imprint of Addison Wesley Longman, Inc.

Reading, Massachusetts • Harlow, England • Menlo Park, California

Berkeley, California • Don Mills, Ontario • Sydney

Bonn • Amsterdam • Tokyo • Mexico City

Many of the designations used by manufacturers and sellers to distinguish their products are claimed as trademarks. Where those designations appear in this book, and Addison-Wesley was aware of a trademark claim, the designations have been printed in initial capital letters or all capital letters.

The author and publisher have taken care in preparation of this book, but make no express or implied warranty of any kind and assume no responsibility for errors or omissions. No liability is assumed for incidental or consequential damages in connection with or arising out of the use of the information or programs contained herein.

Library of Congress Cataloging-in-Publication Data

Fisher, Scott, 1956–
    Creating dynamic Web sites : a webmaster's guide to interactive
multimedia / Scott Fisher.
      p.   cm.
    Includes index.
    ISBN 0-201-44207-8
    1. Interactive multimedia. 2. HTML (Document markup language)
3. World Wide Web (Information retrieval system)   I. Title.
QA76.76.I59F56   1997
006.6--dc20   96-36124
                                          CIP

A-W Developers Press is a division of Addison Wesley Longman, Inc.

Sponsoring Editor: Mary Treseler
Project Manager: Sarah Weaver
Production Coordinator: Erin Sweeney
Cover design: Dietz Design

1 2 3 4 5 6 7 8 9 -MA- 0099989796
First printing, December 1996

Addison-Wesley books are available for bulk purchases by corporations, institutions, and other organizations. For more information please contact the Corporate, Government, and Special Sales Department at (800) 238-9682.

Find A-W Developers Press on the World Wide Web at:
http://www.aw.com/devpress/
Find this book's Web site at:
http://www.living-history.org/dynaweb/

Contents

CHAPTER 1   Interacting with Graphics

Say It in Pictures

Pictures make Web sites exciting. They add visual interest, attract return viewers, convey emotional impact, communicate your message, and fundamentally they're just cool things to have in your page. And unlike some other media, pictures — whether scanned photographs or custom, computer-generated imagery — don't have to be executed, rewound, or restarted: they wait on the screen until someone selects another hyperlink or hits the Go Back button.

Like text, a good picture conveys its message automatically and continually, without requiring the user to do anything to it. In Chapter 7, we'll look at some additional reasons why, and cases when, pictures are really the right choice for the message you want to convey.

But if you're not careful, the way you use pictures can make your Web site frustrating, difficult to use, and annoying — in short, an experience that people won't want to repeat. And the factors that determine the success or failure of your images start from the moment you begin laying out your image, continue through the process of capturing it, and finally come home to roost when you choose how you store it to transfer to your Web site.

This chapter explores the following important questions related to your interaction with graphics over the Web:

- What is the nature of interaction, not merely as a word meaning point and click, but as an understanding of the dynamics of an entire Web site?

- What is good design, not only from the standpoint of how an image conveys information, but also from the standpoint of performance?

- What principles of photography — from the film you use to the way you place the lights — can help you get the best results in your Web site?

- How can you use a scanner not simply as a tool for getting pictures into the computer, but as a support for the overall performance of your Web page?

This chapter also includes an overview of the kinds of tools that you will need, for example,

- Conversion tools — useful for changing graphics from native authoring-tool formats such as PICT, TIFF, JPEG, and others to the common Graphics Interchange Format (GIF) files that Web browsers use

- Image map editors — useful for making "hot spots" on graphical images, so that you can click on to select hyperlinks in pictures and in text

- Photographic scanning and manipulation tools, both hardware—scanners, digitizing pads, video capture cards, and digital cameras—and software—2D drawing packages and other kinds of tools for manipulating images.

Where Does Interaction Begin?

When most people working with computers hear the word "interactive," they think it means point and click: you see something on screen, move the mouse over it, and you click, then something happens. That's one kind of interaction, but your readers experience many others while browsing your Web site.

One of the best pieces of information to remember while designing your Web page is the concept of the moment of truth. I've adopted this key idea from Karl Albrecht and Ron Zemke's book *Service America!* Containing several useful lessons, their book is valuable for anyone in the "information business" because it really suggests that we, purveyors of knowledge, are less in the business of providing a product—namely, information—than we are in the business of providing a service—namely, education. Throughout *this* book, but especially in Chapter 7, we'll work on distinguishing the product, information, from the service, education.

For now, though, let's begin by looking at "moments of truth." These, as Albrecht and Zemke define them, are the countless small, defining actions (or interactions) in a business that help the customer decide whether or not he or she is satisfied with the interaction so far. They talk about "50,000 moments of truth" as being the scope of opportunities to interact with a customer in this kind of make-or-break way. In the following exercise, consider an interaction where you were the customer—at a dry cleaner, buying a car, ordering a bowl of noodle soup, waiting in line at the hardware store, or calling in an order from a catalog.

In a traditional business setting, the moments of truth often begin with what's called "ring time" — how long it takes someone to answer the phone when you call to order a pizza to be delivered, for example. They may begin when you walk up to the information counter at a book store and find the staff engaged in a highly entertaining conversation about their annoying roommates. Later moments of truth involve the attitude of the person behind the counter, the length of time it takes to fill your order, any mistakes you find in your order when it arrives, and others.

Exercise 1: Your Own Moments of Truth

This exercise will be fun — and although it may not seem to have anything to do with Web sites, image file formats, or hypertext, it may well be the most important piece of information you get from this book. If you send me email to complain that this exercise doesn't have anything to do with Web sites, I'm going to ask you one question: did you do it? If your answer is no, you have nothing to complain about.

Do this exercise — do it as though you were getting graded on it. Believe me, your Web site readers will grade you on what you get out of it.

For this exercise, take this book with you so the questions are handy and take paper and a pen so you can make notes. On your next lunch break, visit an unfamiliar restaurant. It can be a chain, a local mom & pop operation, a fancy restaurant or a fast-food dive, as long as it's not your usual place. You want fresh insights and no background (good or bad) to color your impressions.

For each of the following steps, note both the characteristic that the step asks you to note and the emotional impression that this characteristic makes on you.

1. When you arrive, jot down how you're struck by the following characteristics:

   - Access — was it easy to find, easy to get to, easy to see from the street?

   - Parking (if you drive) or access to public transportation (if you take a bus, subway, or commuter train) — did you have difficulty getting there?

   - Appearance — is it clean, neat, cluttered, quaint, dirty, or something else?

2. Note the kind of service provided. Is it a sit-down restaurant where you're given a menu and allowed time to make a choice, or is it a fast-food format where you study an overhead marquee while you stand in line to place your order from a counter person?

3. Note the kind of seating you are provided. Is it comfortable? Was the table clean when you arrived, or did you have to bus it yourself before sitting down?

4. Once you've placed your order, note the time you order it and the time it takes to arrive.

5. When your order arrives, did it meet your expectations? Was it freshly made, nicely presented, and correctly assembled?

6. When you pay (which will probably be before step 4 if you are in a fast-food chain), was the total amount what you expected? Were you charged for any items you did not order?

7. While you have lunch, observe at least ten additional interactions between yourself and the restaurant — the staff, the building, the food, the presentation, the decor, the other patrons, everything that you interact with — and note what insights this gives you into moments of truth between you and this establishment.

8. Here's the fun part: Distill everything into a single grade, pass or fail, based on the simple criterion of whether you would go back to this restaurant again. If you would, it passes; if you would not, it fails.

Several generalizations can be made from studying the moments of truth involved in such a simple, everyday act as having lunch. Perhaps most important is something that you may not see in a single visit: expectations are constantly on the rise. Albrecht and Zemke cite an airline that began by measuring on-time departure as its key moment of truth. The only problem was, passengers began to expect on-time departure as a matter of course; the importance of departing on time rapidly faded into the background once it became the expected norm. If you chose to visit a fast-food joint, you might soon develop the same attitude about the length of time it takes your burger or fish sandwich to be handed across the counter to you. In fact, you may consider (for "extra credit") answering the same questions for your regular hangout, and see where, as Shakespeare said, familiarity breeds contempt.

Even more telling is step 7. How hard was it for you to find additional interactions between you and the lunch spot? Did you struggle to get all ten, or did you end up jotting down everything that happened—the noisy couple at the table across the way, the kids running up and down the aisle playing with the toys from their Super Smile Kiddie-Pak Lunch Value Deal, the homeless person asking for change outside the door?

The point of this exercise is to understand what a moment of truth might consist of in a context you're familiar with, but one that is outside the Web. Once you can distinguish these moments of truth, it's time to take on the second exercise, in which you'll actually identify potential moments of truth in your Web page.

Exercise 2: Who Cares What They Think, Anyway?

For this exercise, you'll be talking (or communicating electronically) with a number of people in your target audience: Web users, readers, and surfers. This is a simple exercise, but one that builds on the previous one.

1. Identify at least five people you know — friends, family, co-workers, students — who use the Web somewhat frequently. (As an added bonus exercise, you might try asking everyone you meet — people at the store, the guy at the gas station, the family next to you when you're getting lunch in Exercise 1 — whether or not they use the Web, and then keep track of how many actually do.)

2. Let these people know that you are designing a Web site and you want their feedback as part of your market research. Be sure to let them know that you are working on a site that doesn't yet exist, and you are looking for their honest responses. Make it clear that you won't take anything personally because you're working on a new Web site, so they can be as critical as they need to be in this exercise.

3. Ask each person to come up with a "top ten" list of things they find annoying about Web sites. If they can come up with specific examples (with URLs), so much the better. If they can't quite come up with ten things, three or four will be sufficient. Some of the ways you can do this include:

   - Set up a mailing list or make the request on a Usenet newsgroup.

   - Set up a reader-response form on your own Web site with categories specified as pull-down form replies.

   - Call a meeting at work (Tip: Order in lunch and you'll get a much better response) and have someone take minutes.

   - Ask everyone you see, everywhere you go, keep a notebook with you at all times, and get a complete cross-section of your community.

4. When you have interviewed your five people, collate their responses. You'll have potentially 50 opinions to work with; some of them will probably be duplicates. ("It takes too long to see pictures" is probably the number one complaint about the Web.) Eliminate the doubles, sort them (if you're feeling particularly detail-oriented) by frequency, but mainly look at them as a portrait of your user base, your customers, your community.

5. Here's the hard part: Look at each complaint from the perspective that there *is* something you can do about it. Even if the complaint is "My modem is too slow," imagine that there is some way you can have an impact on that—that you can control the way your Web site is designed, with the result being faster performance.

The result of this exercise is that you will have a new understanding of what your user base expects, what they dislike, and what constitute their moments of truth as they use the Web. From this, you can develop a way of creating your own Web site to have the maximum impact, the clearest communication, and the most effective sense of community with the people who read it.

How Performance Affects Perception

Now that we've distinguished some of the factors that determine how people are going to perceive your Web site, it's time to look at some of the more specific elements involved in satisfying your audience. In particular, remind yourself that you do have some control over how people perceive your Web site, regardless of the circumstances surrounding their platform's performance.

The issue of Web site performance is universal: It does not respect age, education, or cultural background. When the Disney movie *Toy Story* had just been released, my daughters—then aged eight and four—ran excitedly into my office. "Dad!" shouted the eight year old. "I saw an ad for *Toy Story*, and it had one of those WWW things on it! Can we look at it?"

Since she hadn't yet learned to remember all the parts of "those WWW things," I tried the company's main path, http://www.disney.com, and followed the hyperlinks to the Toy Story Page. We looked at about three pictures, each one taking a minute or so to crawl down the screen over my 14.4 modem (and from what must have been a busy site). The eight year old migrated out of the room, followed a few seconds later by her younger sister.

"Hey, wait!" I called. "Don't you want to see more pictures from *Toy Story*?"

"Naaah," said the four year old. "It takes too long."

So your audience may be more sophisticated, polite, patient, or maybe even captive than my daughters were willing to be that Saturday morning, but when two little girls can't wait for pictures from a brand-new Disney movie to fill the screen, you have to pay attention.

In this chapter, we'll talk about how you can capture your audience's attention and not lose it in the first three pictures. Some of these concerns are design-oriented; some are technical. But if you view all of them from the results of the exercises you did in the beginning of this chapter, you'll begin to shape a different kind of Web site from many of those in use today.

What Kinds of Images Can I Use?

Images on the Web consist of two basic types: images captured from nature and stored in digital format, and images created entirely on the computer. This chapter talks about ways you can make both types work best on the Web.

Although this chapter ends with hands-on tutorials showing you how to achieve specific effects in a couple of popular programs (and provides URLs to some pictures that you're welcome to download for practice and comparison), its primary focus is on program-independent techniques and strategies for creating good-looking graphics with any software. This means that the issues you're learning about here will still be valid when cable modems and T1 lines are commonplace (and when user expectations about speed and performance—as in the on-time departure example—have been modified accordingly).

Getting Started

While you're reading this section, start your Web browser and take a look at the Web site designed to accompany this book:

http://www.living-history.org/media

The examples used in this chapter are all stored there; you can download them for practice and for your own use in learning how these images actually work in your Web environment. Once you have your own copies, you can crop them, convert them, and otherwise play with them, either by following the examples in this book or by trying your own creative ideas.

Image Types

The examples for this chapter all use two basic image types:

- Digital photographs, stored as Joint Photographic Experts Group (JPEG) files; these files all have an extension of .JPG.

- Computer-generated images, stored as Graphics Interchange Format (GIF) files; these files all have an extension of .GIF.

Most filenames used here conform to the Microsoft DOS file-naming convention of eight characters in the filename, a period, and three characters (sometimes referred to as the 8.3 standard); the exception is that text files all end in .HTML. This means you can download the image files to practice some of the techniques demonstrated in this book, whether you are using a Windows 3.1, Windows 95, Windows NT, or Macintosh as your graphics platform.

As with all the images posted directly on the Web page used for this book, you are welcome to use the images, manipulate them, and practice with them for your own Web development work. (Note, however, that many pictures stored at other locations on this book's Web page are the property of their respective authors and should be treated as proprietary and copyrighted unless explicitly indicated otherwise.)

The Basics of Good Design

Chances are good that you weren't a Webmaster a year ago—in fact, the job title probably didn't exist more than about a year before this book was written. This means that, most likely, you did something else for a living. If you're like the Webmasters I know and work with, this could mean anything—one Webmaster I work with was writing advertising copy until he taught himself HTML and got a job designing a major Web site. Another was a high-level Unix systems programmer. Another was a teacher, a fourth was a technical writer, and the list goes on.

Because of this breadth, it's dangerous to assume too much about you, the audience for this book, and your experience. So I'll begin with a short course in design. If you're a highly trained graphic artist, you probably know more about this than I do, but you may not have considered design from a performance standpoint. If you're primarily a writer, a programmer, or an administrator, you have probably never considered performance from a design standpoint. On the Web, the two come together powerfully.

Principles for Design

These basic principles will help anyone who is not primarily trained as a graphic designer to make decent-looking images — photographs and illustrations that convey their message, look good, and attract attention. In the next section, we'll talk about some specific techniques you can use to tweak the performance of your site's graphics.

Note also that these design principles assume that your Web site is meant to convey information, such as background for your company's product or services, the contents of an electronic magazine, or a list of subjects in a Web-based education site. If you visit experimental Web sites, or sites that have been designed by trained graphic artists, you will almost certainly see these basic principles violated to get a particular look or visual effect. In fact, as you develop a sense of visual style, you will probably stray from these basic principles. But if you don't have training in art or design, following these principles will give you decent-looking Web sites that get your message across to the reader.

Know your message. Each image in an informational Web site should be meant to convey a message. It may be the layout of the site, showing the relationship between different files and pages. It may be information about your company's product or service, showing your readers where to go to get more detailed information about ordering from you, using your product or service, or otherwise providing them with value. But make sure that each image has a message, even if it's simple. For a purely artistic site, the images will not have a message so much as an intended emotional reaction. In either case, you might say that you need to know the meaning you intend your image to convey.

Decide on your "visual topic sentence." Basic English composition classes teach that every paragraph needs a topic sentence, followed by several additional sentences that give supporting details. When you design graphics, design them in much the same way. Come up with one central design element that, in the kinds of Web sites we've discussed, is intended to transfer information to your readers. Then, having determined the visual theme or topic sentence, support that idea with additional details (if appropriate) to transfer information more effectively. (The Tutorial section gives some examples of this.)

Draw the viewer's eyes to a particular place in the image first. This ties in with the topic sentence idea, by giving your illustration a logical center. Color, relative size, and composition are some of the ways to place something at the focus of an image. You can also use other elements of the image to draw attention; converging lines, alterations of color intensity, and other elements in the background can be used to make something stand out.

Note that if you are photographing these images, you may be able to move the subjects; if you're taking pictures of people, cars, furniture, flowers, wall hangings, books, or computers, you can move them to make the picture more effective. Don't take a picture of your office the way it looks now; move things so that they work better in the illustration. You can always move them back later so that they function in your workflow. In other circumstances — for instance, the Manhattan skyline, the Golden Gate Bridge, Yosemite's Half Dome — the objects in the image are immovable. But you may be able to take a better angle, one that allows you to line up elements in the background (the horizon, for example, or the way the roads converge into the distance) to attract attention to your visual center.

Keep your images simple — avoid clutter. Cluttered images make it difficult for your users to see the individual components of your illustration. Too many buttons, details, patterns, and shapes distract from the overall meaning you're trying to get across. This principle applies both to illustrations and to photographs, and it ties in with the principle of composition, discussed shortly. And knowing your visual topic sentence often helps reduce clutter because it lets you use a fairly simple test on each element of your image: Does this element support your topic sentence? If not, consider putting it in another image.

Strive for balance but not necessarily symmetry. This is a difficult line to straddle for many beginning designers and layout artists. Layouts and designs that are completely symmetrical don't "move" — that is, there's no sense that the eye is meant to go to any particular place on the screen (discussed previously).

My personal style is to put the visual center about 60% of the way across the image, beginning from the left, and about 60% of the way down from the top. This gives illustrations a certain dynamic appearance; it's just off-center enough not to look like an accident, yet it's not so far off-center that it wastes a lot of space.

Note, for example, that this page is laid out with the center of visual interest — let's call it the middle of the text column — about 60% of the way across from the left. I've kept the left column available, though, for illustrations and headings, but the overall effect is to draw your eye to the right. (If you are designing for a culture that reads from right to left, you may wish to reverse these directions to take advantage of your culture's automatic reading skills.)

Pay attention to your image's composition. In some ways, everything I've said up to this point is building to the concept of composition. Composition in images means having a strong visual or thematic center (your topic sentence), drawing the eye to that center, reducing clutter, having a dynamic balance, and conveying the intended emotional or intellectual message clearly. The composition, however, describes the way that all these pieces work together in the final product.

One way I like to diagram basic composition for my multimedia design students is with a simple nine-patch grid, such as you might use to play tic-tac-toe:

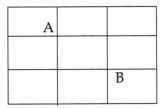

In terms of this simple diagram, the key locations for crucial elements of your image are A and B. There is also a slight sense of order or sequence in this composition: elements placed at location A will typically be perceived as coming before other elements in the scene, while images placed at location B will be perceived as coming later. You can use this implied sequence to add to the sense of relative importance of elements in your scene, or to heighten a sense of process among elements in the scene.

How does it look when it's all in one piece? Whether it's a drawing or a photograph, a still frame from a video or a scanned painting, how it looks is still going to be important—at least as important as whether it does everything I've mentioned here. From time to time, step back and look at the entire illustration as well as its component parts.

For Further Study

In general, the type of design I've described here is called instructional design—that is, design at several levels that is meant to convey information, or more specifically to give people access to knowledge in such a way that they can use it effectively in their own lives. Instructional design for multimedia in particular requires that you look at the micro level as well as the macro level—that you consider what goes into each screen as well as where and how the screens connect to one another.

I've written about this extensively in two previous books, the first of which (*Multimedia Authoring: Building and Developing Documents*, AP Professional, 1994) is used in a number of college courses on instructional design—even though the words "instructional design" never appear in the text. (And if I were Oscar Wilde or Will Rogers, I'd quip that this proves that as long as you know what you're talking about, you don't have to worry about knowing what you're saying.)

For full details on these and other worthwhile references for the multimedia or Web designer, see Appendix B.

The Basics of Web Performance

Web performance is really simple—small files load quickly, big files load slowly, no matter what the connection or browser or computer. If you're looking to get the maximum performance from the media on your Web site, you'll hear over and over that file size is the dominant characteristic. Bandwidth—that is, the speed of the connection between your site and your customer's or reader's computer—is an important issue, true, but that's really a conversation between your network architect and the accounting department. If you can improve your site's connectivity to the outside world, that's great, and in many smaller organizations the Webmaster can recommend enhancements to the system's overall hardware or software performance.

But first of all, for many people raising their bandwidth or their computing performance isn't an option; they've got a 28.8 modem and a 486-66 PC and that's all they're going to get, especially if they're a school, a small business, or a community resource. And second, bandwidth is not really something that you can affect with the design and construction of the information on your Web site. How you construct your Web site, what kinds of media you use, and how you link them together are the subject of this book.

Less (Size) Is More (Speed)

Architect Ludwig Mies van der Rohe, one of the founders of the design movement generally termed the Bauhaus, coined the by-now famous aphorism that I've amended in the heading. He was speaking of commercial building design, in which less ornamentation led to more freedom and usability. Although this led to some spectacularly ugly buildings as interpreted by less talented architects, the basic principle applies to your Web site: less file size leads to more rapid access, and eventually to more hits, more utility, and more satisfaction by your readers.

In the last section, we talked about how design can influence the pictures you publish on the Web, how to focus on the composition and content of your images to get your message through to your reader more quickly and effectively. There, you could say that less (visual clutter) is more (effective communication). In this section, we'll see how less (data in the files) is more (reader satisfaction and interactivity).

Principles for Performance

The following principles can help you maximize the performance of your Web site by generating pictures that load quickly and look good.

Keep it simple. (This is my more polite version of the well-known KISS rule: "Keep it simple, stupid.") The average monitor out there on the Web probably has only 256 colors and manages an image size of 640 x 480 pixels, so using fewer colors and smaller images can help ensure an image that displays quickly — and coupled with the next principle, it can also mean a better looking image.

Use 8-bit files for computer-generated images. An 8-bit image takes one third the time to cross the wires as a 24-bit image does, so perceived performance goes up dramatically. One key to the successful use of 8-bit images is that humans are still better than computers at certain things, particularly where human perception and style are concerned. Why this matters to you is that a graphic artist or designer can almost invariably do a better job of designing an 8-bit image from scratch than a program — even a sophisticated one — can do by converting from 24-bit to 8-bit. This is because the artist knows, during the creation process, which colors work well together. The automated converter only knows which colors in the map are closest to the original RGB values.

Use JPEG compression to store scanned-in photographs and still frames taken from video clips. In Adobe Photoshop, you can control the file size and the image quality with a slider when you save an image; this chapter takes you through several examples of doing this later on. But JPEG compression lets you find the compromise that makes you happiest between download performance and image detail. And all graphical browsers support the display of JPEG images. To give you a feeling for the relationship between image quality and access time, you'll have the chance to play with several different levels of compression in JPEG files later in this chapter.

Crop your image to reduce extra pixels. Look for places where you can reduce your image by cropping the image in Photoshop (or whatever image tool you use). Reducing a 320 x 240 image by as little as 5 pixels on each axis saves you 2775 pixels. On a busy connection running at 500 bytes per second, that saves nearly 6 seconds of load time — and that's if this is an 8-bit image. If you're using 24-bit color, the time saving is tripled.

Assume the slowest performance from your readers' equipment. Although it's encouraging to think of a world made up of ISDN lines, fiber to the desktop, and multi-gigabit links to the Internet backbone, most home browsers are still using 14.4 modems, some 28.8, and it'll be years before the "Internet computer" actually reaches a significant number of homes. When high bandwidth is a given, the sites you design today will perform even better. In the interim, you can help minimize your readers' frustration by designing for hardware that supports the minimum performance, not the maximum.

Use thumbnails set into solid color for opening screens. Large areas of solid color load quickly when compressed with the JPEG standard, because of the way it compresses pixels. If you want to have a full-screen image but don't want the overhead associated with it, use a solid color (typically one of the colors from your logo) as the background, then paste in clipped, reduced-size images (often called thumbnails) for the detail. Better yet, set the background color of your Web page with the BGCOLOR statement in the BODY section of your HTML file. Later on you can make image maps (discussed later in this chapter) that use these thumbnail regions as the links to other parts of your Web site, or to other Web sites.

Digital Sources

Digital cameras come in two basic flavors: those in the under-$1000 range and high-end professional units. The low-price units are great for putting snapshots into your Web site. Kodak, Apple, and Casio all make reasonably priced digital cameras that do an adequate job of personalizing your Web page.

My experience with the lower-cost cameras is that they really require good lighting of your subjects. Although you can adjust the brightness and color balance of images after capture, there's only so much you can do, and it's better simply to make sure that the subject is well lighted in the first place. If possible, a camera with an adjustable zoom (such as some of Kodak's offerings) makes it easy to frame and position each shot precisely without moving yourself or the objects in the scene.

The other advantage to a digital camera is that it's possible to take pictures and download them instantly through the cable supplied with the camera. This avoids the time and cost involved in developing and printing film photographs.

The lower-cost digital cameras, however, are limited in their resolution. While this is not a problem for images that will only be displayed on screen (where resolution is never more than 96 dots per inch), it can be frustrating to photographers looking to use the same image for the Web and the printing press.

What Direct-to-Digital Source Is Good For

The obvious example, of course, is a Web site devoted to the display and potentially the sale of high-quality images. If you're planning to operate a stock photographic image library, either as a vendor or as an Intranet site within your own company, you'll want high-quality digital images made available — but you probably won't want them to be the first thing that people get when they click on your Web site.

Such a Web site should use screen-resolution, thumbnail-sized images as a kind of visual index to the high-quality content. This thumbnail might be as small as 160 x 120 pixels, or even 80 x 60 if that conveys enough of a sense of the image's content. The best way to do this is to shoot the image full-size, scan it at a reasonable pixel resolution, and then reduce it electronically, typically in Photoshop. This process is described later in this chapter.

The next stage would be to link from the thumbnail index to another HTML file containing individual larger size, full-screen images. This way customers can see the entire image in more detail and decide whether or not they want to buy it. This would still be digitized at screen resolution, so your presumed audience—high-end printers, publishers, journalists, etc.—would not find this image useful, and would therefore not bother downloading this image without paying (because this imaginary Web business is designed to make a living for someone, rather than just to provide cool pictures for people to look at for free).

Finally, your imaginary Web customers have found a photograph they want to purchase. They click on a hyperlink that you've placed on the page containing the full-size, screen-resolution image, and your Web software makes the appropriate entries in their virtual cash account and then lets them download a high-resolution image file, one that may be more than 1 megabyte in size.

For examples, look at the Web site. I've stored three versions of the same scanned image: one at 72 dpi, one at 96, and one at 1200. The files in question are located at:

http://www.living-history.org/media/threepix.html

This is a good chance to look at the difference as it shows up on your Web page, and also to time the difference. Note that the 1200-dpi image is approximately 1.2 megabytes when fully uncompressed. (You may want to go make a fresh pot of coffee if you choose to download that one.)

On the other hand, whenever anyone asks me to recommend a cheap digital camera these days, I suggest using a camcorder and a video capture card instead. With Macintosh and PC capture cards alike costing only a couple of hundred dollars, it's difficult to justify buying a still camera for $400 to $600. This is especially so for schools, where chances are the campus already has a camcorder of some kind. A video capture card lets you capture single-frame images from the camcorder or from video tape, just as a digital camera does. However, you'll also be able to make digital movies, record sound effects, make tracks (maybe even in stereo, depending on the equipment you use), and digitize existing material from videotape.

In short, a camcorder and video capture card do everything a low-end digital camera can do, with the added value of being able to capture motion and sound. And if you already have a camcorder, you'll probably spend less on a video capture card than you would on a digital camera. A digital camera just doesn't make sense if you already have a video camera. In fact, in the past few years I've done more with video capture equipment than I have with a scanner. However, if you're planning to sell (or otherwise make available) high-quality image files intended for printing on a dye-sublimation printer or photographic process, the extra cost for a really first-rate digital camera is probably worth it.

The other thing that direct-to-digital image capture is good for, of course, is time. You don't have to wait for your prints to be developed, whether you're having them printed directly to Photo CD or whether you're going to scan them in with a flatbed scanner or some other digitization technique. If you go directly to digital image form, the pictures are already "in the box," ready to be manipulated and uploaded to your Web site.

This, of course, is also possible if you choose to go with a camcorder and a digitizing card. On all video capture cards and systems that I'm aware of, you can go directly to a digital file from your camcorder. Bypassing the analog step of putting the image on tape saves you a full generation of analog-to-digital conversion and results in slightly clearer images. It does, however, tend to limit itself to studio use; I don't know of any notebook computers that run digital capture cards, but I suppose it's possible.

Note, however, that digital video eats file space like nothing else; one of my students digitized a 3-minute video clip with no compression, using a 160 x 120 pixel image at 15 frames per second, and ended up with an 87-megabyte clip. I don't even want to begin to calculate how long that would take to download at 14.4 kilobaud; the answer is probably best expressed in days, not hours. And finally, digital video has its own special requirements and characteristics, especially for the Web; these are discussed in more detail in Chapter 3.

High-Performance Photography

Whether you use a 35mm film camera, an Apple QuickTake, a high-end Kodak digital imaging system, or a video camera with an Apple Video System capture card, photographing images for the Web presents several special technical issues, and one or two design issues as well. The most crucial performance consideration is in controlling—or perhaps more precisely, limiting—the image's size. However, just as important in the long run is the quality and clarity of the image—meaning how distinct each of the components of the picture will be when scanned, digitized, and downloaded, and simply how good it looks on-line. Here are some of the points in the photographic process at which you can make choices that affect an image's size, quality, and clarity.

Setting Up the Shot

Here, composition is the key: look for where your subject fits in the frame of the camera. How much can you get in the picture, and how can you place yourself (or other subjects in the scene) to make the scene compact, but also make it look good? Remember the design concepts: strive for balance but not symmetry, draw the eye toward your visual topic sentence, and keep it simple.

You can impart a feeling of motion by having your subject coming into the picture (or moving out of it), with part of it still outside the edge of the image. This also draws attention to the end of the subject that's fully in the frame.

And although some of this can be done by cropping the image later (either by cutting the photograph or by using cut and paste within Photoshop), remembering this while you're framing the initial action shot can help you turn a fair picture into a powerful one.

Selecting the Lighting

The process of digitizing an image is very susceptible to lighting, or rather to the lack of light. Dark colors often don't look good when digitized because of the way images are converted from analog to digital format. If you are using 24-bit color, this won't be an issue, but because most Web browsers use dithered 8-bit images (depending on the user's system), darker images look muddier and less effective than light ones. In particular, look out for large expanses of dark color; they often get patchy and "noisy" when digitized.

Selecting Film

If you're using 35mm film, look at the ASA number on the box. The ASA numbers (two popular ASA ratings are 200 and 400) determine how long the film must be exposed (that is, the shutter speed) in order to imprint an image on it. For a given lighting setup, there's a linear inverse relationship between shutter speed and ASA ratings: as the ASA doubles in number, the length of time the shutter remains open can drop by half.

But there's a catch. Film with a higher ASA rating typically has a coarser grain, resulting in lower image quality. Kodak has an ASA 1000 film that is spectacular at taking pictures literally by candlelight—but the prints look as though they've already been pixelized, almost like a Monet painting. It can be a beautiful effect if you use it well, but if you're after image clarity and sharp definition, it's exactly the wrong choice.

For photography that is meant to be scanned, a general rule is to use a comparatively low rating ASA—200 is a good all-purpose choice, with crisp images but reasonable lighting flexibility. Then make sure you've got enough light on the set or at the location so that the dark places will show up clearly.

Making Prints

If you have the choice, print your photographs a size larger than you would normally choose for snapshots. Larger images give you a little more flexibility when you scan them in. More specifically, scaling down in size results in a better looking image than scaling up.

If you reduce an image's size electronically, curves and diagonal lines typically get sharper (up to a point); if you enlarge an image beyond its native pixel resolution, the program that enlarges it typically resorts to pixel duplication. This means that, to make an image twice its original size, the program simply doubles every pixel in the original—making blocks of four pixels out of every pixel in the original image. The result is blocky, jagged images, with four-pixel "stair steps" at every curve or diagonal line. Oh, and don't forget that doubling an image's size also ends up quadrupling the number of bytes in the file because you double its width and its height. A 100 x 100 pixel image takes up 10K pixels; a 200 x 200 pixel image takes up 40K pixels (and takes four times as long to load).

Photographic Scanning and Manipulation

Chances are good that at least some of the images you use on your Web site will come from prints. Even if you invest in a high-end digital camera, a top of the line Media 100 digital video system, and a multi-gigabyte array of high-speed disk drives to store all these images, you will almost certainly have existing prints, drawings, and art work that someone—maybe even you—will want to put on the Web page. These existing illustrations are known in general as "legacy documents." In a fully electronic world, legacy documents also include printed letters, manuals, books, specifications, parts lists, and anything else that existed in paper before the shift to electronic publishing (either via the Web or via some proprietary system, such as a bill-of-materials tracking program or a CD-ROM documentation delivery system).

Although the general issues involved in handling legacy documents are challenging, to say the least, the only ones that really pertain to the subject of this book are those involved in getting images out of the filing cabinet and the portfolio and into your computer. For that, the issues are the same as they are for getting in brand-new photographs, prints, and other traditional-media artwork.

After you've taken the picture or you have the image that you want to scan, there are two points in the process at which you can control the image size:

1. When scanning, you can determine the resolution (in dots per inch, or dpi) of the scanned image; this should be as high as possible.

2. When you save the file, you can choose the relationship between image quality and image compression; this should be optimized toward your choice of performance or image quality, depending on the speed of Internet connection for which you're developing your Web site.

Most scanners let you set the resolution of the image that you're scanning in. This way you can tailor the image to Macintosh or PC formats—72 dpi or 96 dpi, respectively. Of course, on the Web, you'll have Mac, PC, and a whole array of Unix systems to deal with. In practice, I've found it's much simpler and more effective to scan at a higher resolution than you intend to publish, and then simply to save copies of your images at 72 dpi regardless of the platform issues; it's always better to capture more information than you intend to use, because you can never regain it.

Saving and Compressing Files

The more crucial point in scanning is how the file is saved once you capture it. Typically scanners today are bundled with an image processing program such as Adobe Photoshop. By loading a software plug-in that interfaces Photoshop to the scanner software, you can scan an image directly into Photoshop. Once there, you can retouch it, crop it, cut bits out of it, color it, and otherwise manipulate it to get it the way you want it to look.

At this point, though, you need to understand a couple of facts about file compression. Here's a print that is stored on my Web site in several formats, with filenames all involving the word "Foom" (self-explanatory from the image!):

This image is a 320 x 240 scan from videotape, made with the Apple Video System. I saved it as JPEG with Photoshop; the JPEG file takes up 33K on disk (or over the wires). The Apple PICT file on which it's based uses 160K. The Encapsulated PostScript file that I imported into the source for this book is 380K. But 320 times 240 is 76,800.

What's the difference? It's all in how you save the file, something that the JPEG format permits you to do within Photoshop. When you click Save As from the File menu in Photoshop, you get the following dialog box:

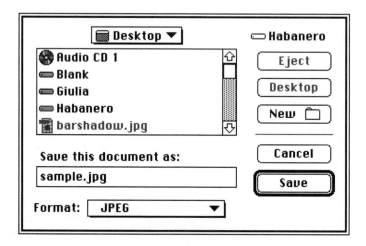

Pulling down the Format box gives you a list of available image formats, such as TIFF, JPEG, PICT, and various other formats. Later on, I've included a tutorial on using Photoshop that takes you step by step through the process of saving this file in several different formats.

For now, note the following slider bar that comes up in Photoshop (version 2.5; later versions look different) when you save in JPEG format:

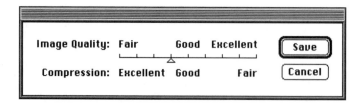

If Photoshop were a Web tool instead of a print tool, the slider would be labeled with "Download Speed" instead of "Image Quality" and "Compression." If it were, the leftmost edge of the bar would be labeled "Fast" and the rightmost edge (the one near the Save button) would be labeled "Slow."

However, your best bet when saving a scanned picture is to save it at a high image quality. Remember, you can always save a copy of it with more compression later on, reducing the file size and therefore improving the page's performance.

And that's the main thing to remember: moving the slider to your left improves the performance of your Web site, whereas moving it to the right slows down your users' load time. (In the Tutorial section, however, you'll get a chance to see how this affects image quality, if that is really what's most important about your particular Web site.)

Creating Pictures for Use in Image Maps

The traditional method for letting people interact with graphics on a Web site is the image map. If you've ever moved the mouse over a picture and seen the pointer turn to the "moving finger," you've used an image map.

To create an image map, essentially you assign a given URL to a specified region of the image. The Web browser reads the pixel location within the image when your reader calls it up, and when the reader clicks within a certain pixel range, the Web browser program jumps to that URL. You may or may not have a background, or default, URL associated with the image—that is, a URL to jump to when the user clicks on the background, outside of any of the specific buttons in the image.

One of the images I scanned to use as an image map for the Web sites I used while developing this book is the following group photograph of all the teachers at Cherry Chase Elementary School.

In at least one way, this image is the ideal visual index to a Web site because each part of the image is clear, self-contained, and easily identified. When you see a teacher's face, you recognize him or her and it's natural to click there to find information about that teacher's class.

What this image does not do, however, is indicate any structural relationship between the teachers (apart from the fact that the school's principal, Alice Pounds, is listed first). You might develop a new version of this picture that listed all the teachers in each grade in their own groups, or all the teachers who have special skills or interests in common. For example, although this is an elementary school, a good grouping for a middle school or high school might be to list all the English teachers together, all the history teachers, all the art teachers, and so on. (One benefit to hypertext is that if one teacher has classes in both English and journalism, for example, you can use the same picture, have it in different locations, but have it mapped to the same URL for that teacher's Web page.) You might also lay out the pictures of the teachers over a map of the school, so that your users could see where the individual teachers' classrooms are located.

Creating an image map is a two-stage process:

1. Creating the image itself — the graphical part.

2. Creating the map of interactivity — the technical part.

The technical part is covered in detail in Chapter 4, where we discuss various ways of adding buttons to your Web site. For now, let's focus on the graphical part: creating images that work well as image maps. For that, let's look at the basics of image map design.

Basics of Image Map Design

An image map is more than just a picture you can click on. In a very real way, it can be a "road map" to your site, or to a portion of the information in your site. The image map is the graphical user interface to your Web page's content — it's the menu, the opening screen, the way people perceive what you have in your page.

When designing the graphical part of your image maps, you need to address two primary issues: clarity and structure.

Clarity. Image maps need to be visually clear so that your readers can distinguish the components from one another. They also need to convey their intended information clearly, which is different from simply being well scanned. The previous example is good in both of these types of clarity: the teachers' faces are easily recognized from the scanned image, and they easily convey the information that was intended (who the teacher is).

Structure. Often the more difficult component, the structure in an image map needs to convey relationships between the information being represented on the screen. There are several ways to do this, depending on the structure inherent in the information. Although the psychological implications of instructional design are covered thoroughly in Chapter 7, they are mentioned here because you need to understand them to some extent before developing your image maps.

By the way, if you're new to designing Web pages or other hypertext structures, you should pay close attention to this section because it's a clear example of one of the places where hypertext would provide a functionality clearly superior to a paper book. Although I can include brief notes about the technical side of image map development, and I can refer you to Chapter 7 for more information about the human issues in instructional design, if this book were on the Web, I could easily put in a URL that would take you directly to the appropriate information. Now consider how you would represent such a structure visually.

Basics of Information Structure

Although this information is covered in more detail elsewhere in this book, it's worth taking a few moments here as you're about to go into the Tutorials to cover the basic kinds of structure that information may take, and to introduce the concept of information partitioning that is key to hypertext and multimedia design.

Information partitioning is the skill of identifying discrete, stand-alone pieces of information, such as those you would put into a single Web page, screen, or image. Information partitioning lets you see the fundamental building blocks of the information you want to convey to your audience.

Depending on your audience, your subject, and the degree of interactivity you want to provide them, information partitioning may proceed to any of several levels of detail: to the level of sentences, paragraphs, subsections, sections, or chapters, using the book model. I prefer to partition information down to the level of subheadings and headings within a chapter; the chapter level is too coarse, the paragraph level too fine, for meaningful partitioning of information—but that's for a book.

For a Web page, you probably want to use smaller chunks of information, for several reasons: they load faster, and they let your reader focus on smaller chunks of information at one time. The rapid-fire nature of interactive, computer-based reading tends to work well with smaller chunks.

When you have a sense of how large or small the information chunks will be, you can begin laying them out in some kind of structure. The structure automatically takes into account the relationship between the individual chunks of information: some partitions will contain smaller chunks, whereas others will contain multiple levels of partitioned information.

Some instructors and authors of training materials on interactive or on-line information refer to information partitioning as "chunking," and information structure as "grouping." These terms may help give you a sense of what you're doing with the information on your Web site: dividing it into chunks, then sorting the chunks in turn into groups.

For now, begin considering that information within a particular subject is naturally related to other information, both in that subject and outside of it. As you consider the pieces of information that stand alone—for example, the individual teachers at a school as used in the example—start to think of other pieces of information that are connected to this.

Although the exercises in Chapter 7 will give you a much more powerful relationship to this concept, the following exercise will help you gain a basic understanding of some of the ways you can "chunk" and "group" information, particularly when you are considering visuals to support a Web page.

Exercise 3: Grouping the Teachers

For this exercise, you'll need to start your Web browser (if it isn't already running) and have two blank sheets of paper for drawing on. This can also be a whiteboard or a graphics program, such as Paintbrush on the Windows PC or a Paint program on the Macintosh, but you will be drawing shapes and relationships, not just typing words.

1. Locate the picture containing photographs of all the teachers at the following URL:

   http://www.living-history.org/cherry-chase/teachers.html

2. On the top of one sheet of blank paper (or empty document), write the title Skills; on the other sheet, write Grade Level.

3. On the Grade Level sheet, draw rectangles (or ovals) entitled Kindergarten, First, Second, Third, Fourth, and Fifth.

4. On the Skills sheet, write Multimedia Specialists, ELD, and Resource.

5. On the Web page, find the first-grade teachers and draw boxes (or ovals) for them in the right place in the Grade Level sheet.

6. On the Web page, find the teachers who are multimedia specialists and draw boxes for them in the right place in the Skills sheet.

This is a very simple exercise designed to get you thinking about how grouping, labeling, and structuring information can let you show how elements of your Web site are related to one another. You'll notice something else, though: one teacher occurs in both the first-grade box and the multimedia specialist box. This is why the third part of the information partitioning and information structuring routine is information linking—and again, this is covered in more detail in Chapter 7.

For now, however, you've had the chance to see how the different pieces of information—in this case, the teacher, the grade level, and the skills they have—help you partition the information about all teachers at a school into manageable pieces. In addition, you've seen how you can use these partitions to help represent and identify the structure of the subject—in this case, the school and its teachers. Finally, you've seen how you can use different visual maps to provide access—out of a wholly separate context—to the same information.

Now consider that your readers will have a different background context when they arrive at Donna Haswell's page, depending on whether they selected her from the first-grade teachers or from the multimedia specialists. It is exactly this background context that is the true nature of interactivity. Your readers will have a different experience—if only slightly—depending on which screen they were reading when they selected her. That context is carried through to Mrs. Haswell's home page.

And you, as the Web site designer, have everything to say about what that background context can be. This is part of the reason the title of this book includes the word "dynamic"—it's more than just multimedia, or high interactivity from using Java applets and Shockwave titles (both covered later). The real reason your Web site is dynamic is that people will access different pieces from different background contexts, and that will change the way they read, comprehend, and act on the rest of your Web site.

Hands-on Tutorials

The rest of this chapter takes you step by step through samples that teach you:

- How to set the scan resolution, and what effect that has on file size.

- How to change the file's compression, and what effect this has on file size and appearance.

- How to convert files from one type to another, including files created on different platforms.

The examples used here may or may not be the best thing you can do with each program used in the tutorial. Experienced users of, say, Photoshop almost certainly have additional, more effective, or more powerful ways of using this tremendous program. This section is designed to get you up and running with a few of the leading tools in the graphical side of multimedia design, with samples you can look at on the Web to see how they come across on your computer (as well as on paper).

Using the Scanner

The following tutorial takes you through the steps involved in scanning an image with Adobe Photoshop, highlighting the points where you can make choices that affect your file's size and therefore your Web site's performance. All screen snapshots for this Photoshop tutorial were taken on the Apple Macintosh; other hands-on tutorials use Windows 95 applications, and some will include Unix commands.

The Web is a completely heterogeneous place, and the more platforms you can learn to use, the more effective your Web page development will be. (I often, for example, scan and save a file on the Macintosh, send it to my ISP on my Windows 95 workstation, then log in to one of the Unix servers at the ISP and use the vi editor to tweak the HTML till it looks right—or sometimes just till it works.)

Scanning a File

To scan a piece of media, follow these steps.

1. Place the media (photograph, drawing, or other flat piece of artwork) on the scanner bed and close the cover.

2. Start Photoshop, if it is not already running.

3. From the File menu, select the Acquire pull-right option.

   This displays a selection of capture options.

4. Select the capture option for your scanner.

   The scanner plug-in displays a dialog box similar to this one (the options may vary depending on the capabilities of your scanner):

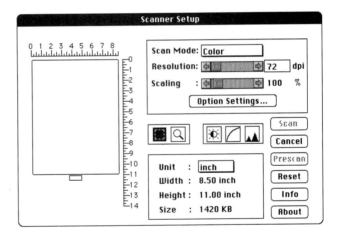

5. For the first exercise, set the dpi (the second row of the box at the upper right) to 150 and set the scaling to 100%.

6. Grab the corner of the rectangle at the left of the screen and move it to represent the corner of the media you want to capture.

Refer to the media as it sits on the scanner bed to make sure that you are scanning the image in the right orientation.

Note: If you scan the image upside-down or rotated 90 degrees out of vertical when it displays in Photoshop, you can use the Rotate option to turn it back to the correct orientation.

7. When you have selected the region you want to capture, click Scan.

    For the next several minutes, the scanner captures data. When finished, Photoshop displays the image you just scanned. At this point, you can rotate the image (if necessary), crop it, and otherwise manipulate it.

Note these points:

- The number at the lower left corner of the image window is the size of the image as it was scanned in, or more specifically, the number of bytes required to display this image. The factors that control this are the bits per pixel used on your system and the number of pixels (determined by the dpi setting you chose) in the image itself.

- You may see the legend "Untitled (1:2)" in the title bar of the image window. This means the image is scaled to one-half its actual size. To zoom in on the image, hold down the Apple key and press the + sign. To zoom out, hold down the Apple key and press the minus sign.

In the next tutorial, you'll save this image in several different compression levels, then compare the file sizes and the way each compression level looks.

Saving a File at Low Compression

1. When you have scanned the image you want, click Save.

   Photoshop displays the Save As dialog box:

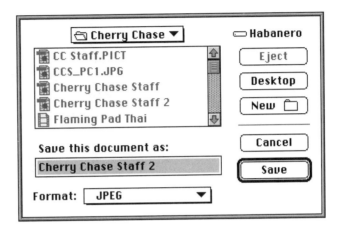

2. Pull down the file format box and choose JPEG (as shown in the previous snapshot).

   Photoshop displays this box:

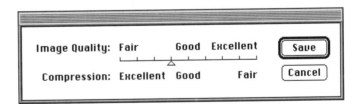

3. Move the triangular slider to the rightmost point of the scale — that is, to "Excellent" image quality and "Fair" compression.

4. Click Save.

   Photoshop displays a progress bar as it writes the file.

5. Minimize (or on the Macintosh, hide) Photoshop.

6. From the Desktop, navigate to and open the folder containing the file you just saved.

7. Click once on the file, then choose the action depending on the kind of system you are using:

   - On the Macintosh, pull down the File menu and select Get Info.

   - On Windows systems, click on the File menu and select Properties.

   This indicates the size of the file at minimum compression. In the next tutorial, you'll save the same file at maximum compression.

Saving a File at High Compression

1. Return to Photoshop, this time clicking Save As.

   Photoshop displays this box:

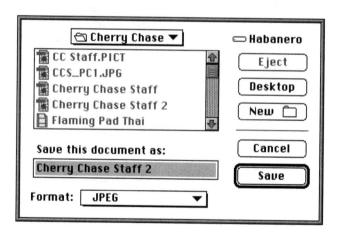

2. Type a new file name in the "Save this document as" box.

Photoshop displays this box:

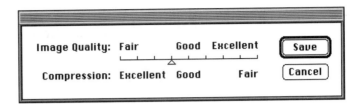

3. This time, move the triangular slider to the leftmost point of the scale—that is, to "Fair" image quality and "Excellent" compression.

4. Click Save. Photoshop displays a progress bar as it writes the file.

5. Minimize (or on the Macintosh, hide) Photoshop.

6. From the Desktop, navigate to and open the folder containing the file you just saved.

7. Click once on the file, then choose the action depending on the kind of system you are using:

   • On the Macintosh, pull down the File menu and select Get Info.

   • On Windows systems, click on the File menu and select Properties.

   This indicates the size of the file at maximum compression.

The point to this exercise is to see the range of file sizes available to you if you pay attention while saving your documents from within Photoshop. For examples of the different image quality levels you get by following the procedures shown here, look under:

http://www.living-history.org/dynaweb/chap1/

Converting Images

For use on the Web, you will want to save your images in either JPEG of GIF formats. These, at present, are the only two still-image file formats widely supported by Web browsers. This means that if a graphic artist or design service provides you with images in another format, you will need to convert them.

Some of the other image formats you may encounter are:

- PICT file—this is the standard Macintosh representation, used by a number of digital video systems (such as Adobe Premiere) and animation packages (such as Macromedia Director).

- TIFF file—less popular now that the Web has moved image generation and transfer into either GIF or JPEG.

- BMP—Microsoft DOS/Windows bitmap format.

- EPS—Encapsulated PostScript.

Photoshop will convert among these files, with the exception that it sometimes will not directly support Save As into GIF format. Under most circumstances, you can achieve better appearance and equal performance by using JPEG files in place of GIF files.

There are three places where GIF files give you something that JPEG doesn't:

1. Transparency. The GIF89a standard supports making pixels of a selected color (typically white or black) transparent when they are displayed on a Web page. This means that background colors or background images display through the transparent portions of the GIF file. This option is not currently supported by JPEG files.

2. Progressive display. GIF files normally display in successive iterations of greater and greater detail, meaning that first large blocks appear, then those blocks resolve into more detail, and finally each individual pixel displays. This kind of progressive display gives the user the appearance that something is going on—a JPEG file simply displays line by line, leaving empty space where it hasn't yet downloaded. On slow connections, this can make a difference in how your Web site is perceived.

3. Animation. The GIF89a standard also supports animation within single GIF images. The good news is that unlike Shockwave or Java, which require specific versions or plug-ins to support their motion, any browser that supports the GIF89a standard displays animated GIFs. You need additional tools to create GIF animations, however; Chapter 4 includes tutorials and examples of how to create animated GIFs.

If you are using Photoshop, you already have a tool for converting files between the various graphical formats used on and off the Web. However, Photoshop can be relatively labor-intensive as a conversion tool; you need to open each file, then select Save As and choose the file type, in order to complete the conversion.

There are other tools available which simplify the conversion, particularly if you have multiple files to convert. For example, if you have been using scanned images in a Shockwave movie, they'll need to be PICTs, but for them to show up as static images on your Web site, you'll need to convert them to JPEGs. That's no big deal if you have two or three, but if you have 40 or 50—or even 10 or 12—it gets tedious.

The solution is something like Thorsten Lemke's GraphicConverter, which lets you convert an entire directory of files to an alternative graphical format in a single operation. It's available on the Web; look for it through your favorite search engine, or check the Web site associated with this book for pointers to some of the mirror sites that make it available.

CHAPTER 2

Three Dimensions

If you really want your Web site to get the attention of readers under 18–20 years old, you'd better prepare to include lots of three-dimensional imagery. That's the single most-requested topic by everyone that I've talked to or taught about the Web, between the ages of roughly 10 and 18 or so.

But what is involved in getting a 3D image to play over the Web? What are some of the techniques you can use to add the illusion of depth to your Web site? When is it worth the extra effort to make this happen? And how can you learn about it without spending a pile of money on software or programming?

In this chapter, I'll walk you through what's involved in adding your own 3D "virtual world" to your Web site — without spending a cent (apart from dialup time). We'll start with a site where you can download a free, save-disabled demo version of a 3D image editor — but one that lets you output code in the Virtual Reality Modeling Language (VRML), the HTML of the third dimension.

And I'll show you how to create, save, and apply your own texture maps to the images you create. (I'll also explain what a "texture map" is, in case you haven't worked that phrase out for yourself yet.)

I'll also give you a brief tour of some QuickTime VR sites. QuickTime VR is really not 3D, but rather a way of creating 360-degree panoramas, yet crucially, all non-Webmasters who see this *think* of it as being a kind of 3D. They certainly see it as a killer tool for 3D virtual environments, for example. So we'll look at the sites currently available for QTVR, as it's known, and discuss a few of the issues involved in this not-yet-mature technology.

What's So Cool About 3D Worlds?

Several things make 3D worlds a great way to add interactivity and excitement to a Web site. Perhaps most important of them, in light of the effect that load time has on user satisfaction, is that they load very quickly, due to the nature of VRML. You see, VRML is like HTML: a text-based language that is very compact. Unlike a video clip (which we'll discuss in Chapter 3) or a Shockwave file (which we'll discuss in Chapter 4), it's possible to have a reasonably cool 3D world in a file that's well under 20K worth of text.

By the way, for the complete specification of the Virtual Reality Modeling Language, check out the following Web site:

http://www.clark.net/theme/vrml/

This site not only has definitions for each of the data types and descriptors in VRML, it also has live examples so that you can use a VRML browser to see what the examples do.

The difference between video and VRML is in the way their respective technologies work. Video stores the individual frames of a moving picture; each second of video requires many, many of these frames (between 6 and 30, depending on the quality of the playback and the amount of time you want to spend downloading the video). To give the illusion of motion, all these frames must be stored (and therefore transferred from the Web server to the client's browser) and then displayed rapidly, one after another, on the user's screen. The vast number of frames required means that even a fairly short video clip can be many megabytes in length, leading to long delays between clicking on the URL and getting the first hint of play from the video window. In short, video places the burden of motion on the file being transferred, with comparatively little cost in calculation at the player. One benefit to this, however, is that video playback is, to a large extent, independent of machine speed (at least for processor speeds in excess of about 30–50 MHz).

VRML, on the other hand, does not store detailed information about the scene in its data files. Instead, it stores only the barest of information — the points in a geometric object, information about the color and transparency of those objects, information about how those objects simulate the reflection of light, and information about any visual textures (which are really patterns; I'll explain more about texture maps later in this chapter) that are applied to the objects. The 3D world I created as an example for this book is 11K worth of straight ASCII text. That's roughly equivalent to about 2200 words of text — say, three times the text in one of my restaurant reviews.

The difference is that whereas video is simply tossed up on the screen as fast as the processor can shift the bytes around in memory, 3D displays with VRML require some fairly sophisticated geometric calculation at run-time. The 3D browser looks at the VRML file to read where the points in a 3D image are located, which points define flat surfaces between the points (an important consideration), and where the virtual light source is coming from. It then constructs a scene based on where you've moved your "eye point" — the spot from which your 3D browser is looking at the VRML world you're exploring.

What's most amazing about 3D images today is that the average low-end desktop computer as I write this (about 100 MHz) is many times more powerful than the top-of-the-line graphics workstations available when I began working in 3D images in the late 1980s. Pentiums and Power Macs make it possible for the average Web browser to play with 3D worlds at something approaching real-time speed, even with fairly complicated images and effects.

The other thing that makes 3D worlds such a draw on a Web site is that they're simply a lot of fun. You can really walk around in them, look at objects, explore all the corners, and check for unexpected objects, items, and areas. You can even create worlds dynamically on the fly, letting your users select, or otherwise be involved with the generation of, individual graphical components of the world.

Before we look at what is involved in this kind of dynamic interaction, let's get a thorough understanding of what goes into the typical 3D world created with VRML. Although there are several ways to get started, we'll look at one of them in detail—a simple, application-driven approach that lets you construct scenes and images easily and export them simply to your Web site.

3D Basics: A Different Kind of World Tour

To understand 3D worlds using VRML, let's look at the components that go into 3D geometry in general and the VRML standard in particular. Although we can break down the components of 3D graphics in many ways, I like to lay them out in four parts:

- Geometry—the set of points that define the shape, surfaces, and locations of 3D objects in a world

- Lighting—the way that the computer display programs model how light interacts with the real world so that the virtual world looks believable (or at least behaves in an expected manner)

- Textures—the patterns of color that give 3D shapes the illusion of reality, as well as pure visual interest

- Transformations—the operations performed on the geometry when you place or move it in a scene, and when you move around in that world

There's one more component, but it's so simple and generally so intuitive that it's not worth discussing after a simple introduction. That is what's sometimes called the virtual camera, but what I prefer to call the eyepoint—the place that simulates what you, the viewer, would see if you were actually in the world you have created or downloaded.

Moving through a 3D world involves moving the eyepoint (which technically is not a point, but a vector, because it has both location and direction). You can change its physical location in the world, and you can also change its orientation—that is, you can turn around "in place," effectively giving you a 360-degree view of your world.

Basic 3D Geometry

Although the details of 3D geometry are beyond the scope of this book, you'll need to grasp several key concepts if you want to get much beyond the simple act of copying in premade graphical components. (If you're familiar with 3D geometry, you can skim the following section and jump back in when we get to the section on writing VRML.)

First and perhaps most important is the concept of a coordinate system. If you've never encountered this term before, it's a way of describing, numerically, the location of a single point in 3D space. One way to visualize this concept is to draw two points on a sheet of graph paper, like this:

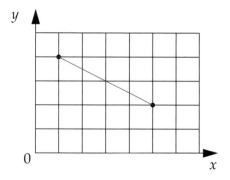

In this diagram, the first point is located 1 mark horizontally from the origin (indicated by the 0), and 4 marks up vertically; the second point is at 5 on the horizontal and 2 on the vertical. In this diagram, I've used the convention of x to represent the horizontal dimension, and y to represent the vertical; furthermore, this convention always lists the x (horizontal) axis first, followed by the y (vertical) axis. One way to define this line, then, is to say that its end points are located at (1, 4) and (5, 2). These pairs of numbers define the coordinates of the points at each end of this line.

Because a point in 3D space has location in breadth, depth, and height, however, we need to identify each point not in two, but rather in three dimensions. Again, the convention is to add a z axis to x and y. In this three-dimensional coordinate system, our line might look like this:

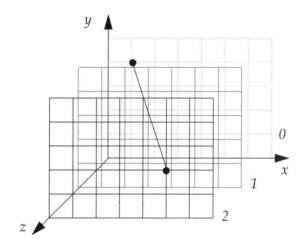

In this image, you can see (if you squint a little) that the line still goes to and from the same x and y coordinates. To help you visualize a 3D object on a 2D page, I've colored the grids a lighter shade of gray as they move away from you (making them fade into the distance). The numbers on the z axis get higher as they get closer to you (in this orientation—if you were standing on the other side of the page, the numbers on the z axis would get higher as they moved away from you). But in this case, the first point also moves from z coordinate 0 to z coordinate 2. In our *xyz* world—also called a three-axis coordinate system— we would say that this line goes from (1,4,0) to (5,2,2).

But lines, even three-dimensional ones, can't create objects. To create something you can see—something that reflects light, takes on texture, and otherwise looks like something other than a transparent jungle gym—you need the next most complex object. Such objects can be created by adding one more point to those just shown. When you do that, you have a polygon. The simplest polygon is the triangle, which has only three points and three lines. The following illustration shows a triangle, made by adding one more point and two more lines to our sample line:

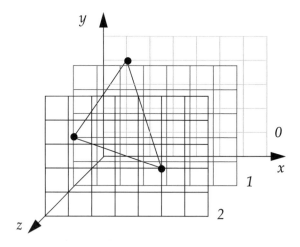

In this triangle, we have three points, which can be identified by the following coordinates:

1,4,0
5,2,2
0,2,1

It may be easier to see the triangle if we shade it in:

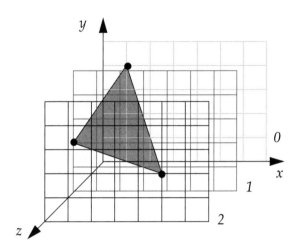

The shaded area of our triangle is the simplest possible kind of *surface* — that is, a flat area that can reflect light (or simulate the reflection of light). The reason it is the simplest is that it uses the fewest number of points possible to create a surface — three, to be specific. In effect, all 3D objects are made up of many such surfaces, which in turn are made up of many points. VRML interprets sets of coordinates as points, which in turn create polygons, which in turn create surfaces.

Where VRML gets fun is that given these coordinates and the eyepoint of the virtual world browser, the computer can calculate the appearance of a surface even as we move the eyepoint. For example, let's move our eyepoint a little forward and to the right, so that we see the same triangle from a different viewpoint, one looking almost (but not quite) directly down the *x* axis of the middle plane:

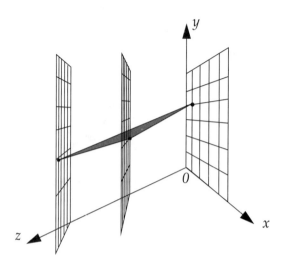

Just to re-orient you, we're actually looking at the underside of our surface here. And this final illustration demonstrates one other part of an interactive 3D world—perspective. The computer can generate perspective automatically, on the fly, while you move through the scene. And it does so within the geometry that you define.

Lighting

The color of your objects varies depending on two characteristics:

- The material characteristics you give your objects

- The lighting

Simply put, a white object with a white light looks white; a white object with a blue light looks blue, and a blue object with a white light looks blue. You can change the appearance of your objects by changing the colors of the lighting you use. (I'll go over the characteristics in slightly more detail when we look at a sample VRML file.)

For the VRML environment, you will primarily be concerned with two kinds of lighting:

- Ambient lighting, which is the light provided by the environment

- Diffuse lighting, which is the light actually reflected off the objects themselves

If you go for high-end 3D rendering, you will also encounter specular lighting, which has to do with reflected highlights. In our simple VRML file, however, we won't be changing any specular lighting components.

Light (and also material) color in a VRML world is expressed in terms of three numbers, each representing one of the three primary colors of the computer: red, green, and blue. This trio of numbers is sometimes called an RGB triple. RGB triples are expressed in terms of a number between 0 and 1 for each of the R, G, and B values, in that order.

For example, the following code fragment from a VRML file defines the characteristics of a directional light used in this world:

```
DirectionalLight {
    on        TRUE          # SFBool
    intensity 1.0           # SFFloat
    color     1.0 0.0 0.0   # SFColor
    direction 25 25 25      # SFVec3f
}
```

In this example, the light's intensity is set to the maximum (1.0), the color is red (with 1.0 as the red value, 0.0 as the green, and 0.0 as the blue), and it comes from the upper right portion of the world (until the eyepoint moves).

We'll look further at VRML, and you can download the sample VRML files from the Web site associated with this book, change the values in your own copy of the files, and then see what happens when you make those changes.

Textures

Textures are somewhat misleadingly named. In ordinary speech, a texture is something you feel, often something with high and low areas. In computer graphics, a texture is a two-dimensional image, like a pattern, which is applied to the surface of a three-dimensional object. This operation is known as texture mapping. (The operation that applies high and low areas to the surface of a 3D object is called bump mapping.)

The best and simplest description I've ever been given for texture mapping is that it's like magic wrapping paper that you can stretch, fit seamlessly, and match up at the edges. In a detailed, high-performance texture mapping system, you can define the way that individual pixel coordinates in the texture (that is, the pattern image) are made to correspond to the coordinates on the object's surface. This forced correspondence is also known as mapping, hence the name "texture mapping."

In the example and tutorial you'll have the opportunity to go through later, you'll see how to take a simple image such as one you've created in Photoshop or some other graphical tool and map it to a 3D object by changing the appropriate line in your VRML file.

Transformations

All 3D objects, no matter where in your world you choose to locate them, are drawn with the intersection of all axes (that is, coordinate 0,0,0) as their graphical center. To understand this, imagine a cube you've created with one corner at 0,0,0 and the other corners each one unit out along each axis, in a positive direction. This gives it the following absolute coordinates:

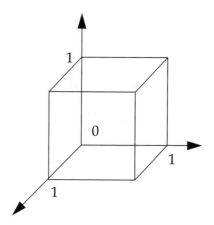

Or, expressed numerically, those coordinates are:

0,0,0
0,1,0
1,1,0
1,0,0
0,0,1
0,1,1
1,1,1
1,0,1

If you drag the object out to another portion of your world—for instance, if you move the object so that its center is now located 25 units down the *x* axis, 20 units up the *y* axis, and -30 units along the *z* axis, the cube's absolute coordinates do not change—the cube is still defined by its 0,1,0 (etc.) combination of coordinates.

How then does the computer generate the cube at its new coordinates? It does so by performing a mathematical operation, called a transformation, to the cube. This is crucial to understand if you plan to code your own VRML worlds: create your objects with respect to 0,0,0 as their visual or graphical center, then perform some kind of transformation to move them out to their desired locations.

You can apply basically three kinds of transformations to graphical objects:

- Translation—moving the object from one part of the world to another

- Scale—enlarging or shrinking the object, expressed as a number or fraction by which the object is multiplied when transformed

- Rotation—turning the object around the center of the world, that is, around coordinate 0,0,0

Note, therefore, that there is a world of difference between two operations that involve translation and rotation. If you translate first, then rotate, the object appears to be orbiting around coordinate 0,0,0 because the rotation operates on the object after it has been translated. If you rotate first, then translate, the object appears to be a certain distance away from coordinate 0,0,0, where it will sit in place and spin around its own axis.

To see if you've got this concept, answer the following question (answer given at the end of this section): What set of transformations describes the way the Earth spins on its own axis once a day while also revolving around the Sun once a year?

For reference, the following selection from the VRML example shows how a typical transform section looks:

```
Transform {
    translation 0 0 0
    scaleFactor 1.0 1.0 1.0
}
```

In this example, the object in question remains at the center of its world and retains its original dimensions and scale.

The answer to the question, by the way, is that to simulate the way the Earth rotates on its own axis while also revolving around the Sun, you would do the following:

1. Let 0,0,0 be the center of both the Sun and the Earth (yes, this means that the Earth is in the center of the Sun — good thing it's a virtual Earth).

2. Rotate the Earth 360 degrees every 24 hours.

3. Translate the Earth 93 million miles from 0,0,0.

4. Rotate the Earth (and the distance of its translation) 360 degrees every 364.25 days.

In the next section, we'll look at some tools that you can use to begin creating VRML worlds without worrying much, if at all, about the geometric concepts or the VRML syntax we've discussed so far (much less the more complex concepts and syntax you'd need to use for rich, interactive worlds).

What You Need to Make 3D Worlds

A quick scan of the AltaVista search engine (located at http://www.altavista.digital.com) turns up hundreds of sites having to do with 3D tools, browsers, or other additions to the family of virtual world construction. What do you need? What do you look for? And how do you make a decision?

Basically you need at least three things:

1. A 3D modeling tool that lets you construct 3D images the way you would create other kinds of illustrations. Depending on the degree of detail and exactness you require, this can be anything from a simple 3D sketch tool to an engineering or CAD package.

2. Some mechanism for exporting the 3D descriptions of your world, scene, or environment to VRML. Most popular 3D drawing packages now have VRML export functions (just as most word processors have HTML export functions), so you can evaluate the ones that appeal the most and select the one that does the best job for your needs.

3. A 3D browsing tool — separate from the 3D modeling tool — which allows you to navigate your 3D world after you publish it on your Web site. You'll need to check its actual function over the Web, which may be slightly different from the way it works when you're using the 3D modeling tool.

Although it is technically possible to create 3D worlds by coding the raw VRML data by hand, I do not personally know anyone who does so on a regular basis; it is exceedingly tedious. On the other hand, if you have written your own computer graphics programs, it is relatively simple to design a program that copies the data points out to a text file in VRML format.

For the examples in this book and on its associated Web site, however, I've stayed with my keep-it-simple model and generated examples in the following way, adhering to the same numbers used in the previous paragraphs:

1. Virtus 3-D Website Builder. This method has several advantages, not the least of which is that they provide a save-disabled demonstration version for free on their Web site (http://www.virtus.com/). Unlike many save-disabled software demos, however, this one has an interesting feature, which pertains to the next paragraph.

2. Virtus 3-D Website Builder. Yes, that is the same program I just described. Although you cannot save the raw 3D worlds you build as graphical files, you can export them to VRML. This means that each 3D world you build is essentially a piece of performance art, as

you can't save it, go back, and edit it later—but you can generate it and publish it on the Web. (I'll walk you through all the steps involved in that process a little later in this chapter.)

3. Virtus Voyager. No, this chapter has not been sponsored by the Virtus Corporation; it's just that they had the most accessible free stuff on the Web, and it all works reasonably well to boot. It also seemed like a logical choice to demonstrate a browser made by the same company that made the VRML export function, although this is probably only because it's been several weeks since I've used my Windows 95 machine, and therefore it's been a while since I've had the joy of Word giving me a General Protection fault as a demonstration of the integration of system and application from the same manufacturer.

Now that you've downloaded or purchased the tools you want for creating your 3D worlds, let's talk about how you can take care of your users by providing them with a set of tools they can use to view the 3D worlds you'll be publishing.

What Your Users Need

To view a 3D world, you need a 3D browser. That seems fairly simple and straightforward, and it's almost that simple and straightforward in practice. If you're using Netscape 2.0 for Windows, for example, several VRML browsers allow you to move through a 3D world. If you're going to create such worlds yourself, you'll want to set up a Web page that guides your users to some popular download sites where they can get free software to view your virtual world.

There's a little more configuration your users will have to do. On Netscape 2.0 for Macintoshes, or for any other configuration where they are required to use a helper application, your users will need to configure the MIME type for VRML files.

Tutorial: Making 3D Worlds

The following tutorial walks you through the steps involved in creating a very simple 3D world. Yet in a way, all 3D worlds follow this basic structure of loading a 3D object into the place you want it, assigning it a texture map, and then exporting to VRML. The key difference is that in complex, visually interesting 3D worlds, the 3D objects themselves are designed from scratch, as are the texture maps. In addition, of course, a really fun 3D world will probably have a lot more than just one eight-sided cone, as demonstrated here.

This tutorial demonstrates how to create a simple 3D world using Virtus 3D Website Builder. Other programs may have different user interfaces, but the fundamental principles of 3D design are all relatively similar.

1. Select a shape from the 3D Galleries window.

   In 3D Website Builder, the initial selection is the triangle (shown here). For the rest of this tutorial, I have used the Octagon, which you can find by scrolling down the 3D Galleries window near the bottom.

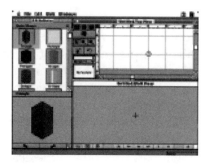

2. Drag the shape you select into the Top View window and position it where you want it.

3. Release the mouse button to position the 3D object where you want it.

    When you release it, the object appears in the Walk View window.

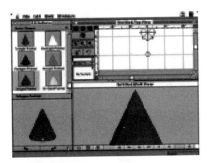

4. Click in the Textures window and drag the mouse to the right.

    This pops up the Texture Map selection tool.

5. Select a texture (Tile Shaded shown).

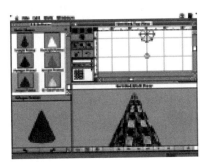

6. From the File menu, pull down and select Export; drag right and select VRML.

This pops up the Export Options dialog box, shown here:

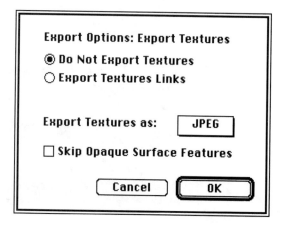

7. Click in the Export Textures Links radio button.

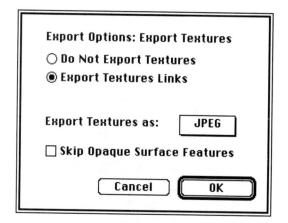

This brings up the Save As dialog box; give it a name that ends in wrl and uses no spaces.

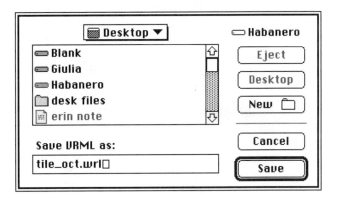

You can now upload this wrl file to your Web site and browse it with either a 3D-capable Web browser or with a 3D viewer helper application.

Now that you've gone through the tutorial on using a 3D builder and what texture maps can do, it's natural to want to create your own texture maps. That's actually much simpler, at one level, than you might think—and much more complex, at another, than it first appears. In the next section, we'll cover some of the pieces that make a difference in creating your own texture maps.

Exercise: Making Your Own Texture Maps

Texture maps make the difference between traveling through the Land of Boring Monochrome Blocks and a world with depth, character, and visual interest. Several programs contain pre-made texture maps, but there's really nothing very complicated involved in making your own.

Before making your own texture map, however, don't forget that the sides of your map will be touching each other, and the tops and bottoms will also be contiguous. This means that if you care about such things, you'll want to make sure that the patterns repeat so that your map looks smooth at the edges. (That's the more complex part of texture map design that I mentioned in the previous section: making sure that the edges of your texture map line up in a way that's visually pleasing.) If that doesn't bother you—as it doesn't for the image I'm using at the texture map in this example—then you can get away with the simple procedure I'm indicating here.

Whatever you decide about the repeated pattern of the texture map you select, you'll need to settle on a size. By opening the sample textures that came with Virtus 3-D Website Builder, I found that they were all sized to 128 x 128 pixels, so I have used that size as a known default value for this exercise. The size of the texture map (in pixels) simply determines how many times the map is repeated in a given 3D object.

1. Select an image you want to use as the texture map.

2. Open the image you selected in an image editing program such as Adobe Photoshop (the sample described in this exercise).

3. In your image editor, crop the image to the section you want to use, then select Save As to make a copy.

4. From the Photoshop Image menu, pull down and select Image Size. Set the longer of the two dimensions (height or width) to 128 pixels—you may also need to select the Units box to the right of the number type-in area.

   For the image shown in this exercise, which is wider than it is high, set the width to 128 pixels. The height automatically adjusts (as long as you remember to click the Constrain Proportions box).

   When you are done, click OK.

5. From the Photoshop Image menu, pull down and select Canvas Size. Set both height and width to 128 pixels. You may need to select the Units box to make sure that the units are pixels, rather than inches or millimeters.

   When you are done, click OK.

6. Save the image file in JPEG format with moderate compression, using the filename TXTR0001.JPG for this exercise.

7. In your .wrl file, add the following lines to the Texture Map section:

```
#TextureCoordinate2
Texture2 {
filename "http://www.yoursite.com/TXTR0001.JPG"
wrapS REPEAT
wrapT REPEAT
} #Texture2
```

This ensures that the VRML browser will use the file called TXTR0001.JPG when it displays this file, and also that the texture map repeats in both the horizontal (*s*) and vertical (*t*) axes. (Be sure to use your site name in place of **yoursite.com**. Likewise, make sure that the JPG file is in the directory you use in the filename parameter of the Texture2 call. Because this is an absolute pathname, however, it can be anywhere on the Web, allowing you to reuse existing textures without copying them.)

8. Start your VRML browser and open the location to which you have saved the test .wrl file.

As an example, here's the picture of my object with the texture maps loaded (notice that the eyepoint was actually inside the object when this picture was taken):

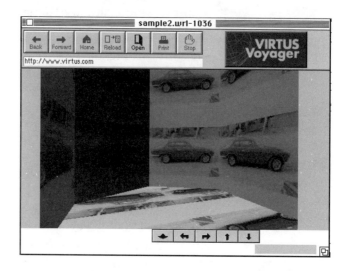

Creating Interactive 3D Worlds

Of course, the real fun in creating a 3D world is in making one from which people can select objects, just as they can with HTML. The procedure for doing this is only a little more complex than the familiar <a href="..."> statement that defines a hyperlink.

You can take two kinds of interaction with a VRML document: you can add new elements to the world, or you can jump to another URL. In either case, you first have to make the element of the world sensitive. The term for doing this in VRML is WWWAnchor.

Adding a new VRML element to your world uses code in this format:

```
WWWAnchor {

  name "http://www.living-history.org/dynaweb/alfa.wrl" #
SFString

  description "Add a new solid" # SFString

  map NONE    # SFEnum
```

```
WWWInline {

  name "http://www.living-history.org/dynaweb/alfa.wrl" }

}
```

Place this block of code at the end of the Separator function that defines the polyhedron you want to make sensitive. (To see how this works, go to the http location defined in this example. If you are running a helper application, Netscape saves the file that you download. Open it with a text editor—any ASCII editor will suffice, such as SimpleText on the Macintosh or Notepad on the PC—and you can see the structure of the VRML code.

The two important lines in the anchor structure are:

```
WWWAnchor {
```

This line introduces the VRML structure of a WWW anchor. If that doesn't make too much sense to you (what are you anchoring?), consider that the "a" in <a href="..."> stands for an anchor. Essentially, this is a link to the site that serves as the anchor, or destination, of the link.

```
  name "http://www.living-history.org/dynaweb/alfa.wrl"
```

This line defines the URL of the anchor being defined. Note that in testing, I was only able to make this work by including the absolute path, including the "http" reference. If you use a relative path, you may find that your VRML browser gets server errors, even if you are sure you're in the same directory as the target.

The inline structure defines the source of any graphics (that is, 3D images) to be used as inline graphics in this 3D space. It's worth pointing out that I was working with an early beta version of Virtus Voyager and some of the behavior I noticed has, I hope, been ironed out in production software. In my testing, however, I had to include both the WWWAnchor and the WWWInline statements to get the add-on-an-item function to work.

When using Virtus Voyager on the Macintosh, I found that moving the mouse pointer over the hotspot image caused it to change from the arrow to a cross-hair. To draw the new 3D image on the Macintosh, hold down the command key (that is, the Apple key) and click when the cursor is set to cross-hair.

You can also use a 3D virtual reality image as your user interface by making the target of the WWWAnchor statement an HTML file instead of a WRL file. For example:

```
name "http://www.living-history.org/dynaweb/index.wrl"
```

This line returns control from Voyager to Netscape and loads the file index.html from the dynaweb directory on my Web page. As with adding images, you need to hold down the command (Apple) key on the Macintosh to jump to a location from a hotspot in the 3D scene.

3D worlds are one of the more exciting and imaginative ways of putting motion, depth, and a certain kind of realism into your Web site. But if you really want to capture the look, feel, and movement of the physical world in your virtual space, you'll want to jump ahead into the next chapter and learn what's involved in serving up digital video from your Web site.

CHAPTER 3

Digital Video for the Web

Lights, Camera, Download!

Nothing says "multimedia" like video. Animation, audio, and interactive images all have their place, but watching movies on your computer—whether they're clips from the latest animated feature on www.disney.com or shots from your company picnic on your employee home page—makes it completely clear that the Web is a new kind of publishing medium altogether.

Video is to multimedia what elephants are to the circus: without either one, all you've got is a tent full of clowns. But like the elephants, video takes up an enormous amount of space, requires meticulous care and feeding, and can turn on its trainer if not carefully watched.

Shooting good-looking video is an art form in itself. But within that art form, there are additional concerns regarding shooting video for digital playback, especially at the comparatively low frame rates required by the technical constraints of the Web. These concerns include lighting, the nature of the motion you choose to capture, the colors of objects in the foreground and background, the speed of pans and zooms used in the video clip, and several other concerns that greatly affect how good a piece of digital video looks when played back on the average computer. We'll look at how you can tame these particular wild elephants later in this chapter.

In addition to the "normal" digitizing issues, making video for the Web introduces a powerful new concern about file size, download time, and its effect on playback and performance. Digital video meant for playback over the Web may also mean making multiple versions of the video source available, or at least pointing your users to public-domain video playback software, to compensate for the different kinds of players, platforms, and Web browsers that your users will be expected to have.

Furthermore, you can use video in your Web pages in two ways: as files to be downloaded explicitly to play later, or (for Netscape users) as embedded images that automatically load when someone clicks on your URL. In this chapter, we'll help you decide which approach works best for you, and what factors you need to consider when adding video to HTML.

Video Formats for the Web

This chapter examines the structure of video over the Web and looks at several different compression and playback methods: QuickTime and QuickTime for Windows, the cross-platform standard developed by Apple Computers for both Macintosh and PC systems (and available on Unix workstations through public-domain software such as xanim); Microsoft Video for Windows, the proprietary format that works on the largest subset of personal computers; and additional compression-decompression (codec) software such as Motion Picture Experts Group (MPEG), Cinepak, and others. Some of the standards bodies, system specification, and vendors involved in digital video production are included in the appendices.

What This Chapter Is Not

This chapter is not a tutorial in how to set up and run an on-line video store, where your users can download movies over the computer. The underlying technology (primarily cable modems and high-speed connections) is still some time off in the future. On the other hand, some of the issues surrounding that technology are being addressed now, particularly in database management systems that permit variables of up to 2 gigabytes, and in Web applications that let these variables be substituted at run time in a Web page. We'll address these issues a little later. We'll also look at how you might set up an on-line catalog for a traditional video store, in which previews, short clips, or trailers for your inventory are stored on-line for Web users to look at and order.

This chapter is also not a comprehensive tutorial in film-making — though it contains many how-to instructions that can help make you a better cinematographer, scriptwriter, or director. Much of this chapter is devoted to the artistic issues of making video meant for display over the Web; I've noticed that it's easier to make a good QuickTime clip than it is to shoot a good video sequence in the first place. As with so many other chapters in this book, the artistic issues are really harder to learn than the technical issues. So if you're the kind of Webmaster who comes from a background of writing code, you may learn even more about what makes movies work than you will about what makes Web sites work.

The 21st-Century Movie Studio

In March 1996, I participated in California's NetDay 96. This event brought together people from technology, education, and almost every other community throughout the state, with the intention of wiring all California's public schools to the Internet. At the end of the day, out of the state's 13,000 schools, 5,000 schools were connected to one degree or another.

My role was as Webmaster for two schools, one elementary (kindergarten through 5th grade) and one middle school (grades 6 through 8). The festivities themselves occurred on campus at the middle school, where teachers, business leaders, and even one or two politicians showed up to take part.

I brought along the video capture system I used to make most of the movies you'll see on the Web site associated with this book: my old but still dependable Macintosh 630 with the Apple Video System. We connected this to a flatbed color scanner, plugged in a VCR, and were ready to roll. I set up a handful of the middle-school students, showed them how to capture movies, and had them digitizing video from the tape they had shot of their teachers, staff, friends, and campus, Columbia Middle School in Sunnyvale, California.

It dawned on me, as I saw the kids sitting around the computer, scanner, VCR and camcorder, that I was looking at a movie studio of the future. The whole thing fit on a tabletop, but it included everything you need to make digital movies:

- Something to capture the images (a camcorder)
- Something to play them back (the VCR)
- A digitizing system (the Apple Video System)
- A frame editor (the Apple MoviePlayer 2.0)
- A viewing screen (the monitor)

There was even a removable hard drive to make it possible to transport the files to a Web server, or to a CD-ROM manufacturing service if you prefer to ship atoms instead of bits.

It's almost pointless these days to estimate what it would cost to duplicate this setup today — either the technology would have since been obsoleted or the price will come down 50% by the time this book hits the stores. But if you

Creating Dynamic Web Sites

did nothing but stack up credit card receipts and canceled checks for the objects on that table, it would come to less than $3500. That's a far cry from the amount I think of when someone mentions a movie studio.

Granted, several options could jack up that price, in return for higher performance or quality in the images, or better speed from the applications used to capture and process images. Alternatively, you could probably delete the scanner, and you don't really need both a VCR and a camcorder, so that'll save you perhaps $1000 or more.

At the upper extreme, you could easily spend $35,000 or more on a higher performance setup and still not have the ultimate setup (particularly in video camera technology, which is critical if you're planning to make professional-looking movies on your computer). But take a look at the images I've placed on my Web site. They were all shot with an inexpensive Hi-8 camcorder, digitized with the $249 Apple Video System, edited with MoviePlayer, and embedded into the HTML files with SimpleText.

On the Windows side, I have used the same camcorder, plugged it into my Intel Smart Video Recorder Pro capture card, used the Asymetrix Digital Video Producer software to edit the frames of those movies, and embedded them into my Web pages with the Windows Notepad program. The Intel capture card costs a little more than the Apple system ($549 versus $249), but it's not a direct competitor. Rather, it's the next niche up in video capture, with more flexibility in image size and frame rate (depending on the processing power of your Windows PC) and a more feature-rich software package (Asymetrix Digital Video Producer) bundled with the card.

Comparing Budgets

How much will you have to spend to create digital video on your own Web page? The answer depends to some extent on what you plan to start with and what your organization's goals are for the movies you produce.

If you're working in a professional organization, you may have professional video—interviews with your management team, marketing presentations, and the like—that you want to digitize and upload for the Web. Because the initial image quality is probably high, you'll want to spend the money on equipment that will do it justice.

As I write this, the best quality video digitizing system I've seen is the Media 100, available from EISI Systems in Mountain View, California. It costs about $10,000, requires a fairly high-performance Macintosh to work best, but is actually used today in broadcast work. Don't be fooled by the word "broadcast quality"—that's the digital video equivalent of the old real-estate line, "Home prices will never be lower." Many systems are advertised as being broadcast quality, when all that means is that under certain circumstances, some aspect of their output matches a specification for broadcast video—sometimes only in the color space of the output, sometimes only in the image size. The Media 100 is responsible for video you've probably seen in commercials, sports presentations, music videos, and other broadcast programs.

Radius also makes a line of broadcast-suitable (meaning they're actually in professional use) digitizing equipment. In particular, their VideoVision Studio products are in professional use by advertising studios, post-processing houses, and other providers of digital video content. They're also at the upper end of the price spectrum, but because these systems have been around for a couple of years, you may be able to pick them up used and save some money.

In either the Macintosh or PC worlds, you can now get enough processing power for about $2500 to do reasonable quality video capture, especially if you're buying a high-end video capture subsystem. The Media 100, for example, has its own processors (multiple) for handling the video streams, so it is even effective with a mid-priced Power Macintosh system.

As for PC systems, a 100 MHz Pentium-powered workstation has most of the speed necessary to do high-quality work with video capture — though I have to admit that the best PC system I've used to date is the Hewlett-Packard Vectra, specifically one with a 133-MHz Pentium, 64 megabytes of RAM, and a high-speed internal 1.2GB hard drive. This was the development and playback system for a project I took on with H-P in 1995, and the resulting video (played from the internal disk, not over the Web) looked like something you'd see on television — just as smooth and as detailed as the evening news.

Shopping List for Your Digital Studio

Because of the volatility of hardware prices in general, I'll give only the broadest of ranges of what you can expect to spend. (I once gave a talk in which someone asked me about hardware prices, and I later found that the price I'd seen in ads that morning had been dropped by $200 in the evening edition of the same paper!)

Video recording system. If you're planning to make your own movies — that is, take the pictures yourself — you need a camcorder or video camera. Camcorders range from cheap to moderately expensive; professional quality video cameras can run more than $20,000. If you really want high quality but aren't willing to invest in the equipment (not to mention the learning curve) required for a full-production video studio, you can rent the services of a video production house. Whether you have them produce the analog videotape or the digital video files is another issue you can consider. For a one-time deal, you may save money having the production house do it all; but if you're going to be creating your own images on an ongoing basis, you will eventually want your own camera, recorder, and the rest of the equipment mentioned here.

Video capture system. The video capture system is the heart of the matter. It's the piece that turns analog images from your VCR, camcorder, or other video signal into digital files on your hard drive. Some Macintosh AV computers have built-in video capture capability; for the most part, you will save money by buying a separate capture system, a special card that you install into your computer (whether Mac or PC) and connect to your video signal. Prices range from about $100 (Connectix QuickCam, a grayscale-only camera that takes low frame-rate images) to $10,000 (Media 100, used in professional broadcast video).

As with the camera, you can rent the services of a production house for one-time or mission-critical work. The real advantage to renting the services of such an organization is not that you'll save money compared to buying the equipment—if it's a good shop, you may actually spend more. But you'll also get a much better product because you'll be working with people who specialize in this skill. I'm all in favor of developing new talents—that, after all, is what this book is about, whether you plan to use it to improve your company's Web site or just to find a new means of self-expression. But don't overlook contacting specialists for critical production work.

Video editing system. For desktop/digital video, the video editing system is most likely a software package—it's probably not necessary to buy a proprietary off-line video editor for doing Web work (at least until cable modems and 20 megabit/second bandwidth becomes universal). A video editing system can be simple; Apple's MoviePlayer 2.0, for example, is distributed free, and it lets you select individual frames and sequences of frames to cut, paste, copy, delete, and move around within the video file. More feature-rich video editing software packages include Asymetrix Digital Video Producer, bundled in with the Intel Smart Video Recorder Pro, and Adobe Premiere, which gives incredible control over what you can do to and with your video clip (at about $500).

Video storage. Remember the elephants? Video files are huge, no matter what kind of compression algorithm, frame rate, and image size you select. You'll need a couple of gigabytes of storage if you plan to do any serious video work. Video files take up storage at three distinct times in the development process, which we'll go over later, but you should keep in mind that, during development, most video takes up two to three times as much disk space as it does when it's completed. Buy storage accordingly.

Video display. You certainly can look at video on a small monitor, but if you're preparing clips that represent your organization, your artistic vision, your product, or your dreams, you want it to look its best. Get a high-resolution, large-dimension video monitor. Shop around and buy the best you can afford. True, the people who read your Web page may have 256-color 13-inch screens with a bad flicker—but that's all the more reason for you to make sure that your images look as good as you can make them.

ISDN, T1, or other high-speed connection. You'll want high-speed connection for either or both of two reasons. First, if you run your own Web server, you'll want to do everything in your power to make sure your viewers can get to your files quickly, that they can download in the least possible time, and that your users—even those with 14.4 modems—have the most rapid possible access to your images. (You'll also want to have a high-powered machine, a Pentium of more than 100 MHz or a high-performance Power Macintosh, or, of course a fast Unix workstation.)

Second, if you use a third-party ISP, you'll want to spend the least amount of time uploading your movies and clips from your development platform to your Web site. If you have a lot of movies to transfer or if you are in a heavy edit-and-recopy loop, a slow modem becomes tiring (unless you do what I do, which is make a pot of coffee while the video uploads; that makes me jittery instead of tired).

Artistic Concerns

Many of the artistic concerns for video echo those for still images, covered in detail in Chapter 1. So if you haven't read Chapter 1 yet, go take a look at it, paying particular attention to The Basics of Good Design, The Basics of Web Performance, and High-Performance Photography.

Video is much like still photography, but with a new picture taken up to 30 times per second. Because of the expense (in terms of time, performance, and storage) of video, you do not want to waste it on something that doesn't make a powerful statement—either artistically or informationally.

Also like still photography, most of the actual creative work involved in video comes before you start the camera. Alfred Hitchcock—who never made a digital video, but who obviously knew a thing or two about making movies that affected people's emotions—claimed in interviews that he never actually looked through the camera. When it was time to shoot the scenes, he explained, he had already set up the shot in his mind by making sketches, worked with the script till he had memorized it the way a conductor memorizes the score of a symphony, and directed the actors, cinematographers, and other professionals on the set so that they could carry out his vision. Hitchcock believed in having an explicit description of every piece of film that would go into the movies he made—before anyone actually loaded film in the camera or turned on the lights in the sound stage.

The tool that traditional video and film professionals use is the storyboard. In my other books, I've talked about how you can adapt the storyboard for interactivity (and Chapter 5 gives an exercise that's derived from my favorite classroom activities on storyboarding for interactive multimedia). Simply put, the storyboard is the visual equivalent of an outline. It not only shows the visual "topic sentences" of your video (to use a term I introduced in Chapter 1), but it also gives a rough approximation (or in Hitchcock's case, a very detailed image) of what you want in the camera.

If you plan to do more than two or three short pieces of video, it's worth constructing a storyboard blank. They're simple enough—here's a sample of one:

Camera View   Notes

You can make these with pencil, paper, and a ruler if you like, or you can do as I've done here and sketch them in with a drawing program on your computer, then run them off as needed. They're simply a way of keeping track of the scene or shot numbers (which you record in the small box to the left of the camera's view), what you want in the camera's view, and any notes about the dialog or action in that scene.

When doing storyboards, you should remember these points:

1. Whether you draw like the reincarnation of Leonardo da Vinci or you still find it a challenge to keep all the color inside the lines, storyboard images should be simple, quickly drawn, and low in detail. The object of a storyboard image is not to produce publication-quality artwork: The object is to compose the image you want in a scene, showing how your players face, where props and scenery are located, and the like.

2. Each frame in your storyboard represents a different cut in the video, a different camera angle, a different shot. The relative length of time that each shot stays on camera affects how your audience feels when watching the resulting video. Lots of short, fast-paced shots, especially with radically different camera angles (such as over the shoulders of two people facing each other as they alternate lines of dialog) can heighten the sense of drama, of excitement, or of action. In my classes, I like to show the scene from *Jurassic Park* in which the tyrannosaurus rex attacks Sam Neill as he's trying to rescue the kids from the crushed Land Cruiser. We keep trying to count how many cuts there are in that 2-minute clip, but it's too exciting and we lose count.

3. Although they're two separate issues, bear in mind that each cut, each separate shot, will almost certainly be digitized as a separate file. You will use a video editing program—whether a simple one like MoviePlayer or a professional-quality one like Premiere—to make the composite clips from a number of individual cuts.

4. You don't need to record your video at the beginning and take it in sequence. Remember that shooting for *Gone with the Wind* began with the burning of Atlanta, a scene that takes place well after the opening of the picture. The following exercise shows you two different ways of recording the same sequence, with two different effects as a result.

Exercise: Variations on a Shrew

If you're planning to shoot any video that includes interviews with corporate representatives, experts giving testimonials in response to questions, or any other dialogue between two people, you'll want to consider two ways of shooting that video. One puts the camera in the audience at a stage presentation; the other puts it over the shoulders of each participant, resulting in two completely different sections of video, and then edits the two tracks into one seamless presentation. Neither one is automatically right (any more than Shakespeare is more "right" than, say, Eugene O'Neill), but they give two different feelings to the resulting piece. We're going to look at how you might videotape each of these treatments of the same scene.

A classic scene in Shakespeare's *The Taming of the Shrew* can help you visualize this. The dialog in question comes from the introduction of Petruchio to Katharina:

Katharina: If I be waspish, best beware my sting.

Petruchio: My remedy is then to pluck it out.

Katharina: Aye, if the fool could find out where it lies.

Petruchio: Who knows not where a wasp doth wear his sting?

(And an additional 50 rhetorical trivia points go to anyone who knew that this particular dramatic device is called "stichomythia.")

Take One: One-camera Shot

So one way to film — er, record — this would be to set up the camera as if it were in the audience at a stage presentation. The next illustration and exercise demonstrate what's called a one-camera shot, made with one camera that's placed in such a way that it captures both actors. You'd frame the actors so that they fill the camera, and your storyboard would look something like this (illustrations courtesy of the Fisher Dramatic School for Expressionless Ghosts — see previous comment 1):

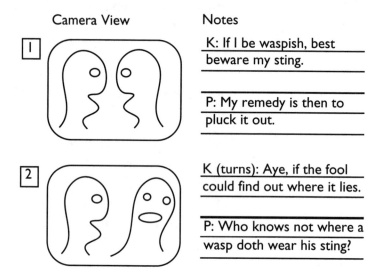

Camera View Notes

1 K: If I be waspish, best beware my sting.

P: My remedy is then to pluck it out.

2 K (turns): Aye, if the fool could find out where it lies.

P: Who knows not where a wasp doth wear his sting?

So let's put one thing to rest right now: you have no reason to be embarrassed about the drawings in your storyboards. They cannot possibly look any worse than these. Yet even these get the point across, which is that the same camera angle — in fact, the same shot — is used to capture both actors delivering their lines.

Your exercise is:

1. Enroll two co-workers, fellow students, or other innocents to assist you.

2. Have each of them learn just these two lines of dialog.

3. Set up the video camera so that they both fit in the image (as in view 1 in the preceding illustration).

4. Videotape them delivering these lines, then play back the tape.

Hold onto this tape because you'll be using it in later exercises after you digitize it.

Now, we'll do what's sometimes called a two-camera shot—except we'll do it with one camera.

Take Two: Two-camera Shot

For the second part of this exercise, keep your volunteers on hand. (I've found that food works well; in some offices it's bagels, in others it's pizza, and if you've got a really free-spirited boss you may be able to use champagne.) This time, however, you'll record them a little differently, following this storyboard:

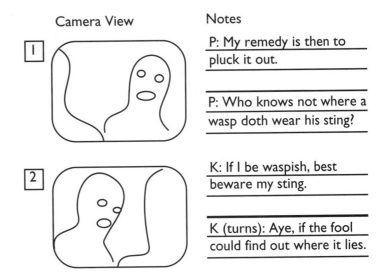

Camera View   Notes

1   P: My remedy is then to pluck it out.

P: Who knows not where a wasp doth wear his sting?

2   K: If I be waspish, best beware my sting.

K (turns): Aye, if the fool could find out where it lies.

Note that this is a shooting storyboard—that is, it indicates which lines of dialog go with which image while you are shooting the scene. (Later on, we'll look at an editing storyboard, which shows the images and dialog in the sequence with which it will be edited into a single clip for distribution.) And this is in fact how you'd shoot this with a single camera:

1. Position your actors and your camera so that you are looking at Petruchio over Katharina's shoulder, as in view 1.

2. Have Petruchio deliver both of his lines, pausing slightly between them.

3. Then move your camera so that it's looking over Petruchio's shoulder at Katharina. (If you move your actors, the audience will see the same set behind Katharina as was visible behind Petruchio.)

4. Now record Katharina delivering her lines, also pausing between them. (The pause is to make it easier to edit the video clips later.)

Later, after digitizing, you will interleave the four lines of dialog as Shakespeare wrote them (and we'll show you how in a later exercise). For now, however, you have all of Petruchio's lines, shot from one viewpoint, in one clip, and all of Katharina's lines, shot from another viewpoint, in another clip.

Several points are to be made here before we move on to other issues involved in making your video look better:

1. Using one camera to do a two-camera shot saves you money on equipment, but takes your actors longer. This means it's a great technique for a garage video or for a video interview to be used by a small business that can't really afford a full-scale video production, but it really isn't going to buy you anything if you're paying scale to a couple of actors while you schlep the camera around on stage.

2. Though I didn't include it in the exercise, it's best if Katharina delivers her lines even when we're looking at Petruchio (and vice versa), so that we get his reaction to her dialog. If he only reads his lines without having hers to respond to, he's likely to look about as excited as our ghosts (or aliens, I'm not sure which) in these illustrations.

3. Yes, I know Katharina's lines come first in the segment of the play that I've used, but I've put Petruchio's first in the illustrations and in the exercise. This is to keep reminding you that, in video, you don't have to record everything in linear sequence.

4. You can also do a three-camera shot, which combines a one-camera and a two-camera shot all at once. That lets you interleave shots of both actors in the screen with over-the-shoulder shots of one or the other (or alternating back and forth between the two). And by now, you can probably figure out how to do a three-camera shot with one camera: do the scene three times, and then edit the clips together.

If you actually got the video camera, plied your friends and colleagues with carbohydrates, and recorded this exercise, you may notice several additional differences between the shots.

The one-camera shot is a great way to introduce a sequence because it establishes both players in the frame at the same time. If there's action between them—say, if this was Romeo and Juliet's first meeting instead of Kate and Petruchio's—the one-camera shot would capture both actors, letting any interaction between the two characters be visible.

The two-camera shot, on the other hand, lets you cut from one character to the other, registering their reactions and emotions in full-face. If you use quick, rapid-fire cuts to go from one character to the other, you can heighten the sense of drama. (You do run the risk of monotony, if you use too many cuts of the same length.)

When you use an over-the-shoulder shot such as those described in the two-camera work I talk about here, you are giving the visual weight to one actor in each scene — the one whose face is viewed head-on. This downplays the other character's role in that scene, for every moment in which we see the back of his or her head.

One typical use for one-and two-camera interleaving is in interviews. Open with a shot of both participants, guest and interviewer, sitting facing one another at an angle, and have the interviewer introduce the guest. You can then cut to the appropriate two-camera, over-the-shoulder shot of each person speaking. You may not want to give the interviewer the full attention of the camera, so you might use the angle from the opening shot for most scenes in which the interviewer is speaking, asking questions, or responding. But cutting from that to the over-the-shoulder shot of the guest will focus the attention on the guest.

Using over-the-shoulder shots also has a more subtle effect: it makes the audience identify, if only slightly, with the person whose point of view we share — even as it downplays their role in the dramatic action taking place. This is part of the power of telejournalism: the audience subtly responds by aligning with the person over whose shoulder we're being permitted to look. If you can wire both individuals with microphones, you may even want to use some shots in which the interviewer's face is not seen when asking a question (but only after you have established the interviewer's voice so that we know who this sound is coming from).

Shooting Attractive Video

Now let's move on from how you set up an entire scene to how you set up each shot to look its best on computer. Several additional constraints apply to video that is meant to be displayed on a computer, especially a Web page.

Lighting

Digitized video requires not only good lighting, but if you want it to look its best, be careful about large expanses of dark colors. Dark colors digitize in a very "noisy" manner, for reasons that the following simple illustration may help explain:

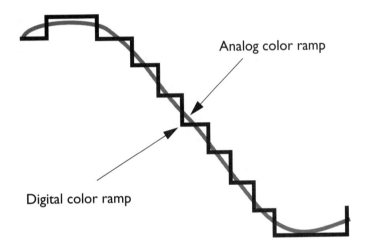

Analog color ramp

Digital color ramp

This figure roughly represents the response curve of the human eye. In terms of computer graphics, this shows up as the gamma correction curve—a way that monitor manufacturers have of modifying the response curve of the phosphors in the monitor so that they more closely represent the response curve of the eye. In this figure, the analog and digital color ramps are shown as two different shapes. The analog ramp (shown in gray) is a smooth curve, with a straight line in the middle and curved ends. When converted into digital form, however, the ramp takes on a "stair-step" effect.

In the middle of the stairs, the steps are fairly linear—that is, there's a predictable distance from one step to the next and there's a fairly constant differential between any two points on the gray, analog line. These are the points in the analog line at which the digital line has taken a sample of the continuous color. In general, this process of sampling is the fundamental transition from analog to digital in color, in motion, and in sound.

But at the bottom end of the curves, notice that the two differ strikingly. What is a smooth curve in the analog becomes a flat line in the digital, and much of the color detail in the analog is lost. What show up as many gradations of color in nature are converted into far fewer digital values. This shows up in images that represent broad expanses of shadow as though they were made up of mosaics of similar, but distinct colors—and what's worse, when viewed in motion, the mosaics can tend to "dance" in the dark backgrounds, as each frame samples the light slightly differently

What can you do about this? One answer is to use more colors in your digital palette. This is one reason why 16-bit and 24-bit monitors typically look better than 8-bit monitors, because the stair steps are smaller. 24-bit color, also called true color, results in 16,777,216 distinct colors, which is many more than the human eye can distinguish. (We typically can distinguish about 80,000 colors, with variations among individuals making it difficult to pin down an exact figure for all human beings.)

However, if you're building video to be displayed over the Web, you'll have 8-bit monitors to contend with in a large number of your users. In practice, it's best just to remember that dark areas in images tend to blotch up when viewed in digital video, and do what you can to design scenes without large dark expanses, and also to light them well so that the colors that *are* present have adequate light for sampling. (It's worth noting that because of the way the eye responds to light, the same sampling problem at the bright end of the curve isn't as objectionable; we're less disturbed by moving highlights than we are by the thought of something slithering around in the darkness.)

Panning and Zooming

Panning and zooming are two cinematic terms you probably already know, but if you don't, a pan—short for panoramic shot—is done by moving the camera from one side to another. Think of what you'd do if you were taking video of the Grand Canyon and only had the tiny viewfinder to look through—you'd want to stand in one place and either move the camera from left to right, or you'd want to turn around on the spot to capture the entire scene.

Zooming means changing the shape of the camera lens so that the effect is as if you were moving quickly forward or backward with the camera. Zooming in results in a close-up; zooming out results in a wide shot.

Novices with a video camera tend to do three things fairly consistently: they don't use a tripod to steady the camera, they pan too much and too fast, and they zoom in and out too often, as though hunting for the right image size in the frame. In analog form, some directors have made a virtue of this vice by creating an intentionally jumpy, jerky style, using lots of jump cuts, camera angles that aren't squared up to the ground, and even shaky images to give their video the feel of spontaneity. However, this can get tiring (as well as tiresome) over long periods—and when you add the element of digital video, you can move from something that's simply ugly (though possibly intentionally so) in analog form, to something that's objectionably difficult to watch when digitized.

Don't forget the previous sampling explanation above—it applies to more than just the digitizing curve of a color ramp. The sampling problem is exactly what you face when you select a frame rate: You're choosing the number of times per second that your movie will take a sample out of a continuous stream of motion. And just as the colors turn into a blotchy mosaic if the sampling rate is too low, panning or zooming too quickly results in a jerky appearance as the objects in the frame appear to hop across the screen, or move toward or away from you in jumps and starts.

When you pan to one side or another, move slowly, deliberately, and carefully. Remember that the images will be moving from one position in the camera to another, and when digitized, any lack of smoothness will be magnified. Likewise, zooming in or out may cause disturbing jumps in size for your subject, between one frame and the next.

Motion

The motion of an object on screen can be just as touchy as when panning the camera. This may be more difficult to control, of course, particularly if you're shooting video in action. Whenever possible, look for smooth motion, asking your actors to move carefully and deliberately across the stage. If you're shooting someone running, playing sports, or another high-speed object (such as the race cars shown on the Web site — take a look for them), you'll have to do what you can to make sure the camera doesn't jiggle or jerk, so that you don't introduce any additional source of sampling error in the picture. Do the best you can with frame rate and image size, and edit it well.

If it's at all possible, track the object that's at the center of your image — that is, pan the camera in sync with the motion of the object you're recording. This kind of attention highlights your visual topic sentence, the object in the center of the frame, because that's what the eye is drawn to. The moving background becomes secondary, and any sampling errors there will be less noticeable and less objectionable. If you can center the moving object in the camera and track it, the object will not appear to move much, relative to the edges of the image, between frames. This avoids much of the visual discontinuity resulting from any sampling error that develops when you digitize your video.

The real paradox of all this, of course, is that motion is exactly what you want to use video to convey. Any basically static image—for example, a city skyline, a person sitting at a computer, or a baseball game—is best portrayed as a single photograph, or a series of photographs. So the answer is not to avoid motion in your video clips because that's what they're best at conveying; the answer is to be careful about how you record your clips, and think about not only what you see, but how it'll look when digitized. And the best way to get good at that is to practice.

Composition

As in photographic images and illustrations, composition is critical to the visual success of your video sequences. However, it takes on a new dimension as you add motion. To develop your own sense of visual style, you should start with some basic rules.

First, having people or objects moving into your scene adds drama, action, and excitement. This is a good rule for static photographs, but it works equally well if an object actually moves into the scene in a video image as well. (Yes, you run the risk of sampling errors that I talked about in the paragraph about tracking shots in action sequences. Are you beginning to get an idea of why good directors are paid so well?)

Something else that's different about on-line video: the colors of objects in your video may need to align with the colors of your Web page graphics. This is one way in which an art director's job is important when recording video; the art director is responsible for designing the overall color of a scene, making sure that everything looks good. If you're producing a high-quality Web page with lots of graphics and video, you'll want to do what you can to make sure it all works together.

Furthermore, if your overall layout has a direction and a dimension—that is, if your art director has chosen a particular balance to the layout of graphics used in your site— it's good to echo that in the composition of video images.

Remember, you can always snag a single frame of video and use that (or pieces cut from it) as GIFs or JPEGs to introduce a section of your Web page. In Chapter 4 we'll look at ways to make portions of captured video into buttons.

Technical Concerns

So far we've covered material that sounds like something you'd need to know when you're sitting in a canvas chair wearing a beret and barking orders through a megaphone—the traditional view of a Hollywood director, using techniques such as storyboards and one- or two-camera shots to design and define the look of your video. From there we covered some issues that cause specific problems for people planning to record images to use in digital form over the Web (or over CD-ROM, for that matter—there's no reason why you can't use the same content in either medium if, for example, you use the Web to market products that you plan to sell for revenue in CD-ROM form).

Now it's time to look at some of the specific technical issues involved in digital video. Although entire books (and some very good ones, too) are devoted to the technical side of digital video, I'll cover just the basics in this chapter. You can always study further by looking into some of the titles in the bibliography.

First, then, let's discuss some terms you're likely to hear as you break into the world of digital video. I'll not only define the terms, but I'll also explain what they mean to you as a Webmaster responsible for the performance, as well as the appearance, of your Web site.

Frame Rate: How Fast, How Smooth?

Frame rate—the number of photographs per second that your video clip displays—is crucial for digital video. A typical frame rate might be 24 frames per second, which is the frame rate of motion picture film; video and television in the United States is recorded and played at 30 frames per second, and in Europe at 25 frames per second (sometimes abbreviated fps).

What makes digital video interesting is that in motion pictures and broadcast video, there's a fixed relationship between the frame rate at which the motion was recorded and the rate at which the movie or video is played back. This is because movies and video cameras use fixed-speed motors to move the media past the playback mechanism (a light and a lens for film, a magnetic read-write head for video).

But digital video uses a computer to find, calculate, and draw a huge number of pixels, many times per second. And especially in the context of the Web, you'll find that computers have widely varying capabilities for such playback. So you may from time to time encounter a digital video clip that "stalls" for part of a second, or sometimes longer, and then jumps to a later portion of the clip to keep in sync with the sound.

In film and video, a higher frame rate—that is, shooting and playing more frames per second—results in smoother looking images. The classic *King Kong* of Willis O'Brien was shot at 6 frames per second, then each scene of Kong and the other stop-motion figures was printed on four successive frames of the movie to work out to 24 fps. (This is known as "shooting on fours" in the animation industry; although shooting on fours is rarely done today, shooting on twos—which results in a frame rate of 12 fps—is common in Saturday morning cartoon shows.)

The paradox here is that in computer-based digital video, a higher frame rate can actually lead to more discontinuity, a jerkier image, and less satisfying video. This is because a high frame rate can put too heavy a load on the CPU of the playback computer, particularly if it's running several other processes (such as the TCP stack, managing the PPP connection, downloading the next Web page, and the like). Oddly, a video clip digitized at 15 fps may end up looking smoother once it's played back than a clip at 30 fps, because the 30-fps clip may pause, freeze for a few seconds, and then resume later in the clip.

All this happens because the standards for digital video are defined so that audio plays in something very close to real time. But to avoid the potential for out-of-sync problems (think of *Singing in the Rain*, where Jean Hagen's head is shaking from side to side while the villain's voice is shouting "Yes! Yes! Yes!," then the villain nods his head up and down while Jean's voice shrieks "No! No! No!"), video playback mechanisms such as QuickTime and QuickTime for Windows drop intermediate frames rather than letting the frames get out of synchronization with the sound track. The player sometimes simply freezes the last image on the screen, then calculates forward to find the frame that fits with the piece of audio that's been running in the background all the while, and the results can be jerky, jumpy, and stiff.

The point here is that although 15 fps isn't as smooth as full-motion video (30 fps) or motion picture film (24 fps), it's better to have 15 fps without interruptions, breaks, and pauses than it is to try for 30 fps and end up delivering only 8 or 10 at your user's desktop.

Image Size

The other issue that has a huge impact on performance is the image size of your video clips. The number of pixels in each frame increases dramatically as you increase the size of the images. Doubling the width of a picture quadruples the number of bits that have to be captured, stored, and transferred to your Web user's workstation. So going from an image of 160 x 120 pixels to one of 320 x 240 can end up with a file that takes four times as long to download.

Sometimes, less expensive video digitizing equipment links frame rate to image size. The Apple Video System that I used to digitize my QuickTime movies for this book's Web page has two fixed settings:

- 160 x 120 pixels per frame, at 15 frames per second

- 320 x 240 pixels per frame, at 7–8 frames per second

These frame rates and image sizes, by the way, were calculated to give images that worked well in standard CD-ROM production (see the next section). It means that clips captured at the larger image size are only about twice the size of clips captured at the smaller image size. In practice, this means that I have a simple choice: go for more detail in the image but with fairly jerky motion, or go with smaller images but smoother motion.

Throughput

Throughput is effectively frame rate times image size. This defines the maximum required throughput for a given video system. It's a bigger issue for CD-ROM development than it is for Web video because video playback from CD-ROM depends entirely on the access time and bits per second that can be pulled off the CD-ROM's surface.

On the Web, the issue of throughput depends on the modem, the server's connectivity, and the client's processor speed. There are two different ways of handling video in a Web page, and we'll cover them in exercises later in this chapter. Both, however, amount to the same thing: downloading the video clip to your user's Web browser, then displaying it from their local workstation.

As a Webmaster, you can't control the effect of your readers' modems on your throughput. You can, however, control (to a certain extent) the performance of your Web site. If you are running a high-demand, video-intensive Web server, you need to look into the following issues:

- *Connectivity*. Make sure you are running the fastest line you can afford between your server and your Internet hookup (whether that is through an ISP or through a direct connection to an Internet backbone site). ISDN is barely good enough for moderately video-intensive sites. T1 is better, and better still are the cable modems that are being announced as I write this book. (For years, I joked that ISDN stood for "I Still Don't Need it." Today that isn't funny any more.)

- *Memory*. No matter what kind of Web server you use—Windows (16-bit or 32-bit), Macintosh, or Unix—the more memory you install on your system, the better its response time and performance will be. In fact, talk to your system administrator (or to a comparable expert on your specific system) about keeping high-demand files resident in memory at all times. One way of doing this is called a "RAM disk," which basically partitions physical memory (as opposed to virtual memory) as though it were a disk. Then, files can be accessed very quickly, without the required seek time and load time that are necessary when a file is on disk. Using a RAM disk means that the files can be kept in RAM, but they can be accessed via URL. (The procedures for doing this vary widely among operating systems, hence the comment to ask your sysadmin.)

- *Processor.* To put it simply: upgrade it. If you think your processor isn't fast enough, your customers are bound to agree with you—sometimes violently. A tremendous amount of computing activity is involved in displaying video, and if you're trying to serve this over the Web on anything less than a high-speed processor, performance will suffer.

- *Modem.* What's the point of paying for an ISDN line (capable of 128K bps) if all you have is a 9600-baud modem to plug into it? Talk to your telecommunications vendor and see what kind of network connection hardware they recommend—what works well with their equipment, and what will help you get the best value out of your relationship with them. Make it clear that this is part of your satisfaction with their overall service, and they'll take it more personally.

Audio Synchronization

Audio synchronization is an important component of digital video. In some ways and for some video, it's the most crucial part of the scheme. If human speech is involved and if you see people speaking so that their lips move, correct synchronization between motion and sound is essential to the experience. (If you don't believe me, watch a badly dubbed horror movie sometime.)

Typically, as in QuickTime, some pain is taken to ensure a strong synchronization between sound and image. In most cases, the video actually drops frames to make sure that the sound does not get behind the frame that's on the screen.

If you are planning to use an animated piece that requires tight audio synchronization, Chapter 6 talks about some techniques for synchronizing sound in Director for use in Shockwave titles. There are several tricks that take advantage of Director's ability to control timing and play on human perception that will help keep your sound tracks in sync with your action.

Compression

Until everyone in the world has 20 mbit/second fiber-optic lines coming into their computers, you will be serving compressed video to your Web users. The only question is how much compression you want to support. The answer depends on what matters the most. Do you just want moving pictures on your Web page, or do you want good-quality images?

In a later part of this chapter, you'll go through the steps involved in digitizing video at two levels of compression, one that permits the best-looking images but requires truly alarming file sizes, and another that permits reasonable images at reasonable file sizes. For now, you'll need to learn a few terms to understand compression in terms of digital video:

- *Compression ratio*. No, this isn't about high-performance cars and 92-octane gas, it's about the relationship between the size of the file without any compression, and the size of the file after it's been compressed. Higher compression ratios tend to result in blotchy images; lower ratios produce finer images. Compression ratio is applied to any video compression standard.

- *Compression standard.* Video compression involves more than just "squeezing" the bits down; it involves a mathematical operation on the bits in a video frame, reducing them to numbers that can later be expanded to their initial state. It should be easy to tell that you have to use the same mathematical operation (or, actually, its opposite) to uncompress the video as you used to compress it. This combination of compression and uncompression algorithms are collectively known as a compression standard.

- *Spatial compression.* Each frame in a traditional video clip, movie, or cel animation occupies a certain space—that is, it has a certain dimension which, when turned into digital form, occupies a certain amount of disk space. The simplest form that this takes is an image map—that is, a grid in which there is a separate number, representing a color value, for each spot in a grid that is the width and height of the image. Spatial compression reduces each frame and thereby speeds the file transfer over the Web. One technique for spatial compression is to keep a count of how many pixels in succession use the same color, then to store two numbers: one representing the color itself, the other representing the number of pixels in that color. For images with solid-colored backgrounds, this can save a tremendous amount of file space.

- *Temporal compression.* This compression scheme tracks pixels that are the same color and at the same location in adjacent frames of a digital movie. If the pixels at the same location use the same color, a temporal compression scheme lets the later frame store nothing in these locations. This way the overall movie size can be drastically reduced.

The MPEG (Motion Pictures Experts Group) video compression standard uses an intense form of temporal compression. This temporal compression is very effective, but at present it requires application-specific hardware for most installations. This changes as processor speeds continue to increase. MPEG movies offer the best compromise between download time and viewing quality, and as the CPUs in PCs become faster, it will be possible to do the decompression at run time.

Video Formats

At this point in the technical development of multimedia, only the most die-hard hobbyist or most relentless do-it-yourselfer actually needs to write applications that handle video streams. For the two major computing platforms, video users have their choice of Apple's QuickTime video system, or Microsoft's Video for Windows. Because Apple's QuickTime is compatible with Windows players, it is the format of choice for many Web pages, because you can post one version of your video clip that viewers on multiple platforms can watch. I sometimes refer to QuickTime as the ASCII of digital video. In addition, several video tools are available for Unix workstations, including the public-domain xanim program, which handles many, many video formats.

QuickTime and QuickTime for Windows

Apple's QuickTime video is available as a system extension for Macintosh and also for Windows workstations. This means that on the Macintosh, you load QuickTime into your System folder (specifically, into the Extensions folder, though dropping it in your System folder causes the Mac OS to "do the right thing" with it). Once there, your Macintosh is enabled for video playback in a number of applications, anything from word processing and page layout programs like FrameMaker to Macromedia Director.

It's a little surprising to newcomers to the Macintosh to see that SimpleText—the Apple answer to the Windows Notepad program—is the way you view QuickTime movies if you simply click on the movie file. You can't edit them in SimpleText; for that, you either need MoviePlayer or a specific video editing program such as Adobe Premiere.

MoviePlayer (in its Version 2.0 form) is also the easiest method for making Macintosh QuickTime movies playable on other platforms. When you save your movie from MoviePlayer, it offers you several options, as shown here in the Save dialog:

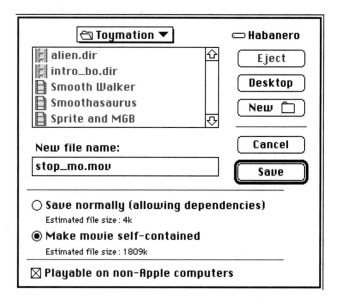

To make your Apple QuickTime movies playable on QuickTime for Windows, you need to do three things:

1. Make sure the filename meets the DOS filename.ext convention—that is, eight characters, a period, and three characters (the last three characters must be "mov," as shown here).

2. Click on the radio button reading "Make movie self-contained." This makes sure that the entire QuickTime movie is in a single file. (The "Save normally" button saves only an edit list—that is, a list of the frames to load, drop from, or add to the original movie. This saves tremendous amounts of disk space, but you will not be able to play the version you saved normally unless the original movie is in the same directory.)

3. Click the box marked "Playable on non-Apple computers." This "flattens" the QuickTime movie, a term you may hear from time to time . What this means is that Apple uses two parts to every file: a data fork and a resource fork. This two-forked format doesn't work on Windows systems, so it's necessary to create a single-fork system in order to run on Windows.

4. You need to make sure that your Web page's users have access to the QuickTime for Windows player. You can locate this at the following URL:

   http://www.living-history.org/media/quicktime.html

   This points you to a number of download sites from which you can find the QuickTime for Windows installation kit. This page also contains a list of download sites from which you can load Netscape plug-ins to handle QuickTime movies embedded in your Web pages (as we will demonstrate).

Later in this chapter, we'll go through some hands-on tutorials in using the Apple Video System to capture, edit, and make cross-platform versions of QuickTime movies. This is still the least expensive way to put color video on a disk; the Connectix QuickCam is less expensive yet, but it has major limitations that we'll get to later in this chapter.

Video for Windows

Cross-platform capability is important if you're developing materials for the Web at large, particularly in the education market where most of the 55 million Macintosh users still predominate. But more and more Webmasters are being asked to provide services for corporate intranets, where an entire organization has made the decision to purchase PCs. For this, you may still want to use QuickTime for Windows if your media has been created by a Mac-based production facility. But if you're shooting it yourself, you'll probably want to create your video directly in Windows, using Microsoft Video for Windows.

Video for Windows files have an extension of .AVI, which is one way to identify them. Depending on the digitizing system you purchase, you may or may not need an audio card (such as the all-but-ubiquitous SoundBlaster) to capture audio. The third piece of the system is the software that drives these two boards. The example I've used here is one of the less expensive options that still provides good quality, the Intel Smart Video Recorder Pro. This card comes with Asymetrix Digital Video Producer, which does capture sound and maintains synchronization with the video images. Both sound and visuals are stored in the same file, by the way; it's just a by-product of the PC's architecture that requires two separate cards in some implementations.

Tutorial: Digitizing Video So That It Looks Good

The following tutorial takes you through the simplest way I know for capturing video: the Apple Video System on the Macintosh. This is an entirely menu-driven hardware add-on that lets you capture individual frames as well as whole movies. The only limits to how much you can capture are the system memory and free disk space.

On the Apple, follow these tips:

- *Place a CD-ROM in the drive* (if you have a CD-ROM drive). The Macintosh system software checks periodically to see if a CD-ROM is in the drive; once it locates one, the system stops looking (until you remove the CD-ROM later, of course).

- *Insert a floppy into the drive*, for the same reasons.

- *Turn off your screen saver.* Most screen savers check for mouse movement or keyboard entry every sixtieth of a second, and this puts a surprising load on the processor's ability to digitize video.

- *Turn off virtual memory.* The results of digitizing with VM turned on are unpredictable; sometimes it just looks blocky, other times the sound sampling rate comes out at half speed (causing everyone to speak slowly and in very deep voices).

- *Close all windows (such as folders) and quit other applications.* Any operation that takes up processing cycles on your computer results in poorer video quality.

- *Turn off your modem or fax modem.* An incoming fax will use up enough system cycles that the video capture process would have a serious jerk at the point when the fax was received. Even if the call is a voice call that you pick up immediately, if it's connected to your computer, it will mess up your movie.

Once you've set your system up this way, you're ready to begin capturing video. To do that, follow these steps:

1. Connect your camcorder or VCR to the Apple Video System, using the appropriate ports/plugs for the kind of video cable you use: RCA jacks, S-Video, or 50-ohm coaxial.

2. Start the Apple Video Player.

    This opens the following windows:

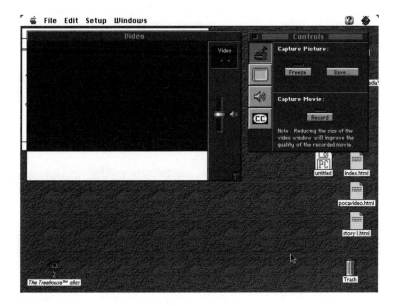

3. From the Setup menu, select Preferences.

   This brings up the following box:

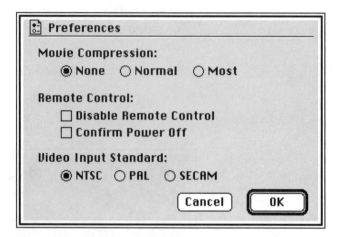

4. Click the None radio button under Movie Compression.

   This produces the highest quality video from the input material you have—but at quite a cost in file size, as you will see.

5. Start playback on the camcorder or VCR.

   You may want to watch the clip you plan to digitize several times before capturing it.

6. Shortly before the action, dialog, or other content you want to capture, click the Record button on the Controls window.

   The hardware takes a fraction of a second to initialize, and this way you will be sure not to miss the frame (dialog, action, etc.) you want to include. The Record button changes to Stop.

7. When you have reached the end of the sequence you want to record, click Stop.

    The video system records the movie you just selected. When it is finished, it displays a file selection box that lets you specify the file and folder into which you want to save this file.

8. Play back your selection.

    Notice the degree of smoothness, synchronization with audio, and other details in the capture.

In the next tutorial, you'll try another setting for compression, one that results in a different look but a vastly different file size.

Tutorial: Digitizing Video for Minimum Load Time

This tutorial takes you to the other extreme, with video that may not have the best detail or smoothest motion, but which takes a very short time to load for the length of video that you capture.

1. From the Setup menu, select Preferences.

    This brings up the following box:

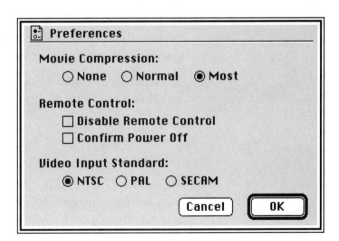

2. Click the Most radio button under Movie Compression.

   This produces the lowest quality video from the input material you have—but at a significant savings in file size, which means in load time as well.

3. Start playback on the camcorder or VCR and play back the same clip or sequence you used in the previous tutorial.

4. Shortly before the action, dialog, or other content you want to capture, click the Record button on the Controls window.

   The hardware takes a fraction of a second to initialize, and this way you will be sure not to miss the frame (dialog, action, etc.) you want to include. The Record button changes to Stop.

5. When you have reached the end of the sequence you want to record, click Stop.

   The video system records the movie you just selected. When it is finished, it displays a file selection box that lets you specify the file and folder into which you want to save this file.

6. Play back your selection.

   Notice the degree of smoothness, synchronization with audio, and other details in the capture.

7. Compare this QuickTime movie with the movie you captured in the preceding tutorial.

   You can have both movies open at the same time (they open in SimpleText). Place the two windows beside one another and play first one, then the other.

8. Close both files and locate them so that their icons are visible from the desktop. Select the first file, pull down the File menu, and select Get Info (or type Command-I). Note the file size.

9. Select the second file, pull down the File menu, and select Get Info (or type Command-I). Note the file size.

From this, you can see what a difference the file compression settings make when digitizing video. When you are looking to purchase your own digital video system, make a point of learning whether it supports different levels of compression. This allows you to tune your video captures for performance or quality, depending on your primary concern.

Tutorial: Editing with Apple MoviePlayer (Mac)

Earlier in this chapter, I introduced the two-camera shot as a technique for interviews, with an example of how you can also simulate this kind of shot with a single camera. In this tutorial, I'll show you how you can use the simplest of video tools—Apple's MoviePlayer 2.0—to create a single, seamless piece of video from two different video clips.

If you want to "follow along" with this tutorial, download two video clips from this book's Web site and see how it works. This tutorial shows you how I used two movies to create a third. You can locate these video clips at the following location:

http://www.living-history.org/chap3/

Three QuickTime movies are used in this example, and they are available from the following links:

- **Smooth Walker**—this is a shot of the tyrannosaurus walking down a deserted street.

- **Smoothasaurus**—this is a shot of the tyrannosaurus attacking an unsuspecting village of toys.

- **absaurus.mov**—this is the resulting QuickTime movie (saved in cross-platform format so that non-Macintosh users can enjoy it as well) made by cutting together frames from Smooth Walker and Smoothasaurus.

Before beginning, you'll want to download at least Smooth Walker and Smoothasaurus (whatever you call the movies on your system—that's the link name on my Web site).

1. Open MoviePlayer 2.0.

2. From the File menu, select Open.

3. Browse to the location on your disk where you've stored the file downloaded from the Smooth Walker link.

    This is the scene with the tyrannosaurus by itself:

4. From the File menu, select Open again, this time browsing to the location on your disk where you've stored the file downloaded from the Smoothasaurus link.

    This is the file with the tyrannosaurus and the villagers, as shown here from early in the movie:

5. From the File menu, select New.

    This creates a blank movie window, as shown here:

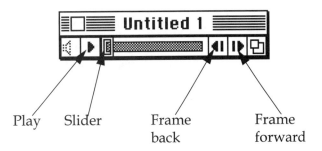

Play   Slider   Frame   Frame
                  back   forward

6. Use the Copy and Paste commands to copy frames from each of the two source movies, then paste them into the new movie you are creating. Here's how:

   a. Copy: To select frames, hold down the Apple key and click on the Frame forward or Frame back buttons. The Slider highlights the region you have selected; the image area displays the most recent frame you have selected. When you have selected the frames you want to copy, pull down the Edit menu and select Copy (or press Command-C).

   b. Paste: Click in the Slider region at the point where you want to insert your frames. Use the Frame forward or Frame back buttons to position the insertion point at the exact frame at which you want to insert the new material. When you have selected the point at which you want to insert your copied frames, pull down the Edit menu and select Paste (or press Command-V).

7. When you have assembled the frames in the order you want, use the slider to "rewind" the movie to the beginning, then press the Play button and watch your movie.

   You can stop your movie at any time by pressing the Play button again.

8. When you have copied the frames you want in the sequence you want them, pull down the File menu and select Save As. . .

This brings up the following box:

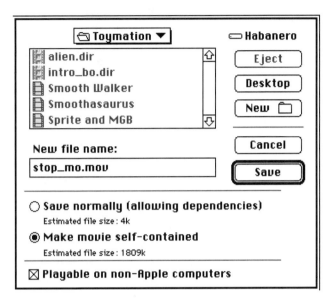

9. Set up the contents of the box as follows:

- **New file name**: Type the name you want to use for this movie. If you are planning to play your movie on Windows platforms using QuickTime for Windows, make sure that the filename is no more than eight characters, a period, and three characters (which must be **mov**, as shown here).

- **Make movie self-contained**: Click this radio button (this automatically deselects the preceding button, **Save normally**).

- **Playable on non-Apple computers**: Click this box if you are creating your movie for playback on other systems.

You can now copy this video file to your Web site if desired, and then you can use it in the following tutorials on incorporating video in your Web pages. Alternatively you can use one of the other source files in your Web page to practice incorporating your own video clips in your

Web pages. (Note that the copyright page in this book contains information about the rights you are permitted when using the video files included on the Web page asociated with this book; in general, you can use any of the video files for your own practice, training and development, but not for resale.)

What did you get out of this exercise? You should now see two things. First, that it's very easy to copy frames of one movie into another, even to create your own movies by editing sources into a single output. Second, however, is that you should see how you can take two different pieces of video—even if, as in this example, they were shot on the same set by the same camera at different times—and interleave them to change the dramatic effect. In the final video on the Web site, absaurus.mov, the cuts from the advancing tyrannosaurus to the peaceful villagers add to the sense of impending doom (or would, if the models were more doom-filled than ceramic penguins and lucky wishing trolls). When the tyrannosaurus actually enters the scene (coming from the direction we've seen him moving in the previous cuts), this action has been foreshadowed by the previous activity, and the dramatic tension is highlighted for much longer than in "Smoothasaurus," where the creature just bursts into the village unannounced.

Obviously the object of these short pieces is to have fun and to demonstrate something; when I teach storyboarding and dramatic development, I take along copies of Hollywood films such as *The Birds* and *Jurassic Park*. But these short and silly pieces can still point out what you can do in your own video productions by using even cheap tools (a $600 camcorder, a $249 video digitizing system, and about $20 worth of my daughters' toys) as long as you pay attention to the human side of the equation.

AB-Roll Editing

Another, somewhat more sophisticated way to edit two separate video clips into a single presentation is with what's called an "AB-roll." Analog video editing systems use two input recorders, one labeled A and the other B. Professional video editors have both tape drives rolling so that the final output shows a smooth transition from one to the other, and all switching is done electronically to control the output tape. A control panel lets you choose visual transitions—from simple cuts to wipes, dissolves, fades, and other special effects—and also lets you choose overlays (such as placing titles or custom graphics on the screen) and play with sound tracks from external sources (such as a seamless musical performance to be played under a series of video clips). In the analog video industry, this is an expensive proposition: video editing systems are very expensive, rent for hundreds of dollars an hour, and require highly trained specialists to operate them.

Digitally, things are slightly different. Instead of separate tape drives, you use separate digital files, one in track A and the other in track B as with traditional video editing systems. You can still select transitions between A and B tracks, you can control the sound, you can make cuts and edits—but you can do this all yourself, in minutes, on your desktop. Many practitioners of digital video like to distinguish between the traditional analog suite and the modern desktop digital suite in the following way:

- The traditional analog method is a *service tool*— that is, the editor provides a service to the director of the video sequence, and the director must explain to the editor what he or she wants in the final product. Because of the high cost of using the video editing system, the director often chooses something that's "good enough," even if it's not quite in line with his or her vision of the finished piece, because enough money has already been spent.

- The modern digital method is a *creative tool* — that is, the creative personnel themselves can use it directly, on their own desktop computer, and with personal attention to how it looks and what they want. Because digital systems cost comparatively little (the one illustrated here retailed for $549, including the capture card), the director can manipulate the images himself or herself, rather than relying on the skills of the editor using the service tool. Best of all, because the operations are relatively fast (depending on the speed of the processor you use), it's possible to try many versions of the same cut, transition, or sequence, playing visual "what-if" just the way that a page layout artist can use a tool like Quark Express or FrameMaker to try sample layouts of a book or brochure.

With that in mind, let's take a look at what you can do with a digital AB-editing system like the Asymetrix Digital Video Producer. (Other digital video editing systems such as the highly respected Adobe Premiere package look and function in much the same way.)

Tutorial: Editing with Asymetrix Digital Video Producer

The key difference between using a dedicated video editing and production tool such as Asymetrix Digital Video Producer (DVP) and a simple frame editor like MoviePlayer as shown in the previous tutorial is that DVP gives you a richer graphical user interface through which you can control the timing and flow of multiple video sequences. In addition, a dedicated production tool such as DVP contains built-in transitions and effects. For example, if you wanted to fade to black with MoviePlayer, you would have to load the desired frames into an image editing tool such as Photoshop, manually alter each frame to the desired level of blackness, and then paste the frames into the appropriate location in the output movie. It's certainly possible, but it's not as seamless or as easy to manage as it is in DVP or Adobe Premiere.

The examples shown here demonstrate how you can edit Microsoft Video for Windows files with Asymetrix Digital Video Producer on a PC running Windows 95. Other video editing tools are similar, although the exact menu options and commands may differ.

1. Download the two AVI files — SUGRPLUM.AVI and CAPTURE.AVI — from the Web site.

2. Start Asymetrix Digital Video Producer.

    This displays the following screen:

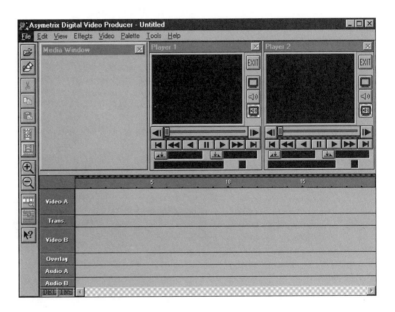

3. From the File menu, select Import Media. . . Browse to the directory into which you downloaded the AVI files and select SUGRPLUM.AVI. Then, repeat this step, selecting CAPTURE.AVI.

    When you have imported both AVI files, they will be displayed in the Media Window, at the upper left corner of the DVP screen.

4. Drag the image of **SUGRPLUM.AVI** from the Media Window into Player 1. Drag the image of **CAPTURE.AVI** from the Media Window into Player 2.

   You can play the movies by clicking on the Play icon (the right-pointing arrow) below the image area.

5. Drag the image of **SUGRPLUM.AVI** from Player 1 into the channel marked Video A in the bottom half of the screen. Drag the image of **CAPTURE.AVI** from Player 2 into the channel marked Video B in the bottom half of the screen.

   Your screen should now look like this:

Instead of copying individual frames as in MoviePlayer, Digital Video Producer lets you locate and mark the start and end frames of the sequences you want from each of the source clips in the two players. To do this, follow these steps (with Player 1 used as the example):

1. Position the video sequence at the first frame that you want to use.

2. Click the Start frame button:

Start frame 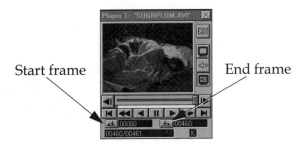 End frame

When you click the Start frame button, the window to the right of the button displays the frame you have selected.

3. Click the End frame button (shown in the previous illustration).

The window to the right of the button displays the frame you have selected.

You have now chosen the Start frame and End frame of the sequence you want to use. You can do this again and again from the same clip, extracting different pieces of the same video and splicing them into a single, seamless project. For example, you can do this to edit from two separate pieces of film created during a two-camera shot, interleaving the over-the-shoulder shots from two separate viewpoints to create a particular effect.

To save your work in Asymetrix Digital Video Producer, follow these steps:

1. From the Video menu, select Build.

   This displays the following box:

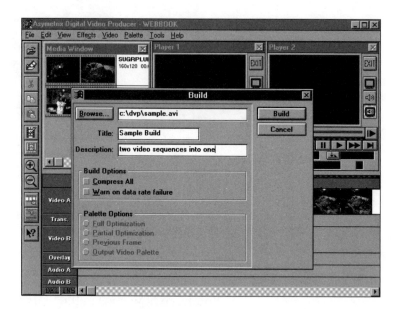

2. Type in a filename, giving also the disk and directory information you want to use for storing the edited video.

   You can optionally include the title and description fields, though these are not required.

3. Click Build.

   Digital Video Producer combines the two video clips into a single AVI file that you can play with the Microsoft Media Player or with any other application that can display Video for Windows files.

In the next section, we'll talk about the final step in the process: how to incorporate the video you've shot, digitized, and edited, into a dynamic and effective part of your own Web site.

Using Clips in Your Web Page

There are, at present, two ways to incorporate a video clip into your Web page:

- As a downloadable document that your Web users can click on, copy to their local machines, and play later using a helper application

- As an embedded image that loads automatically when your users select this Web page

How can you decide which option is right for your Web site? Here are some statements, to which you simply answer yes or no:

1. All of my Web users are on a corporate high-speed intranet, running high-powered workstations, and access time when they click a hypertext link isn't a concern.

2. We're more interested in cutting-edge Web design and multimedia, and users with slow modems (anything under 28.8) don't concern us.

3. We primarily plan to use our video-enabled Web page to demonstrate to potential clients, and then only on specially configured machines and network connections.

If you answered yes to any of these questions, or if you lean toward a yes answer to them, you may want to skip to the procedure outlined in "Embedding Video Clips Directly."

If you answered no—if most of your Web users may still be using 14.4 modems over dialup connections, or if you simply don't like the idea of hiding a potentially unpleasant surprise in an otherwise innocent-looking blue, underlined phrase, you may want to continue with the section "Downloading Video Clips."

Downloading Video Clips

If you want to set up your Web page so that people can download video clips, it's simple: just include the video clip as the target of a hypertext anchor. For example:

<html>

<head>

<title>

Video to Download

</title>

<head>

<body>

<h1>Video to Download</h1>

<p>

Video clip available to be downloaded from a Web page:

<p>

Click <a href="absaurus.mov">here</a> to download the QuickTime for Windows file absaurus.mov.

</body>

</html>

Embedding Video Clips Directly

For the comfort and convenience of your readers who have Netscape 3.0, you can embed QuickTime (and QuickTime for Windows) movies directly into your Web page. Netscape 3.0 plays these movies without additional plug-ins or helper applications. For your readers who are still using Netscape 2.01 (and earlier versions), these versions support embedded video as a plug-in, not as an automatic component. This means that you may want to point your users to the Netscape audio/video plug-in page:

http://home.netscape.com/comprod/products/navigator/version_2.0/plugins/audio-video.html

That lets them choose a video plug-in that works on their platform.

To embed video in an HTML document, set up your file like this one:

```
<html>
<head>
<title>
Video to View
</title>
<head>
<body>
<h1>Looking at Video In a Web Page</h1>
<p>
This is an example of video embedded directly in a Web page:
<p>
<EMBED SRC="absaurus.mov" WIDTH=160 HEIGHT=120>
<p>
This movie is in QuickTime for Windows format. You will
need to have the Netscape QuickTime/QuickTime for
Windows plugin loaded before you will be able to view this
page.
```

It may take several minutes to download the file before you can begin playing it.

To play the video clip, press the Play icon (the right-pointing arrow) in the control bar at the bottom of the image.
</body>
</html>

You can look at this page on line by browsing the following URL:

http://www.living-history.org/live_video.html

Note, of course, that because this example does have the digital video loaded directly in the HTML, it may take several minutes to finish loading this page.

But there's a lot more you can do with a Web page than click on the Play icon in a QuickTime clip. To see some ways of putting in a completely different level of interactivity, put on your beret, grab your megaphone, and get ready for a jaunt through some of the most exciting technology to hit Web design—Shockwave and Java.

CHAPTER 4   # Interacting with Animation

If digital video is to multimedia what the elephants are to the circus, then animation has to be the trapeze act: flashy, entertaining, and seemingly something that ordinary mortals could never attempt. Yet with digital tools, animation can be tremendously simple. And with the advent of the Shockwave technology rising out of Macromedia's popular Director program, your animation can provide game-quality response, interactivity, and speed in a Web-based application.

In this chapter, we'll look at:

- Three technologies for creating animation you can use in your Web page (animated GIFs, Java, and Director/Shockwave)

- Three different techniques for creating animation (point-to-point, path-based, and frame-by-frame animation)

- Strategies for maximizing the speed, performance, and interactivity of your animations while minimizing load time

You don't need to be a programmer to use the technologies I present in this chapter. The most advanced, programming-like part we'll cover is the Lingo scripting language used to control interactivity in your Shockwave applications, but that's really no more difficult than HTML. And if you are looking to hire out a multimedia developer for the content and you're simply planning to integrate their work into your Web site, you'll be happy to know that incorporating Shockwave and Java into your Web page is no more complicated than embedding video or still images.

Furthermore, the Web site associated with this book includes several Java applets and Shockwave files that you can use in testing your own integration of animation and interactivity with your traditional Web documents and structure. It also includes step-by-step tutorials showing you how to use these resources — which you can download for your practice — in your own Web pages. And fortunately, because Director is fully cross-platform compatible between Windows and Macintosh, the Shockwave files here run equally well whether you display them on an Apple product or a PC. And as Netscape introduces the Shockwave plug-in for other platforms, this group of users will grow rapidly.

Most important, both Shockwave and Java really point to a new model of computer use, in which the programs as well as the information are distributed across the Web itself, rather than being loaded into each user's workstation. This distributed model of the Web — putting the complex stuff on your user's workstations, where it can run quickly and efficiently with the least transfer of information across the Internet — is a fundamentally new way of dealing with the Web that promises to provide faster response, more complex interaction, and less intrusion of the control structure into the user's immersive on-line experience (which is expanded on in Chapter 5).

The Big Benefits: Speed and Performance

One problem with clicking on URLs is that when you select a hyperlink that calls for another file, the Web browser has to contact the server, locate the file, transfer the file across the Internet, and then display the file on your local workstation. The overhead involved in contacting, finding, and displaying the file is relatively constant regardless of file size.

Shockwave and Java make possible instant interaction with your screen because they both run programs on your Web user's workstation; all overhead is included in the load time, which is comparable to that of large still images for complex Shockwave pieces. This allows your users to have fast local performance because the processing, image display, and other program operations happen locally instead of over the Internet. Furthermore, both Shockwave and Java are highly compact, in some cases requiring less transfer time than a GIF or JPEG image of the same size as the Shockwave animation that may be many seconds long and have multiple buttons.

What's So Hot About Java?

Java, in some ways, provides even more perceived performance than Shockwave because of the way it's designed. The Java programming language has been designed for optimum use over the Internet, particularly for what are called "applets." An applet is a miniature application: a piece of a program that performs, typically, one function as part of a larger scheme for a Web page or Web site. Where a full application—for example, Microsoft Word or Adobe Photoshop—takes up many megabytes of disk space and performs hundreds of functions, an applet usually takes up only a couple of kilobytes, sometimes even less, and it does usually one or two things. They're the programming equivalent of guerilla troops — fast, light, and specialized, but very effective at what they do.

Teaching you how to create applets in the Java programming language is beyond the scope of this book. Fortunately many other resources are out there; the one I've referred to in developing the applets and examples for this chapter is *Hooked on Java* (Addison-Wesley, 1996). The authors — Arthur van Hoff, Sami Shaio, and Orca Starbuck — were all original members of Sun Microsystems' Java development team, and they've written an effective and compact book about this effective and compact programming language.

Additionally, several Web sites are devoted to the training and development of Java programmers. You should definitely start with this one:

http://www.javasoft.com/

This site is the home page of JavaSoft, which is Sun's division that pertains exclusively to Java. From there, you can browse to links of courses, additional books, and other resources (such as Usenet newsgroups and mailing lists) where you can ask questions and share information with others in the Java programming field. You can also keep track of some promising graphical environments that let you build Java applets by pointing and clicking on menus, imported graphics, and other resources.

What Puts the Shock in Shockwave?

Macromedia's Director multimedia authoring software is easily the most popular, powerful, and widespread authoring tool for creating multimedia presentations, CD-ROMs, and interactive movies. When Director 4.0 was released in 1994, it introduced an unprecedented level of cross-platform compatibility between Windows and Macintosh multimedia titles. You can take a Director movie from a Macintosh, load it into a Windows PC, and edit, compile, and play it on the Microsoft platform. To do this effectively, you need to make very few compromises (mainly in the way that Windows handles color maps, compared to the Mac), but by and large which platform you develop your Director pieces on is completely immaterial.

This made Director a natural for porting to the Web. The Shockwave technology is a joint project between Macromedia and Netscape that permits Director users to put their content up on the Internet and provide playable, CD-ROM quality games and other multimedia directly from a Web page. The way this works is that Netscape provided a plug-in to their Navigator product that permits Shockwave pieces to be played within the browser. Director's compatible source files adapted easily to this scheme, because it meant there was already a well-developed standard for Macintosh and PC users alike; this simplified the process of developing the plug-in. As this book was being prepared for final publication, more than a million Shockwave plug-ins had been downloaded.

One additional piece to the Shockwave puzzle is the Afterburner. This program compresses Director source movies, sometimes by a significant amount. Once compressed, these movies take less time to load over the Web, contributing to the sense of speed and performance that a well-designed Shockwave movie can provide.

To set up your workstation, your site, and your Web page to use Shockwave, you'll need to do a few things; we'll cover all these steps later in this chapter. One worthwhile point is that all of this is free, except for actually purchasing Director; you can download the Shockwave plug-in for Netscape, and also the Afterburner program for both Macintosh and PC, without cost.

As a final note, you may wonder whether I'm talking about Director or Shockwave from time to time. It's simple: Director is the authoring system in which you create multimedia titles, interactive movies, and such; Shockwave is the name of the technology that lets people play these movies after they're running on the Web. You author in Director; you then convert to Shockwave. But it all looks, plays, and works the same no matter what you call it.

What Can You Control with Shockwave?

At one level, Director makes interactivity very simple: if you can see it, you can make it mouse-sensitive—and you can also animate it. This means that Shockwave is ideal for what I like to call dynamic user interfaces. (One specific kind of dynamic user interface is better known under the term "computer game.") In addition to games—or simply providing a sense of play and fun to even the most mundane, professional, or scholarly topic in a corporate or educational Web page—dynamic user interfaces let the developer measure a user's reaction time as a diagnostic for providing additional on-line help, they let you incorporate time-based media such as animation or narration into the user interface, and they let the user interface change as necessary for the user's needs, skill level, or intended application.

Macromedia uses a scripting language called Lingo to control interactivity within a Director title. When you port your Director titles to Shockwave, Lingo for the Web includes scripting commands that let you open other Web pages from within a Director document. You can also run Common Gateway Interchange (CGI) scripts from inside a Director movie as a way of interfacing with applications at your Web site such as database management systems, and you can also link to another Director movie from the same spot.

As with Java, teaching you how to create your own Shockwave pieces is beyond the scope of this book, and also as with Java, several resources are available for learning how to create compelling, exciting movies using Director. One of them is my own book, *Macromedia*

Director: Your Personal Consultant (Ziff-Davis, 1995); in addition, the Macromedia home page provides great information about how to turn a Director title into a Shockwave application. For that, point your browser at:

http://www.macromedia.com/

And, as with Java, this chapter will give you a sense of what's possible in using Director as a tool for animation and interactivity, without really training you in how to develop a Director movie from scratch. However, if your company has Director products (such as CD-ROM titles or corporate multimedia training materials) already, or if you are working with a multimedia production company to create them, this chapter will give you everything you need to put these dynamic, interactive pieces up on your Web site.

The Big Gotchas: Where This Stuff Doesn't Work

So if Shockwave and Java are as cool as they are, how come everybody isn't using them? Well, there are a couple of limitations.

To begin with, at the time that I wrote this book, only Netscape supported Shockwave, and that only for the Macintosh and Windows (16- and 32-bit) browsers. If you're using Spyglass Mosaic, or if you're running on a Unix box, you may have to wait a while to be able to see my friendly alien, the vicious life-or-death struggle between Tobiko and Aji, or the peaceful journey of the Bayou Browser as it steams down Ol' Muddy.

Likewise, if you are relying on Netscape 2.0 for the Macintosh, you won't be able to see the Java applets running. In version 3.0 of Netscape (which has just left beta as I completed this book), Java has been included in all Netscape platforms. If you or your organization has chosen to stay with Netscape 2.0 on Macintoshes, you'll at least have the consolation of knowing that Shockwave isn't really well integrated yet in Netscape 3.0 on PCI-bus

Power Macs. In short, the Web itself is more dynamic than any content you could possibly create for it, so go with the flow and be on the lookout for "not yet implemented" in a product description.

And none of this addresses people running OS/2 Web browsers or many Unix workstations (aside from Sun and Silicon Graphics, which collectively have the most powerful Web packages in the business). If there's a Netscape browser for your platform, you can probably see much of this, but if you're using some Web-browsing package other than Netscape or Microsoft Internet Explorer, you may not be able to view the animations that this chapter teaches you how to make.

That being said, this chapter assumes that you are using either a Macintosh or a Windows PC as your authoring tool—except for the animated GIF section, which works on pretty much any graphics-capable personal computer or workstation. Some of the examples here are from one system or another; when the differences matter, I point them out. And with that preamble, let's dive into the various ways of playing—and interacting with—animated movies over the Web.

But First, the Old-Fashioned Way

Before diving into Director or Java as animation tools, it's worth taking a look at a simpler way of creating moving pictures on your Web site: animated GIFs. The GIF89a standard permits the encapsulation of multiple images in a single file, and Netscape (among other Web browsers) can display these in sequence.

Animated GIFs rely on the traditional method of animation: drawing multiple versions of a scene, with the characters or objects in a slightly different position in each successive frame. When displayed rapidly, the frames give the illusion of motion.

Animated GIFs are a simple but effective way to create small animations that you can incorporate easily in a Web page. To create them, you'll need an image editor capable of storing multiple images in a single file; these are available over the Net, many as freeware applications. In this chapter, we'll go over a tutorial for creating animated GIFs using GifBuilder, a simple and effective freeware application created by Yves Piguet of Lausanne, Switzerland. This specific application runs on the Macintosh, but the Web site for this book includes references to GIF animation packages for Windows and Unix as well.

The key to GIF animation is that speed—and hence the fluidity of apparent motion—is dependent largely on the size of the images. This means that you can animate a whole screen somewhat slowly, but you can animate a thumbnail-sized illustration in such a manner that it blazes along. And with careful design, you can actually create GIF animations that blend into your Web page's background color to give the illusion of depth to a scene— such as flickering candles or torches on a black background to give the appearance of an underground grotto. For now, let's go over the basics of animation— whether you're using Director, Java, animated GIFs, or ink and paint.

Animating 2D Images

The art of animation involves making subtle changes to images in such a way that, when the images are flashed before our eyes in rapid succession, they give the appearance of movement. The changes can be simple— one of the simplest is merely making an object slide across a scene. The changes can be more complex—the artist may want to manipulate perspective, viewing angle, light, and shadow in the scene being created. These changes can be made by talented human beings. The animators who designed, drew, inked, and painted the opening scene of *Pinocchio* (considered by many to be the finest piece of animation yet recorded)—in which Jiminy Cricket hops down the street toward Gepetto's shop and the perspective through the open window changes as Jiminy moves up, down, and closer to the shop—developed this landmark of animation history without the use of computers, scanners, digitizers, or even hand-held calculators. They did it with pure, raw talent and years of hard work.

Fortunately computers offer the rest of us a wealth of shortcuts in making animation, even if we may never attempt something as vast as a Disney feature. Most important, computers make it incredibly easy to copy images, pixel by pixel, from one frame to the next. We can then modify these images, changing their shape or color or location in the scene, to suit the needs of the animation. We can, perhaps most importantly, undo the operation we just performed with a single mouse click, which eliminates potentially hours of redrawing to correct for a simple mistake. And best of all, we can view our animations immediately and decide immediately whether they work or what needs to be changed. With computers, the playback of animation can become part of the drawing process—there's no tedious waiting for films to be developed, prints to be made, and rushes to be screened in a darkened mini-theater. The power to be Walt Disney, Cecil B. De Mille, and Orson Welles all rolled into one is within the grasp of anyone with access to a medium-powered computer, a few good books, and a dream.

So let's start with a short tutorial on the basics of animation. You can follow along with this one in several ways, on any platform that lets you draw bitmapped images. The tutorial is in two parts:

1. Creating the frames, using a drawing program of choice

2. Creating the movie, using a GIF animation package such as GifBuilder

The instructions in each part will be kept general enough that you can use them on a Mac, PC, or Unix workstation as long as you have access to a simple bitmap drawing program (such as Paintbrush on the PC, MacDraw on the Macintosh, or an equivalent on a Unix workstation). If you prefer, you can start with the examples stored in the Web site:

http://www.living-history.org/dynaweb/chap4/

This page contains pointers to all the images used in the creation of the animated GIF that this tutorial describes.

Tutorial: Animating GIF Images

Creating animations with multilayer GIF images is a three-part process:

1. Design the animation and determine its place in the page.

2. Create the individual frames in the animation.

3. Import the individual frames into your GIF animation program and create the single file containing the animation you have created.

To include an animated GIF image in a Web page, use the IMG SRC= tag just as for a still image. At the end of this tutorial, I have included the source HTML for the following Web page:

http://www.living-history.org/dynaweb/flicker.html

Part 1: Designing the Animation

Designing an animation means analyzing the moving drawing into its component parts, determining which parts need to be redrawn in every frame and which can remain constant, and many other issues. Here is a set of questions you can ask yourself as you begin designing a piece of animation:

1. *What is your visual topic sentence?* That is, what is the most important visual element of the scene? Just as a topic sentence in a paragraph introduces the main theme or idea of that paragraph, the visual topic sentence in a piece of animation or video is the backbone on which the rest of that scene's action and imagery is supported. And just like a topic sentence, a visual topic sentence has a subject—the character you are animating—and a verb—the action or motion you are representing.

2. *What is the subject of your visual topic sentence?* Is it an animated character (a mouse, a rabbit, a lamp, etc.)? Is it a corporate logo? Is it—as in the example I use here—a candle?

3. *What is the verb of your visual topic sentence?* Does the character get in a fight with a peg-legged villain? Does the corporate logo fly onto the screen and spin around? Does the candle's flame flicker gently?

4. *What is the nature and purpose of this animated scene?* Is it part of a storyline—either the plot in a piece of fiction or a subject in a corporate marketing or training piece? Is it meant to draw attention to something (like the words "NEW AND IMPROVED!" with a glowing halo around them)? Is it adding atmosphere to a scene (like the flickering candle I've done here as part of an Edgar Allan Poe page)? Is it just to make something look really cool?

5. *How long does or can this action go on?* Do you want it to loop and continue playing as long as the page is displayed? For my flickering candle flame, the answer was yes; for the fly-on of a corporate logo, the answer is probably no (because such a motion would both be too distracting and serve no purpose after the initial introduction—in short, it would look silly). On the other hand, having that logo revolve in place or gleam gently while the page is on view is probably a good way to keep some motion and visual interest in the scene.

For this example, I knew the following:

1. My visual topic sentence was "A candle flickered slowly in a dark room." Apart from setting the stage for a gloriously Gothic scene of suspense and terror, this introduces the subject (a candle), the verb (flickered), and also gives us some information about the setting (we want it to be on a black background).

2. Because I wanted the action to go on indefinitely, I could use the same illustration for the candle and simply make the flame dance from side to side. (If I were really being detailed, I would animate drips of wax running down the side of the candle, but we'll let that go for now.)

3. There were two ways to make the background black. One way was to fill the screen with black and then draw over it with the colors of my candle, the wick, and the flame. The other was to make the background transparent and then set the background of the page to black in HTML. I chose the latter for several reasons, one of them simply being to demonstrate how this works to my readers. Remember also that transparent backgrounds let any background patterns in your Web page show through; you can use this to make an object look as though it's flying, rolling, or crawling across your Web page.

Part 2: Creating the Frames

This section is pure, classic animation—you draw each frame one after the other, saving each one in a different file, just the way a cartoonist would save each cel out of an animated short before they were copied onto film for the finished product. But because you're using a computer, you have a few advantages that the cel animator doesn't:

- You can use your program's Save As menu option to make an exact copy of frame 1, then modify the drawing in it when you create frame 2. This means you don't have to redraw the parts of the scene or the character that are the same in both frames.

- You can easily undo a change you don't like by whatever your drawing program's Undo command uses — probably Control-Z, Command-Z, or pull down the File menu and select Undo.

  As a tip for best use of Undo, remember to let go of the mouse button often — the Undo command erases everything you did back to the last time you pressed the mouse button. Many times I have been frustrated when drawing: my image looks really great, I keep drawing away at it, and then after a 20-second one-line drawing operation I make a mistake or the mouse ball sticks or something else goes wrong and I have to throw away the whole thing. Now I let go of the mouse button the instant I have something I don't want to lose. (This is the counterpart of my advice to use the Save command often so that, in the worst case, you can get back to a previous version of the file if you make mistakes that you can't undo easily.)

- You can easily cut, copy, and paste pieces of an image into new orders, sequences, or locations. Thus, if you are moving an object across the screen, you can draw around it (in most draw programs, select the lasso button for this), then either drag it or cut it and repaste it into the desired spot.

- Another tip with the lasso key: Most graphics programs (I know this works in Photoshop and Director) let you "pin" down segments of the area you select with the lasso by holding down the Alt key (on PCs) or the Command key (on Macintoshes), then clicking at each place you want to become part of the outline you're selecting with the lasso.

- You can fill entire regions with a single mouse click (and the paint bucket icon). This makes it simple and very, very quick to fill in the bare patches in an animated character.

- You can copy the output of another program into your frames. For example, if you are using a 3D drawing tool to create the once-ubiquitous flying chrome logo for your corporate sponsor, you can position the logo at its desired angle, set up the lights just so, and then take a screen snapshot. You can then import that screen snapshot into your paint/draw package, edit out just the logo portion, and create the animated GIF as included in the rest of this chapter.

By the way, remember also that Photoshop may let you antialias (that is, blend smoothly) the edges of the region you select with the lasso. In smaller GIF animations or in Director cast members, this is almost certainly not what you want. (Why not? Because Photoshop antialiases by blending with the background of the picture you are clipping it from. When you put this cutout into a new part of the background, or an altogether new image, the blended colors will look obviously wrong at the edges. In general, I've found that using the lasso in Director gives better results, when the goal is a Shockwave piece, than using Photoshop. But that's getting ahead of myself.)

In short, creating animation directly on the computer has many advantages. On the other hand, if you are more comfortable with the feel of the media under direct fingertip control, or if you're going for a particular look (pencil on coarse drawing paper, for example, or charcoal), you can always draw your frames on paper or paint them on canvas, then scan them into the computer and animate just the scanned images. For certain effects, this may in fact be the method that works best for you. If so, you will be creating the frames on the scanner, retouching them in something like Photoshop, and then saving them as GIF images in preparation for part 3.

For the candle animation used in this tutorial, I created five frames of a candle flame. In each frame, I left the candle and the candle holder as in the original image, then erased the flame and redrew it.

The drawing program I used has a "spray-can" option (on some it's an airbrush); I used this option to get see-through flames that would convey the kind of image I wanted. One of the frames is shown here:

By erasing the flames and redrawing them with a different set of colors, I ensured that the flames would never be too similar in shape, color, or density — exactly the effect I wanted to achieve in this piece.

Now it was time to put them together into my short movie.

Part 3: Creating the Movie

After you have drawn the individual frames, it's time to open your GIF animation package and begin assembling the frames into a movie. At this point, I was glad of two practices I had adopted earlier in the process:

- I put all my frames into the same directory, making it much simpler to find and open them.

- I named my frames in sequence, from candle02.pic through candle06.pic, making it easy to tell which one came when in the movie's order. (There is no candle01.pic. Don't worry about it.)

For this application, I used two pieces of software that run on the Macintosh:

- Symantec GreatWorks, a word-processing/ spreadsheet/database/drawing package I bought when I bought my Mac Classic in 1992. This $99 program handles an amazing amount of work, from writing and setting the type for my first book to drawing the frames for a GIF animation.

- GifBuilder 0.3.2, a freeware package created by Yves Piguet of Switzerland. This program allows you to create multiframe GIFs. You can find out where to download this program on the Web site associated with this book.

On the PC, you can use a drawing program such as Paintbrush to create BMP files that you can then copy into the GIF animation package. Again, the Web site associated with this book has details on where to download PC-based GIF animation packages.

GifBuilder takes individual frames that you have saved as GIF, TIFF, or PICT files. I chose to save my drawings as PICTs, with extensions of .pic. GifBuilder works enough like all other GIF animation packages that it's worth looking at here no matter what keystrokes you'll use on the GIF animation package you eventually select.

1. Open GifBuilder.

    This gives you a blank frame list and a window, labeled Untitled, that shows the individual frames of your animation as you add them:

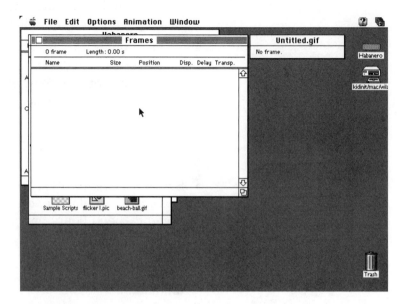

2. Start adding frames. In GifBuilder, you can do this either by pulling down the File menu and selecting Add Frame, or you can type Command-K from the keyboard.

   This brings up the Add Frame dialog, from which you can select the file to add at this point in the sequence of frames you are creating:

3. When you have added all the files you want to use in the sequence you want to create, pull down the File menu and select Save.

   This brings up the Save dialog:

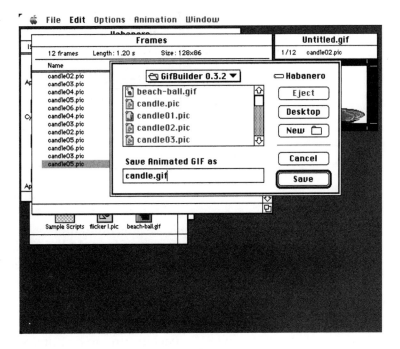

4. Preview the animation by pulling down the Animation menu and selecting Start.

   This lets you check the motion, sequence, smoothness, and appearance of your GIF animation.

Depending on the effect you want to create, you may want to explore the following options in GifBuilder (or their equivalents in whatever GIF animation package you choose):

- Loop: This menu selection brings up the following dialog:

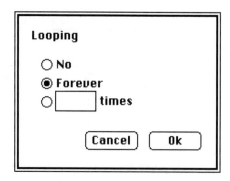

For my animation, I wanted the candle to flicker as long as the image was on the screen. If I had a one-time animation such as a fly-on or a single sequence, I would have selected No. Additionally, GifBuilder lets you select a specified number of times to repeat before shutting off.

•   Background: For this animation, I wanted the background to be transparent. I'd saved the individual frames with white backgrounds because GifBuilder lets you specify white as one of the options to make transparent. Note that you'll need to make sure that any white areas in your image are colored very pale gray or yellow instead of pure white if you choose to make white transparent.

One advantage to transparent backgrounds (rather than choosing a solid colored background) is that if you later choose to use a background image in your HTML file, it will show through your GIF animation's transparent areas. If you set the background of your image to a single, predetermined solid color, it'll be that color no matter what background you select in your HTML file.

Finally, I incorporated the animation into an HTML document, with the usual IMG SRC= statement:

```
<html>

<head>

<title>

Flickering Flames

</title>

</head>

<body bgcolor="#000000" text="ff0000">

<h1>The Cask of Amontillado</h1>

<h2>by Edgar Allan Poe</h2>

<img src="candle2.gif">
```

The thousand injuries of Fortunato I bore as best I could, but when he ventured upon insult, I vowed revenge. . .

```
<p>

</body>

</html>
```

The key to this image's appearance is in the <BODY. . .> line. Because I set the BGCOLOR to 000000 (the hexadecimal value indicating black), this color shows through the transparent areas of my candle-flame animation. Had I set the background of my candle to black, it would look the same in this case, but not if I changed the background of my HTML file. (In later examples, you'll see how to do just this.)

That file, by the way, is available at the following URL:

http://www.living-history.org/dynaweb/chap4/flicker.html

Shockwave: Interactivity for Artists

When I was developing my book on Director, I noticed that many people had serious apprehensions about using Director as an authoring tool. It was "too complicated" for some. It had "too steep a learning curve" for others. For a third group, it was "only for programmers."

So I taught my six-year-old daughter how to create animated cartoons with Director. I sat back with my hands in my pockets, guided her through the menus, and she created the piece—drew it, determined the motion, and animated it—that I've incorporated on the Web site under the following URL:

http://www.living-history.org/dynaweb/chap4/tk_tobi.html

What I suggest is that many people have a particular paradigm with which they view Director—and now, by extension, Shockwave. Under this paradigm, Director—which is a powerful and feature-rich program—is complicated, has a steep learning curve, and is only for programmers.

I'd like to propose an alternate paradigm: that Director is nothing but MacDraw on wheels. If you were working in the computer business when the Macintosh first came out, you probably had a chance to see MacDraw, the simple, bitmap drawing program that let people create surprisingly good illustrations if they had the time and the talent for them. This, of course, has morphed into powerful applications for professional artists and illustrators such as Adobe Illustrator, Macromedia's own Freehand, and many more, but the consumer illustration market all started with the almost ridiculously simple MacDraw.

Fundamentally Director gives you a multicolored version of MacDraw—with, admittedly, a lot of special effects that determine how it looks—but one with a special difference. That special difference is that it lets you move your drawings around on the screen (hence the "on wheels" part of this new paradigm).

In the GIF animation tutorial, you placed your illustrations at different locations on the drawing area in the file you were planning to draw, then you had to redraw the image content in order to make it look as though the flames were moving. In Director, one of the types of animation you can create lets you draw the content once, and then you can instruct Director to move the drawings as you command. This introduces the three kinds of animation that Director supports:

- Point-to-point animation
- Frame-by-frame animation
- Looped animation

In point-to-point animation, you simply specify a beginning and an ending point for your objects to move between. You determine the time value for this movement by choosing the beginning and ending frames of the motion, based on the frame rate you select for this piece. Then Director does the rest. The motion of the boat from left to right across the screen is done with point-to-point animation.

In frame-by-frame animation, you move or redraw or otherwise modify part of the illustration in each frame. This is essentially the same as for GIF animation, except that the program to draw these illustrations and the program to incorporate them into a presentation is the same program. The bobbing of the boat as it moves across the screen and the splashing of the water are done with frame-by-frame animation.

In looped animation, you create a sequence of several individual drawings, one per frame, that repeats over and over throughout a longer clip — for example, the flapping of butterfly wings as the butterfly circles the screen. You create a single element of your Director piece (called a "cast member") that contains all these individual frames. Then you place that into your Director movie, and Director automatically fills out the time that you select with as many repetitions of that loop as are required.

Some Director Basics

Although this book can't do much more than introduce you to the terminology of Director, we need to cover a few phrases and concepts before beginning to use it in the animation tutorial. The following section gets you started understanding Director's fundamental metaphor for creating animated multimedia pieces.

All the Screen's a Stage

Director uses a theatrical metaphor for the components of the multimedia movies you create with it. This begins by using the word "movie" to describe the file that you create with Director. The part of the screen that contains the animation is called the stage. You can have a stage that is as large as the screen of the computer you're using to author your document, or you can scale it down to various sizes. To keep images small and easily downloaded, I've selected half-NTSC—320 by 240—as the stage size for this Director piece.

On a real stage, what moves around and chews up the scenery? The cast members, of course. But in Director, everything that shows up on stage is a cast member — including the scenery, the background, any QuickTime movie clips that you have digitized from video, and even the instructions on what to do when someone clicks on one of the visible cast members.

To determine when and where the cast members move about on the stage, Director has a score. The score keeps track of both time and depth. To determine time, the score shows individual frames, as in frames of animation or of a motion picture. The frames to the right of the screen come after those to the left. You can determine the frame rate individually for each frame, if necessary, to control special effects. Each column in the Director score represents a single frame of the final movie. To position your cast members in the score, simply drag them from their location in the Cast window into the desired frame in the Director Score window. Then you can drag them around on the Stage to position them where they need to be in that particular frame.

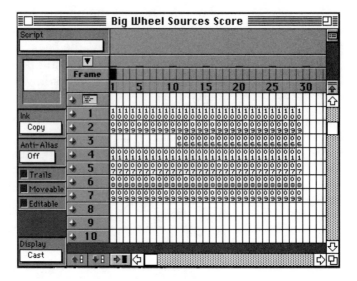

Additionally the score determines whether a cast member is closer to or farther from the audience. Each of the rows across the score is called a channel; cast members in channels closer to the top of the screen appear behind cast members in channels closer to the bottom of the screen. A Director movie has 48 channels, meaning that you can have that many cast members on stage at any time.

You can freely move a cast member from one channel to another in any frame. This, for example, would let two characters chase each other around a bush, or let a satellite orbit a planet in outer space.

And All the Seas Are Ink

The next important metaphor for Director is the concept of "ink styles." Neither inks nor styles, ink styles define how the screen looks when you animate your Director movie—when the cast members actually appear on the stage. Some ink styles are useful mainly for special effects; the ones you'll probably use most often are:

- Copy—this draws the Cast member exactly as it appears, including the "slug" of background color that appears behind the Cast member. This means that if your Cast member is circular (as is the paddle-wheel in the next tutorial), it appears as a circle on a white square when it shows up on the screen. This is probably not what you want, though it is useful for keeping contrasting background for text fly-ons and buttons. The following diagram demonstrates how these ink styles affect illustrations:

**Three primary ink styles—
examples using trapped text**

Copy ink style

Matte ink style

Background Transparent ink style

- Matte—this draws the Cast member without the white slug in the background, following instead the outline of the shape. Any white areas inside the outermost perimeter of the Cast member, however, are kept opaque.

- Background transparent—this draws the Cast member without either the white slug or any trapped white areas.

Of Sprites and Scripts

The last two Director concepts are sprites and scripts. Sprites are the visual representations of Cast members. That is, while you drag a Cast member into the Score window, selecting a given frame and channel as described earlier, it is the Sprite that actually is displayed on the Stage when you animate your Director movie. The Cast member itself is like the template; the Sprite is what actually moves, is acted on, and is displayed visually.

This is how the ink styles work: you specify an ink style in the Score window, associated with a particular sprite. This means that you can use a single cast member to display a Sprite using Matte ink, and then later you can use the same Cast member to display a Sprite using Background Transparent ink.

The other place in which the distinction between Sprites and Cast members is important is when you begin writing scripts. A script, in Director, is not the dialog spoken by the characters: it's the instructions on what a cast member or a sprite is to do under certain circumstances — typically when someone clicks on them with the mouse.

The most common Director script you'll use looks something like this:

```
on mouseUp

    go to frame I

end
```

This tells the Director movie that when it detects that the mouse button is lifted (that is, when someone completes a mouse click), the movie is to start playing at frame 1. This script, then, might be one you associate with a button used to rewind the movie, or to start from the beginning.

Director scripts are written in a scripting language called Lingo. I have been known to say (somewhat tongue in cheek) that scripting languages are to programming languages what "downsizing" is to "layoffs" — in both instances, something that the people in charge think will sound less negative than the more blunt alternative, but equally daunting to someone who is not expecting it.

That being said, the Lingo scripting language is pretty simple. As with HTML, you only really need to know about a half dozen Lingo commands to manage a high degree of interactivity. In fact, probably 90% of a typical interactive movie's point-and-click activity can be handled with a script like the common one just shown. The only real difference is likely to be the frame to which you tell the movie to jump when the script executes.

Lingo and scripting are demonstrated in somewhat more detail later in this chapter. Note, however, that because there are just over 100 Lingo statements, keywords, and commands, the examples given in this chapter are extremely limited and do not represent a significant fraction of what Lingo makes possible. However, they are all you need to know to make interactive movies, on or off the Web.

The generic form of a script is as follows:

on <some event>

  <do something>

end

The values most commonly used for <some event> (and therefore called event handlers) are:

- mouseUp — execute this script when the mouse button is lifted, signifying the completion of a click.

- mouseDown—execute this script when the mouse button is first pressed. For example, this event handler could be used to pop up a menu of selections, just the way a menu pops up when you press the mouse button on the menu bar of a Macintosh or Windows system.

- enterFrame—execute this script as soon as the movie starts playing the current frame. The typical use for this event handler is to perform some scripting operation (such as clearing or initializing a variable) that needs to be performed before a movie (or a portion of a movie) can begin playing.

- exitFrame—execute this script as soon as the movie leaves the current frame. The typical use for this event handler is to pause a movie's action, for example, to keep displaying a menu until the user clicks on one or another of the options.

The most commonly used values for <do something>, at least for the degree of interactivity we'll be discussing here, are:

- go to frame ###—jump to the named frame and begin playing the movie at that point. Director lets you use names as well as numbers for the frames in a movie; this is highly recommended, as you can add frames inside a movie at any point (much the way you can splice film into a motion picture when editing). If you add or remove frames, the frame numbers after that point change, and a command to go to a given frame causes a jump to the wrong part of the movie.

- **pause** — suspend the movie operation until another event handler detects something. This is most typically used with the event handler on exitFrame, as a way of keeping the movie on a given frame (such as a menu or other choice) until the user selects something.

- **go to the frame** — keep executing *this* frame. This has a similar effect to "pause," unless you have some calculation or some other scripted operation that this frame performs. In that case, a script reading **on exitFrame pause** executes its script once, then holds at the end of the frame; a script reading **on exitFrame go to the frame** executes its script every time the frame is executed.

- **play frame ###** — begin executing the movie at the frame indicated (by name or number), but remember what frame you jumped from and return to the frame immediately following it when play is completed. This works in conjunction with the next value, **play done**.

- **play done** — terminate a jump previously set up with a **play frame ###** script, and return to the first frame after the frame containing the **play frame ###** script.

For example, consider the following two scripts:

Script connected to a button in Frame 100:

```
on mouseUp
    play frame 200
end
```

Script connected directly to Frame 200:

```
on exitFrame
    play done
end
```

When you click the button in frame 100, the movie immediately jumps to frame 200, but it remembers where it came from—in this case, frame 100. The movie plays frame 200, and when it exits the frame, it executes the **play done** script and returns to frame 101—the first frame after the **play frame** script.

This is very useful for branching to and from menus, such as you might do for a pop-up. We'll go over the specific commands you can use to go to other URLs and other Web resources a little later in this chapter. Right now, however, it's worth taking a look at how Director lets you select an on-screen object: through one of three kinds of scripts.

Director's Script Types

For the purposes of this introduction, consider the following three objects with which you can associate a Director script:

- A frame of the Director movie
- A Cast member
- A sprite

Frame scripts are useful for pausing the movie at a certain point—for example, when you want to present a menu of choices for the user to select from. To create a frame script, use the Script channel from the Score window—that's the channel immediately above channel 1.

A typical frame script to pause your movie while the user reads a menu (or reads instructions before continuing, or stops for any other reason) looks like this:

```
on exitFrame
    pause
end
```

This is about as simple as a script can get: when the movie exits this frame—that is, when it completes all the actions defined in this frame and is ready to move on to the next one—it pauses. A pause in Director has no predetermined limit. Unless you do something, the Director movie that executes this script pauses until the machine shuts down.

A cast member script is associated with the cast member every time it is displayed in your movie—with certain exceptions, which we'll get to next. To create a cast member script, click on the Script button from the Paint window. Although our typical frame script tells the movie to do nothing until further notice, a typical Cast member script *is* the further notice. For instance, the following script might be associated with the Quit button—which could either be the word "Quit" in a fancy font or might be the ubiquitous red octagon meaning "STOP" in every country that uses traffic signs:

```
on mouseUp
    quit
end
```

This script waits for the event mouseUp —meaning that the user has clicked on the mouse inside the boundaries of the Cast member for which this script is in effect. If the mouse goes up anywhere else on the screen, this script does not execute; the mouse has to be inside this cast member for this script to run.

Finally, there's a sprite script. A sprite script works much like a cast member script, but with two differences:

- You create a sprite script by clicking on the frame and channel that has a particular cast member loaded; then you click on the Script window (in the upper left corner of the Score window) and select New from the pull-down menu that appears.

- More important, a sprite script is associated only with the sprite in that frame—not with any other sprite in any other frame, even if you use the same cast member somewhere else in your movie.

It's this last point that makes sprite scripts so powerful. You can change the sprite script on a frame-by-frame basis so that different actions occur at different times in your movie. For example, in a twitch game, you might give more points for clicking on something as soon as it appears, and fewer points when it's been on the screen for longer. This ability lets you create Director movies with a high degree of interactivity, in which literally everything that you can see on the screen can be interactive.

For the moment, let's go on with Director as an animation tool. You can create a pretty dynamic Web page with straight, linear Director movies and HTML to control the flow and direction of play. But if you can manage HTML, you can manage Lingo—it's not that much more complex.

Tutorial: Big Wheel Keep on Turnin'

In this tutorial, you'll see how to use Director to create an animation of an old-time stern-wheeler riverboat. I picked this image because it introduces you to the two most fundamental concepts in animation: motion in a scene and motion in place. In addition, this subject makes it easy to copy whole images within a motion loop, where an action is repeated many times—a bird's wings flapping, for instance, or in this case a paddle-wheel turning over and over as the riverboat heads across the screen.

For this simple animation, I wanted to use these distinct pieces of the main character:

- The riverboat itself, or specifically its hull and superstructure for boat enthusiasts

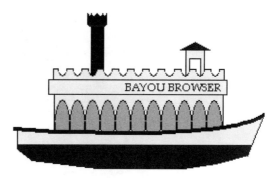

- The paddle-wheel, drawn as four separate components of a movie

- The water line, several opaque wavy lines that could be moved and modified individually to simulate the motion of the river's surface

- A background that would show through the spokes of the paddle-wheel

First, let's make a film loop of the paddle-wheel rotating:

1. Drag the first cast member of the paddle-wheel animation into any empty frame of the Score window.

2. Drag the second cast member of the paddle-wheel animation into the next frame after the one selected in step 1.

3. Drag the third cast member of the paddle-wheel animation into the next frame after the one selected in step 2.

4. Drag the fourth cast member of the paddle-wheel animation into the next frame after the one selected in step 3.

   If you had more than four frames worth of animation, you would simply continue this until you had all the cast members loaded into consecutive frames this way. The longest movie I've ever made this way was 15 frames, but I don't believe there is a practical upper limit.

5. Select all four frames from within the Score window, then pull down the Ink Styles menu (at the left of the Score window) and select Bkgnd Transparent.

6. Test your movie by rewinding the movie, clearing the Stage, and playing the sequence. To do this, type the commands Control-1, Control-R, Control-P (or on the Macintosh Command-1, Command-R, Command-P, where the Command key is the one with the apple shape on it).

   If you are satisfied with your movie, continue with the following step.

7. Select all four frames from within the Score window, then pull down the Edit menu and select Copy Cells.

8. Click on an open Cast member, pull down the Edit menu, and select Paste Cells.

   Director presents the Name Cast Member dialog:

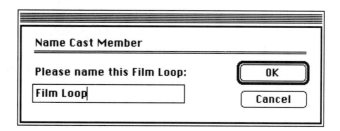

9. Type a name for the film loop, then click OK.

You're now ready to move this animation across the screen. To do this:

1. Drag the film loop cast member into the first frame of your movie—drag it directly into the frame in the Score window.

2. Clear the stage by typing Control-1 (on the Macintosh, Command-1).

The first frame of the film loop cast member is displayed in the middle of the screen.

3. Drag the film loop cast member to the leftmost edge of the stage, so that it is not visible at all. When it is positioned as you want it, type Control-1 (Command-1 on the Macintosh) to redisplay the Score window.

4. Assuming that the frame rate is set to 30 frames per second (the default), set up a 2-second animation by dragging the film loop cast member into frame 60.

5. Type Control-1 (Command-1 on the Macintosh) to clear the stage, then drag the paddle-wheel to the rightmost edge of the stage, so that it is not visible at all. Then type Control-1 (Command-1 on the Macintosh) to redisplay the Score window.

6. Click on the movie in frame 60, then scroll back to frame 1 and shift-click the movie in frame 1 (that is, hold down the shift key and click with the mouse).

7. Type Control-B (or Command-B on the Macintosh).

    Director fills in the intermediate frames between frame 1 and frame 60.

8. Play your movie: type Control-1, Control-R, Control-P (or Command-1, Command-R, Command-P on the Macintosh).

    You should see the paddle-wheel rotating as it moves from left to right.

To move the riverboat as well, follow the same procedure but make the riverboat's alignment the same, with respect to the center of the paddle-wheel, in frames 1 and 60. Then perform steps 6 and 7 of the preceding sequence to generate the intermediate frames for the riverboat as well. Now when you play your movie, you will see the riverboat moving from left to right, and the paddle-wheel turning as it moves from left to right.

Some things to look out for:

1. Is the paddle-wheel in front of the boat or behind it? If you've made your riverboat a stern-wheeler, the paddle-wheel should be in a channel closer to the top of the screen than the boat's channel. If it's a side-wheeler, the paddle-wheel's channel should be closer to the bottom of the screen so that it's visible in front of the hull.

2. Do the hull and the paddle-wheel retain their alignment all the way through the movie? If not, you can select one frame at a time, choosing either the paddle-wheel or the hull, and "tweak" that sprite's location on the stage with the arrow keys. Each time you press on an arrow key, the sprite you selected moves one pixel in the direction of the arrow. This is a great way to fine-tune your animation.

If you do nothing but animation like this, you can develop exciting, dynamic multimedia content for your Web page. There's a lot more—but what's particularly exciting about Shockwave is that once I ran my own riverboat movie through Macromedia's compression program, the entire animation resulted in a file of only 22 kilobytes. And what makes that so exciting is that the candle animation that I created for my animated GIFs example is 17 kilobytes—and there's no opportunity to put additional buttons within the candle animation. This means that load time is short and animation/interactivity is fast—just the combination Web surfers and Webmasters alike have been looking for.

What's involved in converting your Director movie to a Shockwave movie? Only about four mouse clicks and a call to your system administrator (or a little file editing if you're comfortable working in Unix). In the next tutorial, we'll see exactly what's involved in converting Director movies so they'll run from your Web page.

Tutorial: Adding a Shockwave Title to Your Web Page

To use a Shockwave title in your Web page, you need to take the following steps (detailed instructions for each activity come next):

1. Set up the correct MIME application types on your Web server's home page directory. (Must be done once per site.)

2. Run your Director movie through Macromedia's Afterburner program to compress it for faster loading. (Must be done once per movie.)

3. Copy the compressed Director movie to your Web site. (Must be done once per movie.)

4. Embed the URL for your compressed Director movie into the appropriate Web page using the correct HTML tag and format. (Must be done once per HTML page using this movie.)

5. Download the Netscape Shockwave plug-in for your Web browser so that you can view your Shockwave movie on your Web page. (Must be done for every browser that wants to view the Shockwave movie.)

In order, then, here are the detailed instructions for each step of setting up your site and your Web page for Shockwave.

Set Up the MIME Application Types

MIME is a multimedia encoding technique supported across multiple platforms as a way of distributing media types. Your Web server needs to have an entry in your top-level directory indicating that your Web server supports all three primary Director file types—.DIR (plain Director files), .DCR (compressed Director files), and .DXR (locked Director files).

To do this on a Unix system, you need to create a file called .hdefaults, with the following three lines in it:

```
x-application/dcr
x-application/dxr
x-application/dir
```

On other Web servers, you need to locate the appropriate MIME encapsulation settings (whether in system files or in a menu) and give permission for these application file types to be served.

Run Your Director Movie Through Afterburner

The Afterburner program is a utility (distributed without cost by Macromedia) with which you can compress Director files, significantly speeding their load time. The Director movie that produces the riverboat animation used in this chapter is 116 kilobytes uncompressed; after running the file through Afterburner, the output is only 22K.

To run a file through Afterburner, follow this procedure:

1. Double-click on the Afterburner icon to open it.

2. From the File menu, select Open. Browse to the Director file you want to compress, and double-click on it.

3. Afterburner displays a Save As dialog box. For safest results across platforms, save your file with a name that uses no more than eight characters, followed by a period and the letters DCR.

4. From the File menu, pull down and select Quit.

Copy the Compressed Movie to Your Web Site

Follow the steps you use to copy files to your Web server. If your Web server is the same machine with which you authored this Director piece and compressed it using Afterburner, simply copy the file into the appropriate directory on your server.

If you use the Macintosh to develop your Shockwave files, you'll have to make sure to use several settings when copying your compressed Director movie. The notes here apply to the popular Fetch FTP program.

1. In your FTP program, make sure you select Binary as the file transfer type. In Fetch, for example, the transfer dialog has three radio buttons: Automatic, Text, and Binary. Select Binary.

2. Click on the Put command to begin the transfer, then navigate to the appropriate directory for the Director movie you converted with Afterburner.

3. Double-click on the Director movie you converted with Afterburner. Fetch displays a dialog box from which you can select the filename at the destination, and also the file transmission format.

4. Make sure the filename ends in .DCR, and select Raw Data as the file transmission format. (The file transmission format list is available under the pull-down box at the bottom of this dialog; it typically reads MacBinary by default for binary files.)

This setting copies the Shockwave file in a format that other computer systems can read and play.

Embed the URL into the Appropriate Web Page

Now that you've got your Shockwave file uploaded to your Web server, and your Web server knows how to deal with the MIME type, all that's left is to embed the Shockwave movie in a Web page. The following line of HTML shows how to do this for our riverboat example:

```
<EMBED SRC="riverboat.dcr"  WIDTH=480 HEIGHT=360
TEXTFOCUS=onStart PALETTE=foreground>
```

In this line, the **EMBED** tag sets up Netscape to embed a media element at this point in the page. (Note that **EMBED** is one of the few HTML tags that does not have a corresponding /EMBED tag to turn it off. Like the <P> tag, the **EMBED** tag is self-contained.) As with images, the SRC="riverboat.dcr" parameter tells Netscape to look in the same directory (because no alternate directory is named) and to load the riverboat.dcr file.

Next come the **WIDTH** and **HEIGHT** parameters, which tell Netscape how much room in each axis to leave for the image when it is loaded.

TEXTFOCUS=onStart tells Netscape that the Macromedia file you want to load will have text focus—that is, will be listening for input—as soon as it starts running. (For other values, see the Macromedia Web page, at http://www.macromedia.com.)

PALETTE=foreground tells Netscape to use the movie's color palette for the movie, not the entire page. Omitting this parameter can cause interesting results if you play a Macintosh-generated Director movie on a machine running Windows. Be sure to save the palette you want to use as an explicit part of your Director file. (Briefly, Director lets you incorporate specific color palettes, which lets a talented art director optimize a series of palettes around a particular object, color scheme, or other motif.)

If Your User Doesn't Have Shockwave

You can use the **NOEMBED** tag to set up an alternative for users who do not have Shockwave loaded on their browser. This way they can at least see some images—and if you use animated GIFs, they may even be able to see some motion as well.

The **NOEMBED** tag works as follows:

<NOEMBED>

<IMG SRC="replacement.gif">

</NOEMBED>

If this Web page is read by a browser that does not support the Shockwave plug-in, that user's screen displays the file replacement.gif (or any other file that you include in the IMG SRC= line).

Of course, if you're really being considerate (and if you really think your Director movies are the coolest things since sliced bytes), you'll include a hypertext link to Macromedia's download site so that your users can easily obtain the Shockwave plug-in.

Download the Netscape Shockwave Plug-in

To download Shockwave, browse to the following URL:

http://www-1.macromedia.com/Tools/Shockwave/Plugin/plugin.cgi

This page lists the currently available servers for downloading the Shockwave plug-in for all supported platforms. Note that Windows 16-bit and Windows 32-bit versions are different; be sure you download the correct plug-in.

After you download the plug-in, it's stored as a self-extracting archive document that automatically uncompresses itself. When the plug-in is uncompressed, you must install it as indicated in the README file that comes with your system's version of Shockwave.

There are no surprises—PC users will find the familiar setup.exe, which installs the appropriate .DLL files and all the other information necessary to run Shockwave, whereas on the Macintosh, the files are automatically copied into the right directory. In either case, you will need to restart your computer after you have installed the Shockwave plug-in.

For More Information

The best source of information on Shockwave at this time is Macromedia's own Web page on the subject:

http://www-1.macromedia.com/Tools/Shockwave/Director/contents.html

Be sure not to break the line in your Web browser—that should all be typed in without a carriage return to get to the right place within Macromedia.

Using Shockwave as a Dynamic User Interface

So far, we've covered how to make dynamic pieces with Director and Shockwave, and how to incorporate them into your Web site. It's one thing to have an animation running at the top of your Web page, drawing people's attention to the main features of your site or your organization's primary function, service, product, or benefits. But you can also make the Shockwave portion of your Web page the user interface to your entire site. Doing this requires that you learn a little of the Lingo scripting language.

As mentioned earlier, Director lets you make any visual element into a button—that is, into an object that you can click on as a way of controlling the flow of the Director movie. This level of interactivity is carried over completely to Shockwave, which means it is available within your Web page.

This provides the developer of multimedia for the Web with two specific benefits. First, it means that if you have time-based media or interactivity-based products or services (and CD-ROM games are the most obvious, but by no means exclusive, example of this), you can now incorporate those directly on your Web page. For example, if your company produces interactive CD-ROMs using Director, you can create "trial versions" of your company's products, previews if you will, that run on the

Web. And just as obviously, one of the buttons that will be included in the preview that is not in the consumer version is a button to order your company's product over the Web.

But more important, especially for companies that deliver their product or service directly over the Web, is the second benefit: you can use Director as the guide to other locations on your Web site by linking the buttons in your Director title to specific URLs. For example, you can have a visual table of contents to your site's services or to other information elsewhere in your hierarchy. This, of course, you can do with an image map.

But there's more. Because Director is a powerful multimedia package on its own, you can add sound, animation, or other effects to the table of contents itself. For example, you can associate narration with each button, allowing your Web users to hear a description of the information available at the destination of each link. You can have a short demonstration or sample image of what's available when they choose a destination from your table of contents. And, of course, you can simply put in wicked awesome cool special effects when people click on something. This *is* supposed to be fun, after all, right?

Reference: Shockwave Commands for the Web

The key to Shockwave as a user interface for your Web page is that it supports running asynchronous activities (meaning they can be started independently without requiring synchronization with some other activity such as the completion of a file transfer) over your Web connection.

Examples of these asynchronous activities are:

- Getting the contents of a URL

- Preloading the contents of a URL into the Netscape disk cache

- Retrieving a separate Shockwave movie from the network

- Retrieving text from the Web (using HTTP) to be interpreted by Lingo as text

Shockwave supports only four such asynchronous operations at one time, however, so be sure to manage your Shockwave titles so that no more than four operations can be selected from any given location.

Interacting with the Web Via Director

In addition to the standalone Lingo used in Director movies, Shockwave supports the following Lingo commands as ways of interacting with items on the Web:

getNetText

This command uses HTTP to fetch text from a file somewhere on the Web. The text will be available to another Lingo function, netTextResult(); you can then use that text to display information within a Director movie, as the contents of a text field.

To use getNetText, follow this format:

on mouseUp

    getNetText "http://www.foo.com/intro.txt"

end

This Lingo script retrieves the contents of the file intro.txt at the URL www.foo.com. This way, you can use Director as a dynamic way of getting at text information, displaying it in an animated or interactive form, or possibly even displaying the results of another activity (such as the output of a database search called from a CGI script).

preloadNetThing

This command preloads some object from the Net—a Director movie, a graphic, a Web page, or anything else that HTTP can transport. This asynchronous command operates while the current movie is playing, making it possible to display an animation or play a sound while your Shockwave movie downloads the next chapter.

To find out whether a **preloadNetThing** operation has finished, use **netDone** (described later).

To use **preloadNetThing**, follow this format:

```
on mouseUp

    preloadNetThing "http://www.foo.com/movie.html"

end
```

This Lingo script preloads the movie embedded in the HTML page found at the URL in quotes. While that movie preloads into Netscape, the current movie — that is, whichever movie was displayed when the user clicked on the object associated with the script shown here — continues playing.

You could also preload a graphic, a video clip, a sound file, or any other object, including an entire Web page with its own graphics, video, and sound. Why this is so cool, however, is that you can leave a sound clip or an animation playing while the loading goes on, giving your audience something to do while they wait (kind of like the music playing while they're on hold, only one hopes not quite so annoying.) Then, the user's copy of Netscape can display the preloaded item immediately, as it's already on your user's local disk cache instead of out on the Web somewhere. This is the way to display video clips, for instance, or to give people something entertaining to do while downloading.

gotoNetMovie

This command retrieves and begins playing a new Director movie from the network. The current movie continues playing until the new movie is available. When the new movie finishes loading, the Shockwave plug-in quits playing the first movie immediately, without warning, and begins playing the new movie inside the same display area as the current movie. (This means it's a good idea to standardize on a screen size for your Shockwave movies; I like 320 x 240, which is large enough to get some good content yet small enough to load quickly and fit inside a typical Web page.)

This command takes a URL as its parameter, but note that it can be either of two kinds of URL:

1. A filename, in which case it takes the entire movie

2. A filename plus an anchor, in which case it begins playing the movie at the frame indicated in the anchor.

Here is an example:

```
on mouseUp
    gotoNetMovie "http://www.foo.com/movie2.dcr"
end
```

This script loads movie2.dcr from www.foo.com, beginning to play it from the first frame as soon as the movie finishes loading. (This is the network equivalent of the traditional Lingo code,
goto frame 1 of movie "movie2".)

Here is another example:

```
on mouseUp
    gotoNetMovie "http://www.foo.com/movie2.dcr#Part2"
end
```

This script loads movie2.dcr from www.foo.com, but begins playing it from the frame named Part2 as soon as it finishes loading. (This is the network equivalent of the traditional Lingo code,
goto frame "Part2" of movie "movie2".)

You can only run one gotoNetMovie statement at a time; if one gotoNetMovie statement is in progress and you issue a second before the first one finishes, the second one cancels the first.

gotoNetPage

This command opens a URL, which can be a shocked Director movie or any other MIME type. On completion, this command opens a new page in the Web browser. As with **getNetText** or **preloadNetThing**, you can check the status of **gotoNetPage** with the netDone() function.

netTextResult()

This function returns the text result of a **getNetText** statement. You cannot call **netTextResult** until the **getNetText** statement completes; to test for this, see the netDone() function.

netDone()

This function returns a value, either true or false, depending on whether **getNetText**, **preloadNetThing**, or **gotoNetPage** are finished. By default — that is, if none of those other Lingo commands has been executed — netDone() returns TRUE. Once you have started a net operation, and while that operation is in progress, netDone() returns FALSE. It returns TRUE again once the operation is complete, or when the operation has been terminated by an error in the browser.

You must check **netDone()** and it must return TRUE, before you can put the text retrieved by **getNetText** (and then returned by a call to **netTextResult**) into a variable or a Cast member. For example:

```
--cast member script:

on mouseUp

    getNetText "http://www.foo.com/intro.txt"

end

--frame script:

on exitFrame

    if netDone() = TRUE then
```

```
            put netTextResult() into field "Intro text"
            go to the frame + 1
        end if
        go to the frame
    end
```

When your user clicks the button to which the cast member script is attached, the Director movie begins loading the text stored in the file intro.txt at the location www.foo.com. The frame script then checks netDone as it exits the frame. If netDone returns FALSE (as it will till the getNetText call completes), the script jumps out of the if and executes the next line, which is go to the frame—meaning it loops on this frame until netDone returns TRUE. When netDone returns TRUE, the script loads netTextResult into a field titled "Intro Text," and then the script passes control to the next frame, terminating the loop.

getLatestNetID()

This function returns a unique identifier for the last asynchronous operation that you started. This way you can check netDone() for each individual process by storing the unique identifier for each of the operations you have running.

What You Can't Do

Although most Director functions are supported in Shockwave, a few are impossible to provide at present, because of the physical nature of the network.

The most crucial absence from Director is linked media. In standalone Director movies, you can link a Cast member—rather than importing it directly into the movie. In particular, QuickTime movies work this way, meaning that QuickTime is not supported in the 1.0 release of Shockwave. In the interim, you can do one of two things:

- Import each frame of the QuickTime movie as a separate PICT image and animate them individually using Director.

- Use Netscape 2.0's QuickTime plug-in to play video elsewhere in the Web page. You can even use **preloadNetThing** from Lingo to ensure that the video gets preloaded while your Director movie plays.

You also can't run a movie-in-a-window as you can in standalone Director applications. (For more information on this feature, see the Director documentation.)

Shockwave files cannot use any of the Wait For options in the Tempo channel. This means if your Director movie waits for a mouse click, you must write a simple Lingo script that listens for a mouse click rather than using the Tempo channel.

One final feature of Shockwave is that you can play more than one movie on a page; users can scroll up and down through the HTML page while the Director movies play. The movie can also access information on the Web, using the Lingo commands outlined here, and can also open additional URLs if you've set the movies up to do so.

This leads to two suggested restrictions, one on the number of movies to include in a given page and another on sound tracks:

- Although the number of movies you can include on a given Web page has no technical limit, Macromedia recommends a limit of three movies per HTML page.

- To avoid technical conflicts when trying to resolve multiple sound track issues, use sound in only one movie per page, and program the movie so that your users activate the sound track by clicking the mouse (that is, with a button that reacts by going to a frame in which the sound track is present) rather than having it automatically begin playing.

Finally, you can program a Director movie to repeat infinitely simply by writing a Lingo script that goes to the first frame at the exit of the last one. This can, however, cause problems for your users, as well as tying up processor time. Macromedia strongly recommends that you program the movie to stop playing after a certain number of loops, or better yet, provide some way for the user to stop the movie at any time.

Java: Interactivity for Programmers

Unlike GIF animation and Director, Java — the third way of adding high-performance interactivity to your Web site — is a programming language. This doesn't mean you have to be a programmer to use it; it just means you have to be able to learn a programming language. And no, that's not entirely as smart-alecky as it sounds.

Java is a very simple form of a programming language, at least as programming languages go. It handles many of the ugly, difficult concepts for you (like memory reallocation) automatically. It's a very safe language, meaning that its structure does not permit operations that can cause problems on the client machines. Specifically it's a byte-code language rather than a machine-code language; this means that all Java applets compile to a series of byte codes, which in turn are interpreted by the Java browser at run time. The Java instructions are never executed by the microprocessor on the client machine, and the Java interpreter makes sure that only safe operations (such as writing to local memory) are performed.

If you want to get into Java, refer to one of the books I've mentioned in this chapter, or check the Appendix under On-line Resources to learn where you can find out more about Java. If you're not reluctant to dive into a new programming language, Java offers you the power and flexibility that only writing your own code can give you. In addition, Java compiles into very compact applets, meaning that they cross the Net swiftly and perform rapidly, saving both download time and performance time.

If you don't particularly want to code your own Java applets, you can still use already coded applets from some other source, whether from the comp.lang.java newsgroup or from a hired programmer. Incorporating a Java applet into your Web page is no more difficult than doing the same task for a Shockwave file. The following tutorial shows you how to add a Java applet to a Web page, using an example on the book's Web site.

Tutorial: Adding a Java Applet to Your Web Page

This tutorial uses one of the Java applets written by James Gosling and included on the CD-ROM distributed with *Hooked on Java* (Addison-Wesley, 1996). Gosling's animation applet, called ImageLoop, plays a sequence of images in much the same way as the GIF animation we did earlier. In fact, you can use the same images to generate animations, and you can compare the animated GIFs to the Java version of the same scene.

For this tutorial, you'll need to create a series of five small image files, 160 pixels wide by 120 pixels high, in GIF format, and store them on your Web site. For their names, call them T1.gif, T2.gif, T3.gif, T4.gif, T5.gif, and T6.gif. Note the directory in which you stored them—that will become one of the parameters you need to pass to ImageLoop when you build your sample Java-powered Web page.

1. Download the Java applet titled ImageLoop, which you can find at the following URL:

http://www.living-history.org/dynaweb/java/imageloop.html

2. Put this Java applet on your own Web page (or in a directory that you can then open with Netscape).

3. Copy your five GIF images into the same directory on your Web page (or on your workstation's local hard drive) that contains the Java applet you downloaded in step 1. Then, at that same level, create another directory called frames.

4. In the same directory that contains the Java applet and the directory called frames (but not in the frames directory itself), create an HTML file with the following lines in the <BODY> portion of the file:

```
<applet code=ImageLoopItem width=160 height=120
align=right>

<param name=nimgs value=6>

<param name=img value=frames>

<param name=pause value=100>

</applet>
```

That's all there is to it; these lines pass parameters — special values that control the way the applet works — to ImageLoop when someone loads this Web page. Here's what each line of HTML does:

```
<applet code=ImageLoopItem width=160 height=120
align=right>
```

> This line loads the applet called ImageLoop at this point in your Web page. It reserves room for an image 160 pixels wide by 120 pixels high — 1/4 the size off a standard NTSC screen — and aligns it with the right edge of the page.

```
<param name=nimgs value=6>
```

> This line sets up the nimgs (short for number of images) parameter to the ImageLoop applet. The nimgs parameter tells ImageLoop how many individual images are in the loop, so that it can set its counters for any number of images.

In this case, the value is 6, the number of frames used in this tutorial. Later, use the number that corresponds to the actual number of frames you have created.

```
<param name=img value=frames>
```

This line sets up the parameter that tells the applet where to look for the images. In this case, you created a directory called frames in which all the images were stored. This is why you need to name your individual frames so carefully: ImageLoop expects files called T1.gif, T2.gif, and so on through the last frame. Furthermore, it expects a number of frames equal to the value you specified for the nimgs parameter on the previous line.

```
<param name=pause value=100>
```

This line tells the applet how long to pause before displaying the next image; the pause is measured in milliseconds (thousandths of a second). Therefore, this line pauses the applet for 1/10 of a second between frames.

```
</applet>
```

This line ends the applet tag.

Other Kinds of Buttons

Using Thumbnails as Hot Links

You can use any image as the contents of a hypertext link by following this format:

```
<a href="jump.html"><img src="jumpthumb.jpg"></a>
```

In this example, jump.html represents the file that acts as the destination of the hypertext jump; jumpthumb.jpg is the JPEG file that is displayed as the contents of the jump. By default, this shows up with a blue border around the image. You can turn this off by adding the parameter BORDER=0 to the end of the IMG SRC= tag.

And, of course, you can combine this with the GIF animation technique presented earlier in this chapter. By combining the two, you can create small, animated buttons that flicker, blink, or otherwise move to attract your users' attention, but which are themselves hyperlinks to other places on your Web site.

One way to build a kind of image map—and possibly a dynamic one at that—is to build up an array of several animated GIFs, using the <BR> tag at the end of each line and making a kind of animated mosaic. Not all the GIFs have to be hypertext links. It's possible to have them act as placeholders, as alignment markers, or as noninteractive visual content (that is, pictures you don't click on). For example, you could come up with a standard bottom-of-the-page menu bar using something like this:

```
<hr>

<a href="index.html">

<img src="home.gif" border=0>

</a>

<img src="decoration.gif" border=0>

<a href="screen2.html">

<img src="right_arrow.gif" border=0>

</a>
```

To set up your Web page for an example like this, you'd need the following files:

- index.html—the basic home page for your Web site.

- home.gif—an icon representing home, such as a house (and with animated GIFs, you could have some fun with this, making smoke curl out of the chimney or making the door open and close to display odd goings-on inside).

- decoration.gif — a file containing some graphical motif, but in this case one used solely as a placeholder to position the next image at the right edge of the screen. There's no reason why this could not be animated as well, however.

- screen2.html — whatever the logical destination for a "next" button would be from this screen.

- right_arrow.gif — a graphic of an arrow pointing to the right. As with the other GIF files, this could be animated, either blinking on and off or containing some motion.

The first time you try this with multiple thumbnails as a pieced image map (call it an "image quilt" if you like), you'll notice that Netscape 2.0 does something ugly. If you have spaces or line breaks — that is, if you press the Return key — between two image maps used as the display portion of a hypertext anchor, Netscape shows a single, tiny blue underline between the pictures. The solution to this problem is to remove the line breaks and spaces — just put everything on a single line in your HTML file. (You'll need to open the file in a text editor, such as Notepad, SimpleText, or vi, to make this kind of change — it's not something you can do in any of the WYSIWYG HTML editors I've used.)

For an example of how to compose an HTML page with not only a graphical menu bar, but an animated graphical menu bar, take a look at the following UTL:

http://www.living-history.org/cchase/

This is the Web page for Cherry Chase Elementary School, and each of the animated images represents a different hypertext link. If you browse to that link and View Source, you'll see the following text:

```
<html>

<head>

<title>Cherry Chase Home Page</title>

<body bgcolor="#ffffff">

<center>

<img src="ccicon.jpg">

<h1>

Cherry Chase Elementary School

</h1>

Check out some of the great activities we have on our Web
page!

<p>

<a href="http://www.living-history.org/cchase/kids.html"><img
src="kidsnaps.gif" border =0></a><a href="http://www.living-
history.org/cchase/staff.html"><img src="staff.gif" border =0></
a><a href="http://www.living-history.org/cchase/commu-
nity.html"><img src="pizza.gif" border =0></a><a href="http://
www.living-history.org/cchase/calendar.html"><img
src="tree.gif" border =0></a><a href="http://www.living-his-
tory.org/cchase/activities.html"><img src="donna.gif" border
=0></a>

<p>

<font size=-6>

Copyright (c) 1996 Scott Fisher/Sunnyvale School District

</font>

</body>

</html>
```

This doesn't make for the most readable HTML code in the world, but it has the desired effect in the browser. Each of the GIF animations appears directly adjacent to its neighbor, with no space, borders, lines, or other blemishes to mar the menu bar.

If you click on any of the animated GIFs, you'll notice that the destination page retains the same GIF animation at the top and center of the page. This isn't technically an animation issue, it's a human-interface issue, but one that is worth pointing out here. It reinforces the sense of where in the Web page's structure you've ended up, and helps build additional understanding for repeat visits. And since this Web page is meant to be used again and again by students, parents, teachers, and other people associated with the school, it's a good way to build this kind of usability.

We noticed one other problem while creating some of the GIF animations used elsewhere on the Web site as examples for this chapter:

Netscape 2.0 for the Macintosh does not correctly handle GIF animations that set the background color to transparent. Instead, the background was transparent on the first frame of the image, but then turned black afterward. (You'll notice that this doesn't appear as a problem in the Edgar Allan Poe example, where the background of the HTML file is set to black.) This caused something of a sleepless night, because I was sure I'd done something wrong in GifBuilder — chosen an incorrect disposition method, set some value to the wrong option, or something like that.

It turned out that on Windows and Unix workstations running Netscape 2.0, and on Macintoshes running Netscape 3.0, the GIF animations did "the right thing" — displayed the Web page's background correctly through the transparent background of the GIF, as originally intended. So don't be too hasty to assume, in these days of rapid Web development, that every mistake on your Web page is your own fault.

In the next chapter, we'll move away from a strict reliance on technology and into a part of Web page design—and for that matter, multimedia design in general—that gets very little attention, yet can make the single biggest difference in how you develop your multimedia title and what effect it has on your audience. For the coming chapter, we'll put programs and coding aside for a while and concentrate on something a little different. So let's gather around the digital campfire, listen to the crackling of electronic logs, pull our windbreakers a little closer around our shoulders as protection from the strange noises of the night that trickle in from outside the lambent golden pool of light from the fire, and get ready to dive into a question that's as old as language: what makes a good story?

CHAPTER 5   # Interacting with Story

"What do you mean, 'Interacting with Story'?" asked one of my early reviewers of this chapter. "Don't you mean 'Interacting with *a* Story'?"

Not at all. I've chosen this odd way of phrasing the chapter title intentionally, to catch your eye and to propose something new: That just as film is a medium and *a* film is an example or instance of that medium, story is also a medium, and *a* story is an example or instance of that medium. And just as in other chapters where we've inquired into interacting with graphics and with animation, two of the media that go into multimedia, this chapter is an inquiry into interacting with the medium of story.

Let's begin by inquiring into the nature of this medium called story. What does it consist of? What are its fundamental principles? How can we design for the medium of story, much the way we design graphics or animation? What makes one story succeed where another fails?

Much has been made of the "immersive" quality of computer-generated images, such as those associated with virtual reality. The truth is that the ability to engage one's audience so that they become lost in the tale has existed for as long as a storyteller has had the ability to capture and hold people's imaginations. Homer, Shakespeare, and Dickens knew how to draw their audiences into a story without the benefit of Pentium processors, special glasses, or datagloves.

In this chapter, we'll look at how you can structure your information—independent of the sophistication of your display tools—in ways that capture and hold the imagination of your audience. We'll discuss techniques for creating, within the story medium, techniques you can use in instructional multimedia, in entertainment, in sales and marketing, or in any other kind of communication that you plan to put in place over your network. And, of course, if you apply these principles to high-performance visuals, the experience will be even more impressive.

What Is Story as a Medium?

At the heart, storytelling is the most fundamental way of communication between human beings. Although it's impossible to verify because of the absence of records, most anthropologists believe that storytelling is the oldest human medium, even older than petroglyphs or cave paintings—which, when combined with the story they represent or depict, qualify as the oldest multimedia.

In fact, consider a leading anthropological theory about one of the cultural uses of cave paintings. Many anthropologists propose that cave paintings such as those at Lascaux represent a ritual of passage into adulthood in the tribe or clan: that adolescents passed into the cave, underwent a ritual involving a retelling of the clan or tribal myths, were exposed to the images on the cave walls under conditions of high psychological excitement, and emerged from the other side as fully initiated adult members of the group. The rituals were given meaning by the tribe's agreement on what they represented, but they

Creating Dynamic Web Sites

had their effect in large part due to the use of several media—story (in the form of tribal mythology), visuals (in the form of the paintings and petroglyphs), and tactile interaction (being guided through a dark cave by one who knew the way). The result was a personal transformation, from youth to adulthood—in terms of personal behavior and self-identification, and also in terms of social expectations and treatment.

Today, digital multimedia has the power to make a similar impact on people's senses. That it does not do so is due more to the lack of a coherent cultural set of expectations than it is due to the nature of multimedia. Today's world is too diverse, encompasses too many different cultures for any single computer-based experience—no matter how powerful—to have the same depth of effectiveness that such a tribal ritual would have on people who had been raised in the culture since infancy, and whose entire world outlook was shaped by the beliefs expressed in these rituals.

Yet, the potential is there in multimedia. Human physiology hasn't changed that much in the past 40,000 years; the nervous system still responds to light, sound, and touch in the same way. The most profound difference between us and the Cro-Magnon people who used the caves of Lascaux for their social and religious activities is that they believed—completely and without reservation—in the story that went with the pictures and the journey.

Consider that it may be the story that gives power to the shapes, sounds, and movements in the cave. It's the story—or more correctly, our belief in it—that moves us today, makes us take action on something. When we believe a story, even if we are only pretending to believe it (as in fiction), that story gives us our view of the world, our way of being. By changing the story—by introducing a new story that gives a different view of the world—we change how we relate to the world and to ourselves. And this is the medium I invite you to participate in with me now.

Story is the medium through which we convey our hopes, dreams, wishes, fears, anger, joy, and self-expression. Sometimes story shows up as a structured event; sometimes it's simply a natural outpouring of our emotions, our thoughts, our ideas. Stories make us see ourselves in others; stories engage our curiosity; stories stir up old dreads and insecurities; stories wash away our sorrows and our regrets. Stories are also complete, in their own way—at least the best of them are. (We'll examine these and other characteristics of story as a medium in a few pages.)

Something that isn't always realized is that, at the heart, story is inherently interactive because it is inherently part of human language, and thereby requires communication in both directions—sending and receiving. At the 1996 Writer's Connection conference on Writing for Interactive Multimedia, one of the presenters who preceded me was Sam McMillan, instructor at San Francisco State University's highly respected multimedia studies program. Sam is also a very active scriptwriter in the interactive multimedia field, and his presentation, "Interactive Scriptwriting for Marketing and Business-to-Business Communication," ended with a slide that everyone in the interactive communication field should pin to the wall:

> "The most interactive thing you can do is have a conversation."

And in the guttering light of torches against a cave wall, or the 72-Hz flicker of a high-resolution monitor, the most powerful conversation you can have is to tell a story.

Where Is the Story Medium Useful?

The power of story as a medium is perhaps most visible in fiction, where the story is completely imaginary and yet causes responses in its audience that are as real and as moving as any actual event. Audiences in nineteenth-century England wept at the death of Little Nell in Dickens's *The Old Curiosity Shop*. More recently, television viewers were kept breathless with suspense over the question, "Who shot J.R.?" after the season finale of the series *Dallas*. And 14 million people were moved to buy Robert James Waller's novel, *The Bridges of Madison County*, because the story evoked a powerful emotional response from them. (You may begin to observe something else about story—critical success and objective standards of quality have nothing to do with the effectiveness of a story in reaching out to people's lives. Later in this chapter we'll look at some of what makes a story effective.)

But story doesn't have to be excluded from nonfiction. Stories can be true and still be powerful. Do you remember Baby Jessica, the little girl who fell down the well in Texas and kept us all in suspense until she was finally rescued? That this story happened to be true was certainly no impediment to our ability to respond with our hearts. Or the Bay Area man who donated his annual salary to start a fund for victims of the Oklahoma City Federal Building bombing—consider that what moved him to give up his income for 12 months was the way he responded to the stories of the survivors and their families.

Stories can be useful, powerful, and effective in different ways in different fields. Training and education can benefit from the effect of story, which is to engage and command the attention of the audience. One of the ways I like to distinguish this in classes and seminars is to ask the following questions:

1. How many of you follow a soap opera regularly, or know someone who does? Can you explain the current plot(s), including enough background information to have it all make sense that Don is sleeping with Jessica, who's married to Raymond, but Raymond got Sylvia pregnant, and she's trying to convince her ex-husband that—you get the point.

2. How many of you know how to program your VCR?

3. Which of these tasks is really more complicated— programming the VCR or explaining the plot lines in *Days of Our Young and Restless Hospital Lives*?

Story is the fundamental difference between the answers to question 1 and question 2. We have an almost infinite capacity to follow a story, as long as it's presented in a way that captures our interest. Consider what would be possible if you could use the medium of story to teach people a subject, whether geography or algebra.

How about marketing and corporate communication? Certainly advertisers know the power of story. Consider a recent internationally known series of television commercials where the two people fall in love after one goes to borrow some instant coffee from the other. This was a piece of purely inspired work on the part of the ad agency—the commercial became a phenomenon in its own right, and better yet (from the agency's perspective), it led to an entire series of commercials in which we followed the budding romance of these two people.

What it really comes down to is an understanding that story is one of the most effective tools you have in your multimedia toolbox for conveying any information you want people to remember and be able to use powerfully. Story engages, motivates, immerses its audience, and in the end, provides them with something that can lead them to take action.

Just as graphics, video, and interactivity have certain design principles for effectiveness and performance, story has its own design principles. Let's look at them next.

What Are the Characteristics of Story as a Medium?

The characteristics or design principles of story-as-medium are the key to using story powerfully in your own multimedia pieces—whether those pieces are corporate marketing statements, interactive games, or some form of interactivity that doesn't exist yet as I sit typing this book. The following design principles are by no means exhaustive, nor are they all mandatory. I encourage you to inquire into what makes a story great, and what design principle—whether it be one of these or a different one—that greatness speaks to.

1. *Story engages people's interest.* It touches their lives in some way; it evokes an emotional response in them; it deals with something that is fundamental to the human experience, and it does so in a way that makes us care about the story and its outcome.

2. *Story is personal.* "Experts agree" or "Studies have shown" are not part of the medium story; quite the opposite, statements like this distance the events from the reader, turn them from story into anecdotes. Story deals with individual human beings, represents their actions in detail, makes the audience identify with one person (or one person at a time) and relates the events of the story or the purpose of the story with that person's life.

   I gave my Web Club students a short exercise on personalizing their writing not long ago. They were working on a project involving a series of interviews we'd made, along with the video club, and the students were writing up the text for their Web page. To get them to put some vitality and personal interest in it, I had them imagine they were reporting on a fight between a cat and a dog, but they were going to write two stories about it, one for *Cat Lover Magazine* and one for *Man's Best Friend, The Noble Dog*. What would they do differently in one than they did in the other? What kind of descriptions would they use? It's a simple exercise, one geared for fourth-grade students, but it made a powerful difference in what they wrote that day.

3. *Story has characters*. The characters are almost always multiple, if only because story is fundamentally about relationships between people. Some stories (that is, the individual instances of the medium story) deal with intrapersonal relationships — how we feel about ourselves and what kind of a world and a life this relationship gives us. Hemingway's *The Old Man and the Sea* is a classic story in which most of the dramatic action involves only the title character and an assortment of fish, but the engaging, personal, and conflicting part of the story deals with how Santiago relates to himself, alone in a small boat on a very large ocean filled with hungry, impersonal things.

4. *Story has conflict*. Conflict is what drives story. If nothing ever goes wrong, if there are never any obstacles, there's nothing to engage and command the reader's attention and interest. Once, many years ago when I was much more arrogant than I am now about other people's pleasures, I asked a friend why she liked to read romance novels when they always started out with the two main characters hating each other and ended up with the heroine yielding to the hero in a misty, rose-covered bower. "Oh, I know they'll end up the same way," she replied. "But I like wondering how they'll manage to get from hate to love in 150 pages. It's like a challenge." That's what conflict provides: a sense of wonder, of not knowing how it'll work out.

5. *Story has a setting*. Sometimes the setting is crucial to the plot — in Poe's *The Cask of Amontillado*, the setting is almost a character, having a specific, unique, and irreplaceable role to play in the dramatic action. Montresor (the narrator) couldn't immure poor, sad Fortunato if the story were set on a beach, at a forest summer camp, or in an airport.

Creating Dynamic Web Sites

Other times, the setting may not be irreplaceable to the plot, but it provides a critical part of the atmosphere, the background, and the emotional impact of the story. Many of James Herriot's lovely tales of a Yorkshire vet fall into that category—the Yorkshire Dales provide a rich background to all his stories, but it's the fundamental simplicity of human interaction that gives his stories their charm, their depth, and their touching warmth, and many of the stories themselves would work as well in the rolling hills of Iowa farmland or the steppes of Russia.

At the same time, note how even the replacement settings I selected have much in common with the Dales—rural areas and farm communities far from urban life. You can't tell a story about a country veterinarian and the simple, honest farmers with whom he works if the setting is midtown Manhattan or the jungles of Burma.

6. *Story is whole and complete in and of itself.* The old Hollywood saw is still the best generalization about story: "Boy meets girl, boy loses girl, boy gets girl." That's story in a nutshell—characters, conflict, and resolution. A specific instance of story may or may not have resolution—in fact, some of the most engaging, immersive stories leave certain elements unresolved (though increasingly, this is to leave an opening for next summer's blockbuster, *Unresolved Stories II: The Alignment*). But each episode of a Dickens serialized novel, or a Perils of Pauline short, or a TV miniseries is whole and complete unto itself—as well as being part of a larger, overarching structure—even if the overall resolution of the conflict doesn't happen till the final episode. Easily the best-known example of this in recent years is George Lucas' *Star Wars* trilogy—each film itself has complete dramatic integrity, yet they all set up the events of the next film, either through dramatic action or through foreshadowing.

7. *Story makes us want to know what happens next.* It's more than just leaving us hanging, as principle 5 hints. Later in this chapter I'll go through an exercise in how to keep people wanting to know what happened next, and how to engage them in actually selecting what happens next—the fundamental difference in a truly interactive story. In this case, the audience has a stake in the overall outcome, but even in a non-interactive story, it's this characteristic that makes us refer to thrilling books as "page-turners." (I have yet to hear anyone refer to an especially exciting CD-ROM or Web site as "a real mouse-clicker," but it's only a matter of time.)

8. *Story has the 5 Ws (and an H).* For those who skipped journalism, those are the six key inquiry words: who, what, when, where, why, and how. Who was there? What did they do? When did it happen? Where did it take place? Why did they do it? And how did they pull it off? This is part of what makes story personal, part of what makes it whole and complete, and part of what makes us want to know what happens next. One crucial difference between this design principle and the rest is that this one is actually something you can measure as a way of reaching the others: you can look through your story and see whether it addresses who is acting, what action they're taking, where it's happening, when it took place, why they did it, and how it happened.

More than just asking these questions, good story uses them—in the way I've done at the beginnings of the chapters of this book—as the starting point for an inquiry into what excites us about the answer to this question. One of my Web Club students, a fourth-grade boy, was writing his part of a project the whole club worked on. The kids had chosen to write individual HTML files answering each of the 5 W's and an H, and this boy had picked "What We Did" as his part of the project. He put down a single, direct, but fairly flat sentence, and then told me, "Mr. Fisher, I wrote down what we did, now what do I do?" So I sat down with Mark and had him continue to ask himself the following questions: What was exciting about what we did? What would my readers like to know? What would make people enjoy hearing about what we did?

Within a few minutes, Mark had written four more sentences that brought a lot more life into his report, and most important, he completely changed the way he was being in class—from a distracted, disconnected kid to someone who was completely lit up by what he was doing.

9. *Story combines linear and nonlinear communication.* Linear communication is something we're all familiar with: it's the beginning, middle, and end that we were all raised knowing that stories have. It's the way the different reels in a motion picture follow one after the other, resulting in the movie that the director wanted to create. It's the way Act I introduces the characters and conflict, Acts II through IV develop subplots and build tension among the characters, and Act V offers climax, resolution, and completion. Or it might be the way a training class begins with introductory concepts, builds on those to form more complex ideas, and finally ends with mastery of the subject matter on the part of the students.

Nonlinear communication is often described as something completely different, something most people think is new and mysterious. Yet it's neither new nor mysterious—if anything, it's more natural as a way of human expression than strictly linear story is. But nonlinear communication, in the context of story, is the conveying of information that is outside the strict, linear sequence of time, logic, or the flow of events. And when used properly, it can provide a richness, a depth, and a contribution to the overall impact of a story—whether that story is a traditional motion picture, a book, or an interactive CD-ROM. Let's take a look next at a few questions that will open up a new understanding of nonlinear communication for you.

What Is Nonlinear Communication?

Occasionally, when I talk about nonlinear communication with newcomers to interactive writing, they tell me that they don't "get it." The first thing to "get" about nonlinear communication is that it's actually a lot more common than we realize. Many instances of what we think of as linear communication are often nonlinear; it's just that we don't think of them that way because of the way we perceive time.

For example, two common dramatic devices—foreshadowing and flashback—are ways of introducing nonlinearity into a story. So are multiple points of view, including the two-camera shot described in Chapter 3. In the case of foreshadowing and flashback, we break the linearity of time; in the case of two-camera shot, we break the linearity of location.

The concept of nonlinear communication isn't new; only the ability to click on part of the screen and change what we're looking at is really an invention of the past decade.

When people ask me what my favorite nonlinear story is, I say *Citizen Kane*. Then they furrow their eyebrows and say, "But that's a movie. It can't be nonlinear."

"It can't?" I ask. "Consider this: it starts out with the title character dying, then it shows us his life story. That's not what I think of as linear; most people don't die, and then have their lives. Then it breaks the story among three or four different reporters, each one in turn asking two or three people in Kane's life what they remember about him, and each one has a slightly different viewpoint about the man. That's a far cry from direct, continuous, linear time, like the time we spend in the theater or the sequence of the frames of the movie. And finally, at the end, only the audience knows the whole story about what Rosebud meant and what Kane's life was about; the characters in the movie never figure it out. So in that sense, it's not only nonlinear, it's also interactive."

At this point, people do one of two things: either they walk away with a very skeptical look, or their eyebrows shoot up over their hairline and they jump back and say something along the lines of "Aha! I get it!"

So that's one way of getting access to nonlinear communication: by seeing that it's a fundamental, already existing part of stories you probably already know. But when you add in computers and HTML and the Web, nonlinear communication takes on a new dimension, as the basis for hypertext and multimedia.

In this new dimension, nonlinearity lets you jump from concept to concept at will, at your own choice. In fact, consider the following assertions (not as though they're the truth, necessarily, but for what access they provide for creating your own stories):

Citizen Kane is a nonlinear story, for the reasons already mentioned — it starts on the main character's deathbed, it jumps between different characters and what they meant to his life, it covers a vast number of years in a 2-hour stint in the theater. It is clearly not strictly linear, detailing the events in a one-to-one relationship between time in the world and time on the screen. (For an example of that, see the early Hitchcock film *Rope* — the entire film was shot without camera cuts, jumps, or interruptions; even the breaks when a roll of film ran out were managed to keep up the semblance of absolute linearity.)

Citizen Kane is also an interactive story — the audience has an important role in the film, as the only people who can actually figure out the entire story. Only the audience sees all the reporters' interviews, observes all the flashbacks; and while *The Rocky Horror Picture Show* probably has a higher degree of audience participation on a given evening, *Citizen Kane* requires the audience to interact, to track plot events and flashbacks alike as they come to their conclusions about the story.

Out of these assertions arise some questions. If *Citizen Kane* is both nonlinear and interactive, what fundamentally new element does hypertext provide? Hypertext presents users with a choice of where they want to go next. Hypertext and multimedia let people choose what follows, what precedes, and where a story goes. Sometimes, to distinguish a linear story such as a movie from a nonlinear story such as a CD-ROM (since I've already asserted that all stories have nonlinear components), I talk about "plug-and-play" stories—unalterably linear, front-to-back stories such as movies, plays and books, borrowing from the metaphor of plugging in a videotape and pressing the Play button—and "point-and-click" stories—stories in which the linearity is, to some extent, under the control of the audience, borrowing from the metaphor of using interactive CD-ROMs.

What does the ability to choose provide that wasn't present in the domain of the "plug-and-play" story? For that, let's look at what this new twist on nonlinear story—that is, user-selectable story—makes available to its audience (and therefore what the medium makes possible for its authors).

What Does Nonlinear Story Make Possible?

The most crucial distinction of nonlinear story is that the context—that is, the background behind which the action takes place, the characters occur, etc.—can be shifted dramatically. In the past, each scene led to the next; authors, directors, and playwrights carefully crafted the sequence of events in their stories to lead the audience down a well-thought-out path. This result has created great works of art—plays, novels, films, short stories, all using this design principle: that the author chooses the order in which the events are displayed, projected, or presented.

Before we continue, I want to make it clear that I am not proposing dumping the unidirectional principle of design. Would *Pride and Prejudice* be more effective if we could choose to learn about Lydia Bennett's disastrous elopement early in the novel? Or would the irony of Lizzie's un-courtship with Mr. Darcy (who turns out to be Lydia's benefactor) be any richer if we knew when she found out about it? Face it—we *know* she's going to find out about it sooner or later and they'll end up together; this is Austen, after all, not the grim irony of Dickens. But part of what makes Jane Austen so enjoyable is that she makes us wait in agony before Lizzie finally understands, accepts, and comes to terms with Darcy. And this ability the author has, to control pace and flow and the sequence of events, is part of what makes fiction so enjoyable.

But what else is possible? I am convinced that a generation of new authors, brought up in the domain of interactivity, can develop new ways of relating to story, new ways of providing entertainment, that we can't yet imagine. I can't imagine them myself, certainly—but I know some of the mechanisms with which they'll be created, and I'm committed to getting these mechanisms into as many creative minds as possible.

The most crucial mechanism of interactivity is that the readers themselves select the context they carry from one part of the document to the next. This, I believe, is even more important than the ability to choose whether the character goes to the right or to the left (which is more exactly a game metaphor than a nonlinear metaphor)—the ability for background, context, even setting to be dynamically selectable. Think about it: irony, foreshadowing, flashback, suspense—all depend in the linear model on an absolute, inviolate succession of scenes, events, and actions. In the nonlinear model, these characteristics will be dynamic, depending entirely on what the audience has encountered before coming to each scene. How would you, as an author, use this knowledge to create powerful drama, comedy, suspense, or other fiction?

One key result of this new way of interacting with context is that each new concept in the presentation, or each new scene in fiction, depends entirely on the context you had before going there. Juxtaposition becomes a run-time phenomenon, not something the author or director can control completely. Is this a good thing? I am convinced it can be, in the right hands. I am less convinced that those hands are already on the keyboard somewhere, making possible new forms of art. But if not now, then soon, the artists of this new medium will begin working. Who knows — maybe one of them is holding this copy of this book right at this moment. Yes, *this* copy — the one you're reading, not some other copy in another corner of the world. If not you, who? If not now, when?

Does it sound confronting, frightening, overwhelming to engage in the exploration of an entirely new medium for communication, art, literature? Consider this, again not like it's the truth, not that it's something that experts agree or 4 out of 5 doctors recommend, but as though it's an idea you can try on like a coat and take off if it doesn't fit: that nonlinear communication as I have been elaborating on here is not strange, new, or difficult, but rather is the fundamental mode of human communication and human perception. It's simply so fundamental, so automatic, that we don't see it.

Think about the staggering, truly awe-inspiring ability of human beings to pick up the story in the middle. We are born into an existing story — our parents met before we were born; the town we lived in existed before our emergence; the state, nation, continent, culture, and world had all been here for anything from decades to centuries before we popped onto the scene. Our job has been to pick up what's going on, to learn how to speak, read, write, and interact with other people — and with the stories of their lives.

Later in life, we move yet again into existing stories. We go to school and meet 30 or so other children, all of whom are the centers of their respective worlds. We are drawn to some of them, and so we pick up their stories—in the form of their name, their family life, what they like and don't like—and begin collaborating with these coauthors of our lives in the creation of a new, interactive form of art. Usually we call this art form "friendship." Sometimes, when it's particularly powerful, we call it "love." In either case, it's really a collaborative, shared story we tell ourselves, a story that our collaborators—friends and loved ones—believe in with us.

In some cases, we actually get many others to participate in the same story; sometimes we publish our collaboration, in the form of a marriage announcement—a form of official recognition of the story we've collaborated on together. Sometimes these stories involve sequels—our children. And the people we meet later on pick up that story in the middle, when they meet us.

But fundamentally, human beings are so naturally adept at jumping into the middle of a story that we don't even know we're doing it—it's the water we swim in, a metaphor that is made clearer by, what else, a story:

> A man once walked by the side of a clear stream on a hot day. The water looked cool and inviting, and down in the shallows he saw a fish, its flanks rippling with silver scales. It looked like birch leaves in the moonlight, the sharp clarity of a winter evening breeze glinting in stark contrast with the dust and the heat of the streamside path.
>
> "Hey!" the man called, for he lived in an age when people and animals had not yet lost the art of speaking to one another. "How's the water in there?"
>
> "Water?" asked the fish. "What do you mean?"
>
> "The water!" the man shouted. "You know, that stuff you're swimming in."

"I don't get it," called the fish, looking confused.

"Here," said the man, and reached in to grab the fish. He lifted the fish out to look it in the eyes.

The fish flapped, gasped, and pulsed open its mouth and its gills in desperation, choking at the thin air.

"See?" the man told the fish. "Up here we live in air — but where you live it's water. Get it?" Then, sensing the fish's discomfort, he dropped it back into the stream.

"Water!" shouted the fish, doing a little dance. "I get it! I live in water! That's what these fins are for, and that's why I've got gills and this smooth shape and these scales that let me bend and flex to shoot away — like this!" And the fish bent and flexed and shot away to tell his friends.

"Hey!" the fish called out as he swam up to a group of his pals, wiggling with excitement. "I just learned the most incredible thing — we live in *water!*"

"Water?" said his friends. "What are you talking about?" They looked around at one another, their fins lazily waving against the current, unaware of what they did.

But because the first fish had no hands, he could not lift his friends out of the stream to show them the water. He tried to describe it, but they didn't get it. Eventually his friends decided he was just being goofy and they swam away shaking their heads, the water rushing past their gills.

So if this chapter sounds a little like that goofy fish, consider that what I'm doing is trying to introduce you to the water you swim in — the ability that we as humans have to pick up a story in the middle, to make sense of nonsense, to invent at the drop of a hat the background, context, and events of the stories of our lives.

Whether or not this fish story helps you visualize the transparent nature of our ability to navigate through nonlinear events in our lives, it's worth taking a few pages to look into where the concept of linear story—the belief that events in a story must unfold in direct sequence—came from.

Where Do Nonlinear Stories Differ from Linear Stories?

The format and rules of linear story dates back to Aristotle, or specifically to his *Poetics*. One of the most crucial pieces of critical thinking in this work was his belief that the drama—the highest form of art in his day and his opinion—needed to observe a number of rules, which he called "the unities."

From our perspective, the Aristotelian unity that affects us in this conversation is the unity of time. Aristotle believed—and for hundreds of years, playwrights and authors alike followed suit—that for a play to succeed, it had to follow the restrictions of linear time in at least the following two ways:

- The play had to proceed forward in time, not jumping back to an earlier age (though characters could of course introduce plot elements from the past, otherwise Oedipus would never know that Jocasta was his own mother)

- The play had to proceed in a strict one-to-one relationship with time, so that every moment on stage corresponded exactly to an equivalent moment in the world being imitated.

This is of course a fundamental offshoot of how we perceive time; our ability to navigate through time is strictly limited to a unidirectional path.

But nonlinear story predates Aristotle. Some six or seven hundred years before the unities, a blind poet named Homer started his tale about a ten-year-long war by placing the opening scene of his poem in the last weeks of that war, just as the Greek's greatest hero was about to pull up his tents and return home. This, by the way, simply makes good dramatic sense: it gives an exciting, engaging, powerful first scene, one that draws the audience in and makes them want to know what happens next.

(Centuries later, Homer's dramatic sense was made into a principle of epic poetry by the Roman author Virgil, who said that all epics start in the middle, *in media res.* Although the word "media" here means middle, it's noteworthy that this is related to the modern word "media" — something that is slightly ironic in the context of this discussion.)

So one distinction that nonlinear story gives us is the ability to jump immediately into the action, then fill in the details later as required — even *if* required, because some audiences may not want or need to fill in background details from the document. Again, unidirectional story does this as well. The difference in an interactive story is that the author needs to make explicit the ability to get supporting information, rather than embedding it in character development or plot exposition. But because of the ability that human beings have to pick up a story in the middle, it may in fact be unnecessary for everyone to know the background. Many readers may breeze right past that, content with what they can pick up for themselves about who did what and why.

The good news is that finding things out for ourselves — which is the fundamental design principle behind interactive nonlinear story, whether by inference or by explicit search and discovery — can be much more engaging, much more entertaining, and in the case of education in particular can lead to much higher retention of the subject matter. We always remember most strongly that which we find out for ourselves.

What Skills Apply to Nonlinear Stories?

The good news is that many of the skills that writers, journalists, and storytellers have developed for centuries apply directly to developing this new breed of nonlinear story. There are just a few new design principles to distinguish that can make hypertext stories interesting, effective, and immersive.

The chief difference is the organizational metaphor. Linear stories used the organizational metaphor of flow—that is, they provided a sequence in which events happen, as already mentioned, in an unalterable order determined by the author, playwright, or director. Furthermore, this flow was managed by using transitions between events, by creating or including explanations, and by an almost innate sense on the part of the storyteller of what comes first.

This sense of what-comes-first is especially critical in nonfiction, in education, and in training, but it's every bit as critical in fiction. The author of an instructional handbook gives careful thought to what people need to know before they can move on to the next subject, what information is prerequisite, and what is complex. The author of a novel gives no less careful thought to revealing new information in a certain sequence: lining up the actions and reactions of characters to build the plot, to make subsequent actions plausible, powerful, and effective in telling the story.

Take the Hollywood cliché I mentioned earlier: Boy meets girl, boy loses girl, boy gets girl. Change the order and the story changes: Boy meets girl, boy gets girl, boy loses girl. The first sequence describes every movie that Fred Astaire and Ginger Rogers ever made; the second describes *Love Story*, at least at a macro level.

The sequence is no less critical at the micro level. The author or director uses the individual scenes as a way of building to a dramatic climax. Each new piece of information revealed to the audience adds to the momentum, the effect, and ultimately to the emotional impact. The effect of this in the flow of the story can be critical, as each scene leads to the one that follows it. This kind of flow-based writing is almost musical, where the different elements form a kind of melody in the imagination.

Exercise I: Fixing Holes

The following exercise illustrates several of the concepts I've been writing about so far in this chapter. In it, we'll look at how people fill in the background to stories (and how we make up stories to fit what we're given), and we'll also look at how the sequence of individual scenes within a story—even when we may not think of it as a story—contribute to our emotional response to it.

Anyone who grew up with the Beatles, as I did, is familiar with the sequence of songs on the *Sgt. Pepper's Lonely Hearts Club Band* album. Much has been written already about how this was the first rock album in which the entire album, rather than a simple collection of hit (and not-so-hit) songs as previous albums had been, was instead a cohesive creative work. Certainly, over the past 25 years or more, it's taken on a kind of life in the minds of its listeners as a single entity, due in large part to the sequence of songs chosen by the Beatles' producer, George Martin.

What is less well known is that this order is not the original sequence, at least for side one. The sequence of songs on side one, as originally conceived, was (with the song's published sequence in parentheses):

Sgt. Pepper's Lonely Hearts Club Band (1)

With a Little Help from My Friends (2)

Being for the Benefit of Mr. Kite (7)

Fixing a Hole (5)

Lucy in the Sky with Diamonds (3)

Getting Better (4)

She's Leaving Home (6)

The following exercise will be most effective for those who have already spent many hours listening to *Sgt. Pepper* as it was published. If you're not familiar with the album or if you don't already have powerful emotional connotations to the songs, this exercise may not have the intended impact, but it may be valuable in any event.

So your exercise, should you choose to accept it, is:

1. Locate a CD of *Sgt. Pepper's Lonely Hearts Club Band*.

2. Find a friend who also has memories of listening to the album, as it was published.

3. Program your CD player to play the songs in the sequence shown in parentheses in the previous list, or so that the following track numbers are played in this order:

    1 2 7 5 3 4 6

4. Play the CD in the original, unpublished sequence that you programmed in step 3.

5. What is your emotional reaction to this sequence? Discuss this with your friend. What emotions go through your mind as each new song comes up?

6. Now go back and play the CD in its published sequence.

7. What is your emotional reaction to the CD as you know it? What emotions go through your mind as each new song comes up?

The intention of this exercise is for you to distinguish the degree to which you have invented a story to go along with the music of *Sgt. Pepper*. "In the published sequence, ever since I was a kid I visualized the band giving a performance, leading from one song to the next," said one of my students when we did this exercise. "In the unpublished sequence, it sounded like just any rock album."

"The songs just sound flat in the (unpublished) sequence," said another. "There's no connection between them."

"When I listened to it the real way," said a third—a very telling word for expressing the published sequence—"I got goosebumps before each song came up because I knew what it was and where it fit in the whole album."

Once again, if you don't have a long experience listening to this album—if the Beatles weren't part of your cultural development for whatever reason, whether time or space or inclination—this exercise won't have such a powerful effect on you. But for those people with whom I've engaged in this exercise, their reactions were fairly consistent: Listening to the songs in the unpublished sequence highlighted the degree to which the listeners had constructed something very much like a story. How much like one? To find out, answer the following questions about your own vision of what's going on during the play of *Sgt. Pepper*:

1. Who is involved in your vision of the event?

2. What are they doing?

3. Where are they doing this?

4. When is it happening?

5. Why are they doing this?

6. How is it accomplished?

I suggest that if you have answers to more than even two or three of these questions—much less to all of them—then you have constructed a story out of the songs, and specifically the sequence, on the album.

The counterpart to this exercise, of course, would be to introduce the album in its unpublished sequence to people who had never heard it, let them listen to it in that way, and then introduce them to the order in which the songs were originally published, but that would be too long an experiment for most of us who need to come up to speed in nonlinear story immediately.

Structure as Organizational Metaphor

I mentioned earlier that nonlinear, or point-and-click, stories have a different organizational metaphor—that although linear stories have a sense of flow that gives them their being, nonlinear stories have no such guaranteed flow. Each part of a nonlinear story must stand alone, must itself be whole and complete rather than taking its wholeness from the overall story, because there's no intentional dependency from one part to the next—they're like the songs on an album (or at least some album other than *Sgt. Pepper*). When the users can select the "next" piece arbitrarily, there's no guaranteed, predictable flow as there is while watching a movie. Does it matter, then, how you organize a nonlinear story? Yes, very much. You just need to use a different organizational metaphor.

What replaces overall flow in nonlinear story is structure. This concept is gradually working its way into the general public. A few years ago, I had to spend a long time in each book, class, or consulting agreement getting people to understand the concept of structured documents. Today, more people already know the term, and some of them actually know what it means and how to build a structured document.

Whether you already know how or not, the next few sections of this chapter will offer some powerful ways of arriving at a document's structure, out of several stages of information analysis that will lead you, quickly and efficiently, to an understanding of how the information in any subject—whether a nonfiction how-to or reference work, or an interactive novel or virtual storybook—relates to itself.

My chosen technique for analyzing a document for its structure involves three primary activities, the result of which is a structured document design—a kind of outline, blueprint, or overall plan showing what information needs to be included, where it belongs, and how to get to it. These three activities I describe as:

- Information partitioning
- Information layout
- Navigation design

Information Partitioning

Analyzing information structure begins with information partitioning, a term I've used for the past four or five years to define the process. Information partitioning begins with study, with developing a good working knowledge of the subject you're writing about. You will probably not have the time to become the world's leading expert on the subject before you begin working on the document, but you must know it well enough to be able to describe it, off the cuff and without notes, and to outline it at a fairly low level of detail.

Note: A low level of detail means a lot of detail, whereas a high level of detail means very little detail. The analogy here is to how high or low you are over an object—flying over a city at a low elevation would let you see details like license plates on the cars, street numbers and signs, and individual people's faces, whereas flying over at a high level would let you see buildings, roads, and open spaces like parks and factories.

When you have a good understanding of your subject, partitioning the information is very much like partitioning a large open-floor building into cubicles—you look for what needs to be distinct, what needs to have its own unique space and contents, and what can stand alone. Then you divide the information in the overall subject into the individual partitions that will represent the pieces of your document. In addition, just as in the open-floor office, the partitions in your information serve both as ways of keeping each space distinct, and also as ways of guiding people around within the overall space.

An additional concept that I have found to be useful in information partitioning is to consider that different pieces of information belong naturally in information communities — that is, that certain characteristics of some kinds of information make them naturally related in some way. Communities of information, in this way, fit within the same kind of partition. As for how the different pieces of information in a community relate to one another and to the whole, that is part of the next section, so put that thought aside and let's do an exercise on how to see, sort, and partition different information communities.

Exercise 2: Identifying Communities of Information

The following exercise is also available in slightly different form on line, at the following URL:

http://www.living-history.org/nc5talk/ex-sort.html

As such, it's part of a presentation I gave the Northern California Community College Computer Consortium (NC5) in early 1996. From the URL given there, you can navigate back to the opening page and follow along with it on-line, if you like.

For this exercise, consider the following businesses and organizations that you might find in part of a city:

- Vietnamese restaurant
- Grocery store
- Toy store
- Bookstore
- Card and stationery shop
- Tax preparation service
- Comic-book shop

- Exercise studio
- Pizza restaurant with pipe organ
- Fast-food place with clown
- Pet store
- Discovery Zone
- Six-screen theater complex
- Gas station/smog check shop
- Library
- Elementary school

In the following exercise, don't worry too much about being really critical in your analysis of the kind of people to whom these businesses would appeal. The goal of this exercise is not to be exhaustive, accurate, or politically correct; it's to get you thinking about how the same object—whether a pizza parlor or a home page—can be linked to many different communities.

Which of the previously listed businesses and organizations:

1. Would primarily appeal to kids under 14 by themselves?

2. Would primarily appeal to adults?

3. Would primarily appeal to families (kids & adults together)?

4. Would appeal to active people?

5. Would appeal to quiet people?

6. Would appeal to people with a lot of education?

7. Would appeal to people who like excitement?

With luck, you've drawn some circles on a sheet of paper and connected them in different ways. Many of the businesses appeal to more than one kind of community; many are more tightly focused on a single market.

Creating Dynamic Web Sites

When you analyze, structure, and then map your information, be looking for similar kinds of connections—some information only links one way, some might be linked to from many directions. In the next section, we'll see some specific ways of laying out information that take these connections into account.

Information Layout

When you have partitioned the information in your subject matter, it's time to lay it out so that other people can use it. But what goes together? What needs to be separate? Are there some pieces of information that really have to come first—even in a point-and-click environment like the Web?

The truth is, as the Web page designer and Webmaster, you have a great deal of control over where people go on the Web. Although it's possible to type in a URL and jump to it without any existing context, background, or structure, that's not how most people use the Web. By and large, people use the hyperlinks on a page (at least once they've clicked on the page). As Webmaster, you control the hyperlinks; with some software, you can even track how your readers use them, if necessary.

Thus, although you are providing your readers with the option of nonlinear story (whether fiction or nonfiction), you can still define pockets of linearity when someone needs to know something in a particular order, and you can provide links out to related information. You can, in short, control what your readers see, when they see it, and what they see first. And you may not choose to set up your Web site that way. The choice depends on the members of the information communities you identified in the previous exercise, and on where they fit in the following model of information layout styles.

When defining information layout, you can choose from three primary structures:

1. *Procedural*—where the sequence is critical; the instructions for defusing a bomb, for example, or performing surgery, are examples of information that has a critical procedural nature.

2. *Hierarchical*—where one piece of information contains many parts, all related by whatever the overriding information structure is, but not necessarily by sequence or procedure.

3. *Flat*—where everything is related to everything else with neither an implied sequence or an implied structure, like the entries in an index.

In the real world, your information may include bits and pieces that go back and forth between these three layout styles. In fact, individual partitions within your information structure may well include examples of all three styles. In the next exercise, we'll look at how this can work.

Exercise 3: The Virtual Mall

In Exercise 2, I had you group the different businesses and functions of a city by the communities they served—age groups, education, and other demographic data or character traits.

In this exercise, you're going to consider how you might lay out a large mall or shopping center with these businesses in it, according to several different design criteria. (You don't have to fit every business into each design layout—for example, the gas station/smog test shop will probably not fit into an enclosed mall, though it might be present at the corner of the parking lot.)

1. Write each of the following design criteria on a sheet of paper (or a separate file in Notepad, SimpleText, or vi):

   • Maximum audience concentration

   • Minimum traffic concentration

   • Likelihood of impulse purchase

2. Use the same audience/demographic categories from Exercise 2, as well as the same businesses.

3. Draw a sample layout in which you are trying for maximum audience concentration. That means all the businesses that cater to people under 14 go in one corner, all the eating establishments in another, all the businesses that specialize in well-educated customers in another part of the mall, and the like.

4. Now draw a sample layout in which you are trying for minimum traffic concentration. That means that you don't want all the food-service businesses in the same place because it'll get too crowded at lunchtime; you don't want all the kid-oriented businesses in one place because you'll draw both the kids and the parents.

5. Draw a sample layout in which you are trying to maximize the opportunity for people to make impulse purchases. For the record, people make impulse purchases—that is, small to moderate purchases without much planning or preparation—while entering or leaving a store; the classic impulse purchase is a pack of gum at the cash register.

You'll notice several things about the sample layouts you selected. When you were going for maximum audience concentration, your mall layout was strongly hierarchical—everything in a given area was grouped there because it shared a common characteristic, in this case, the audience. This mall layout might have had several different wings, corners, or even buildings, each of which catered to a distinct audience; this is a hierarchy, in which wing 1 contained the food-service businesses, wing 2 the kid-oriented shops, wing 3 the adult services, and the like.

On the other hand, minimum traffic concentration is a flat architecture. Adjacent businesses have very little in common — they're businesses, and they are in the same mall. But there's no real dependency among them, no reason to put one beside another. When you divide the businesses to keep the traffic concentration to a minimum, your mall layout may still include related businesses (the comic-book shop and the Discovery Zone, for example, both relate to kids), but they will not be laid out together.

Finally, the impulse-purchase design really looks at procedural layout. You want to put the stores that attract the greatest impulse buyers where people can get at them first or last on their shopping trips — at the entrances to the mall, most likely, where people enter and leave while going to and from the parking lot.

What you've done here really involves some fairly complex reasoning. In the impulse-purchase layout in particular, you must — for each store — consider what they sell, whether people would be likely to see something and pop in to buy it, and then position those stores near the entrances — which assumes a sequence or flow to the traffic through the mall. This is the kind of complex reasoning you need to do when laying out your information. Fortunately it's not difficult; it's just a different way of looking at information than from the classic beginning-middle-end approach.

Navigation Design

At this point you've partitioned the information, you've decided on a structural layout—now you have to move people through it. The trick isn't in doing it:

`<a href="file.html">This is all it takes to navigate the Web</a>`

The trick is in keeping track of your information, and in having (and executing) a scheme for doing this in a visually compelling way that enhances the experience of story. And the way to do that is to look at your information layout and determine a navigational metaphor that best supports the layout that your information requires.

Navigational Metaphors

Navigational metaphors are at their best when they reinforce the feeling, mood, or effect that the story is meant to have. Additionally they are at their strongest when you use them with a graphical user interface, rather than with a typical text-only hyperlink. Typical activities that could serve as the metaphor for navigating a Web site (or any other information space) include:

- Driving—using the wheel to turn left, the pedals to go and stop, even turning the radio on and off or changing the station to get different audio tracks

- Sailing—whether a detailed point-of-view animation including a ship's wheel that turns when you click on it, or an antique treasure map on which you can click different destinations and watch an animated sailing ship move from island to island

- Rooms in a building or hallway—you could walk down the middle of the hallway, turn right or left, or back up depending on which part of the screen you clicked

- A desktop—the original Macintosh pioneered this, and the opening screens of both the Mac OS and Windows 95 are still called desktops

- A bookcase—you could click on different volumes, have them fly out toward the viewer, and then open them, turning the pages by clicking on the edges

- A physical space represented in 3D and/or in maps—Myst Island (from the record-setting CD-ROM game *Myst*) is easily the best known of these

The best navigational metaphors, however, should all but go unnoticed. You'll notice that although I talk about a hierarchical information structure, nowhere in this list do I mention hierarchical menus, pull-downs, pull-rights, or lists of selections, buttons, or dials. For any information that you must convey, there is a visual, naturalistic representation that will provide a powerful and enjoyable access to it. Resist the temptation to have simple screens of text, menus, and other computeroid interfaces.

The whole point with multimedia—whether standalone or over the Net—is that your audience can interact with the visuals. At its best, such navigational metaphors don't appear to be an interface at all, in that there's really nothing to learn, memorize, or negotiate; navigational metaphors like this are something I call "Interface-free Design," and they're the highest form of user interface.

Keeping Their Interest

The interface, the navigational metaphor, guides people into your information set, it's true; but it does more than that. The main reason you should use a graphical navigational metaphor is that it attracts people's interest; it engages them in what your Web site has to offer. Once your users get past the initial screen, however, you'll still need to concentrate on keeping them at your site. This final section of the chapter includes some suggestions on specific techniques taken from literature and film that can help you gain and keep an audience's interest. The chapter ends with one final exercise, intended to bridge the gap between story as plug-and-play and story as point-and-click.

For now, let's look at some story elements that filmmakers, novelists, and playwrights have long used to catch and keep the interest of their audience.

Suspense

Alfred Hitchcock is arguably the all-time master of the suspense film. In movies like *Psycho*, *The Birds*, *The Man Who Knew Too Much*, and many more, "Hitch" used a careful combination of story, pace, and visuals to keep audiences on the edge of their seats, practically from the beginning of the picture through the final credits.

Hitchcock once told an interviewer his secret to making suspense movies. He had the audience imagine a movie in which Hitchcock and the interviewer were assassinated by a spy, who put a bomb in a briefcase and left it under the table between them. In an action film, the bomb would go off, the explosion would use expensive special effects, and Hitch and his interviewer would be blown to pieces. The whole scene would probably last no more than 30 seconds.

In his own movies, Hitchcock insisted, the audience would see the bomb being placed a good ten minutes before the event itself. The interview would go on, with cuts every few minutes to a shot with the briefcase as the center of attention, possibly with an interior shot of the briefcase showing the timer counting down. (Fans of the original James Bond films will recognize that the movie *Goldfinger* actually uses this—there's a nuclear device in the middle of Fort Knox, and the digital dial on the front counts down the seconds till detonation.) For even more intensity, Hitch might show us a third character who knew about the bomb, and he'd cut to scenes of this character trying to make it to the studio to warn Hitchcock and the interviewer, but being thwarted by the everyday elements of life—traffic, slow elevators, people blocking the halls, and the like.

The climax to Hitchcock's assassination scene—whether he and the interviewer were blown to bits, or whether they were saved by the third character—would come only after several minutes of excruciating tension, in which we the audience knew the impending disaster and were powerless to stop it. That, in Hitchcock's view, is the difference between suspense and violence. The violence of the explosion lasts (and keeps the audience's attention) for perhaps 30 seconds, maybe a minute with the aftermath. The suspense of not knowing whether or when the explosion would come lasts (and keeps the audience completely riveted on the action) for 10, 15 minutes or more.

The other classic example of suspense is Edgar Allan Poe, the best of whose stories begin with a narrator in prison or in the madhouse, writing about the events that brought him to this sorry condition. We know from the first line that the narrator has done something hideous; we then spend the rest of the story reading, breathless with anticipation, to find out what horror, what unthinkable monstrosity, the character has done—walled his wife's corpse up with the maimed body of a one-eyed cat, or cut an old man into pieces and buried them beneath the floorboards of his room, or immured his old enemy in a damp chamber at the disused end of a catacomb.

Can you use this technique in nonfiction writing? Of course—it just takes a little work, and a little adaptation. In some ways, the classic structure of an expository essay uses this mechanism: you tell them what you're going to tell them, then you tell it to them, and finally you tell them what you told them. Although the typical use of this structure is meant to reinforce a mental model of the information being transferred, a few minor changes can move the mood from one of knowing what's coming (a key to instructional design) to wondering what's coming (a key to engagement, attention, and suspense). And one of the keys to that is the subject of the next section.

Not Saying Everything

"The poetic art is not to say everything" (*ars poetica non omnia dicere est*). So said the Roman poet Horace (as long as we're quoting the classics). Suggestion, indirection, a barest outline with shadows that tease out the imagination and make us wonder—this is a way to keep readers (or watchers or listeners) enthralled.

Not saying everything is a technique particularly useful as a means of achieving suspense: it invokes the reader's imagination by giving only part of the story, by setting up a tension between what the audience knows and what the characters know. But this tension is useful in any situation where you want to create a feeling of apprehension, of anticipation, or of excitement. And the longer we can maintain this feeling of apprehension, as long as it's created in a context that delights the reader, the more satisfying the story will be when it is finally resolved.

And that leads to another technique for keeping the reader's interest: withholding the resolution of a story, asking unanswered questions, and drawing out the conclusion.

Withholding Resolution

Rudyard Kipling's fable about the Elephant's Child (*How the Elephant Got His Trunk*) is one famous, simple instance of resolution withheld. In this story, the Elephant's Child, known for his insatiable curiosity (though it's called "his 'satiable curiosity" in the quaint, slightly childlike wording Kipling uses for his story) keeps asking the question, "What does the crocodile have for dinner?" His aunts and uncles all spank him and send him off without an answer.

By about the fourth or fifth aunt or uncle who spanks him with his or her hard, hard paw, claw, beak, bill, or hoof, we are positively overcome with our own 'satiable curiosity about whether the Elephant's Child will ever find out what the crocodile has for dinner. (Of course, the answer is very nearly Elephant's Child, and this leads to the dramatic conclusion of the fable.) But for the duration of the story (about as long as a child's story ought to be), we identify with the Elephant's Child in wanting to know the answer to this question, and in wondering about how the story will turn out.

Of course, while we're wondering, a good author can drop hints—oblique references that, when seen with the clarity of hindsight after the resolution is provided, tie in the dramatic elements of the story powerfully. This, of course, is the literary effect known as foreshadowing.

Foreshadowing

Foreshadowing is the technique of giving a taste of something that's going to happen (and you'll notice that I did this back in my design principles, when I said we'd do this exercise later in the chapter). Foreshadowing is a way of violating the inherent linearity of time in a story, a way of tying events forward—a counterpart to flashbacks, in which the action ties events backwards.

What's most curious about foreshadowing is that when it's done well, which is to say subtly, it isn't something that we know is being done because we haven't experienced the event being foreshadowed. It isn't till the final event itself that we are jerked back—very nonlinearly—to the instance of foreshadowing.

There's a difference between foreshadowing and giving away. In *Macbeth*, for example, the three witches prophesy that Macbeth will be king, and that his friend Banquo "shalt get kings, though thou be none." This isn't truly foreshadowing—it's more giving away future action, at least to the audience. But it decidedly sets us up to keep our attention on the rest of the play. How will it work out? If we've never seen the play before, we watch to see the action; if we've seen the play dozens of times, we look for new interpretations, new details in the interactions between Macbeth and his wife, little ironies in what they say to Duncan, to Banquo, and to Macduff.

There is an opposite to foreshadowing, of course, and I've mentioned it before in this chapter, but it needs to be included here for the sake of completeness, and to provide a full set of literary (or cinematic, or poetic, or dramatic) techniques. And that technique is the flashback.

Flashback

What a flashback really is—when it's used well—is a way of filling in details that give the present story more richness, more depth, and make it more personal. In addition to the *Citizen Kane* example I've given already, one of the classic uses of flashback is in *Casablanca*, where Rick (Humphrey Bogart) remembers his time in Paris with Ilse (Ingrid Bergman).

Fundamentally what this does is leave space in the readers' world for them to create their own back-story, to decide for themselves what else went on, what motivated people, why they did what they did. In this sense, flashbacks are also an excellent tool for providing the beginnings of interactivity because they present the audience with a technique for visualizing characters— making them more personal and making the story come to life more effectively, all of which helps keep people engaged in the story.

There's a huge difference, however, between keeping people wondering what happens next in a film, book, or play, and doing the same thing in a CD-ROM or interactive story. In a film, the screenwriter chooses one action for the character to take. There are two important points to that sentence:

- The screenwriter chooses.

- The character takes one action.

In interactive drama—the drama of point-and-click— neither of those is true. The author of interactive stories needs to consider all the actions—at least all the plausible ones—that the character might take. Then, from these, the audience chooses the action.

Here's a thought for people developing interactive fiction: consider a flashback button in the menu of each scene of your interactive movie. That is, whenever appropriate, your users could watch a scene, then click on a flashback button to see an event out of the past that added richness, depth, or character development to the scene they'd just watched. Likewise, you could include a foreshadowing button, one that played or highlighted individual parts or elements of the scene they're watching, with the intention of outlining the elements that foreshadow future events. Although I can imagine this being done in a very heavy-handed way, it could also provide tremendous insight to the character, great resonance to the plot, and fabulous interest to the story line and the interactive piece in general.

There's one final issue involved in interactive fiction, particularly interactive fiction that heavily borrows from role-playing games in which the characters make one of several choices in a scene and the story line alters slightly depending on their choice. This is the part of interactive fiction that many authors find incredibly daunting. "I have enough trouble writing one plot," I was once told by an author who was attending one of my seminars on writing for interactive multimedia. "How am I ever going to find the time, energy, or creativity to write three, or five, or ten?" I gave that some thought for a few months and came up with the following exercise.

In the next exercise, you'll go through the one of the classes that I most enjoy teaching—a brainstorming session on how to generate interactive storyboards for multimedia.

Exercise 4: The Interactive Storyboard

My favorite class is the hour or so I spend on storyboarding for interactivity. First, I introduce the idea of the storyboard, a kind of visual outline for setting up the scene as the camera will record it (and as outlined in more detail in Chapter 3). In the class, we watch pieces from several movies that make the point clearly. I start with *The Birds*, specifically the scene where Tippi Hedren sits outside the schoolroom as the crows collect behind her. This makes it easy to visualize the storyboard because there are essentially only two views—Tippi sitting on the bench looking nervous, cut to the birds gathering behind her; Tippi smoking on the bench looking more nervous, cut to even more birds behind her; and so forth till you see the playground equipment covered with hundreds and hundreds of crows.

For the next part, we move on to *Alien*, the scene where Tom Skerritt crawls through the air duct in search of the creature that's been killing his crewmembers. For this scene, I point out how the fast cuts add to the feeling of tension and drama. In my class, I simply have the students make hash-marks on a sheet of paper each time the camera shifts position. Depending on where I start and stop, the scene (which lasts about 2 minutes) has between 27 and 32 camera cuts (or at least that's how many the students count; I'm not interested in getting the right answer, I'm interested in them getting the point).

Finally I move to *Jurassic Park*, and we study the scene where Sam Neill rescues the two kids from the overturned Land Cruiser being tossed around by the tyrannosaurus rex. I do two exercises here; the first one opens up your sense of visual style, the second one provides a breakthrough in plot development. (At least it does in class, where the group dynamic and direct interaction with me can help guide the students in the direction I'm committed to taking them.)

So for this exercise, set yourself up in the following way:

- Rent, borrow, or otherwise obtain a videotape or laser disc of *Jurassic Park*.

- Get together with four, five, six, or more of your most creative friends, colleagues, or fellow students and make an evening of it.

- Make sure that each of you has several blank sheets of paper and a pen or pencil; you'll be doing some sketching and note-taking.

- Advance the tape (well, if you really want to, you can also just watch it) up to the point where the tyrannosaurus eats the lawyer, then start paying attention—the assignment starts here.

1. Watch the movie for the next 2 minutes; stop the tape when the Land Cruiser falls over the edge of the embankment and the *t. rex* roars again. (You may want to take a few minutes to catch your breath if you haven't seen the movie before.)

2. Sketch out the scenes as you remember them. Don't worry about details—check Chapter 3 for notes and suggestions on storyboard development. Just get the sense of the scene as you remember it—was the camera looking up or down? Was it a still shot or did the

camera move? What was the action — did someone run or jump, did the *t. rex* shove the Land Cruiser around? Most important, don't try to draw what you know — draw what you *see.*

3. Rewind the movie to the point just before step 1 and watch it again, stopping it at the same point. This time, follow along with your storyboard.

    What was the same? What was different? What did you change? What did you remember just as it was in the movie?

At this stage in the class, I intervene and make sure the class is completely clear on one point: wherever they differ from Spielberg's vision, they aren't wrong. This is not a test to see how well they can remember the movie; it's not a test to see how quickly they can draw. It's an exercise to develop their sense of visual style. And I propose that the differences between their storyboards — or yours — and the actual movie is the first sign of their own personal style of moviemaking.

Then we have some *real* fun. For the next part of the exercise, you're going to pretend you're designing an interactive CD-ROM to go along with *Jurassic Park* (and if you pitch one and it sells, remember to send me 10%!). Rewind the movie back to where you started for step 1, get everybody into the room again, grab the remote control for your VCR, and take it from here. From this point on, it's audience-participation time, with one of you (whichever of you had the good sense to buy this book, naturally!) leading this exercise. Play the movie, pressing Pause at the following points:

1. Just as the *t. rex* spins the Land Cruiser.

2. After the Land Cruiser spins or twists again, and Sam Neill and Lex dodge it.

3. Just as Sam and Lex jump up onto the ledge, nearly slipping in the mud.

4. As they hang on the cable, just after Sam Neill says "Lex, you're choking me!"

Each time you press Pause, turn to the group and say, "Now, what else can Sam do at this point?" Tell your friends and classmates to just shout out whatever comes up. Pick one person to write them down. Each time one person says something, acknowledge it and ask, "And what else is possible?" Keep asking "What else is possible?" till the room doesn't answer for five or ten seconds, then press Play again and go on to the next pausing point.

At the end of this exercise, you should have between 12 and 20 different actions to take, at each of these critical stages of the story. You can now diagram the actions you've generated and see how you could develop an entire interactive movie based on making the choices you've identified in the past two or three minutes.

You'll also get an idea — given the cost to produce the single, plug-and-play version of *Jurassic Park* — just how expensive it would be to do this really well. This just means that when you write that proposal for the interactive home game version of the next hit movie, remember to ask for more money!

CHAPTER 6   # Web Sound

How much does sound add to a great multimedia experience? In the right hands, sound can be everything. Yet only digital video is more bandwidth-intensive than audio as a way to drag out the time between stimulus and response, between user interaction and system delivery.

This chapter discusses a number of issues involved in the effective use of sound in a Web site. It includes:

- Tips for synchronizing sound effects with motion in Shockwave movies

- Suggestions on looping sounds to minimize load time

- A discussion of the issues involved in selecting a sampling rate for performance versus quality

- Suggestions about using MIDI versus captured or sampled sound

- Suggestions on great ways to capture and create sound effects

As with most of the methods of animation, adding sound to a Web site typically (as of Netscape 2.0, at any rate) involves the use of helper applications or plug-ins. The exception, of course, is to use a Java applet designed and written to play sounds. Although instructing you on the design of such an applet is beyond the scope of this book, we'll look at some of the alternatives and search for some public-domain applets you might be able to plug into your Web page.

The Four Stages of Adding Sound

Before going on, however, it's worth taking a look at the four stages involved in adding sound to your Web page:

1. Capturing

2. Editing

3. Processing

4. Publishing

After an overview of where each of these steps fits in the entire process, we'll look at what's involved in each stage. Following that, we'll go through how to use and include sounds in Shockwave pieces, how to set up RealAudio on your Web page, and how to include short button sounds for use on helper applications.

The process of adding sound to a Web page is similar to pressing a record or a CD. First, there has to be a sound that you want to keep; it may be a musical performance, an interview, a dramatic presentation, a special event, or a sound effect. That sound needs to be captured. The technology has progressed far since the days of Edison and his wax cylinders. Today, the options include recording digitally, mixing multiple audio tracks, and using other sophisticated techniques to ensure the highest quality.

When the sound has been captured, it's time to edit it. I like to think of editing for any (or all) of three reasons: editing to fit the time available editing to clean up the sound quality and editing to combine with such effects as mixing voice-over with music or interleaving different tracks of audio (much the same as the two-camera work described in Chapter 3).

Processing involves any conversion, alteration, or modifications required to fit the sound you have recorded and edited — which may involve several different pieces of software — into the format and tool you're planning to use to publish the sound on the Web. Again, this may be a new tool that you haven't yet used, or you may have captured or edited the sound directly in the package you're planning to use for publication. Some sound tools make this simpler than others; Macromedia, for example, does a good job of integrating their SoundEdit program with Director, and the result is an easy import of sound files into the finished multimedia project. When you convert the Director title to Shockwave, the sound follows along pretty much automatically.

Finally, there's publication itself. The tool you choose for publication depends to a large extent on what you plan to do with it. The tools we'll look at here fall into four categories:

- Sound files distributed for playback with helper applications on the user's platform, such as .WAV and AIFF files using the Windows Media Player or SoundMachine on the Macintosh

- Sound included as the synchronized soundtrack in a piece of digital video, such as QuickTime audio tracks

- Sound files meant for long, relatively uninterrupted play, with RealAudio being the premiere example at present

- Sound files meant for incorporation in an interactive multimedia piece, such as effects, dialog, and feedback cues in a Director/Shockwave piece

After you've published the sound in your Web page, there's one other step: supporting your audience in getting to the necessary resources to play and hear your sound. Consider adding a Plug-ins page to your Web site, one from which you can direct your audience to all the necessary FTP sites where they can find and download anything they may need to experience your site in its full multimedia glory. You may also want to include instructions there on how to set up helper applications, and possibly recommendations on helper applications that you know work on each of the platforms (with, of course, links to where those applications can be downloaded).

Before we go much further, however, I should point out that although I base all the examples in this chapter on experiences I've had editing, digitizing, and publishing sound (much of which you'll be able to hear on the Web page), there's a good chance that you are more of an audiophile than I am. I bought my first audio CD player in December 1994; before that, I listened to records (remember records?) on my ten-year-old turntable (remember turntables?). No, I didn't have to crank it up and place the megaphone horn directly on the disk, but I will admit that—although I love music, and I'm a huge fan of both Treg Brown and Carl Stalling—I'm one of the least audiophilic people I know.

So if you're looking for a technical dissertation on mu-law acoustics or on how to simulate Dolby noise reduction in software, well, you've come to the wrong place. Check out the Webliography for references on the highly technical side of acoustical engineering. In exchange, what I offer here is intensely practical advice on how to get sound into, and out of, your Web page, on a shoestring budget and with little technical assistance.

Creating Dynamic Web Sites

By the way, if you wondered who I'm a fan of in that last paragraph, they're the two guys responsible for the great sound of the classic Warner Brothers cartoons of the forties and fifties. Treg Brown was Warner's sound effects man, responsible for everything from the crunch of Bugs's carrots to the "eeobbidy-obbidy-obbidy" noise that Elmer Fudd *et al.* make when Bugs shakes their heads. Carl Stalling was the music director for the Loony Tunes gang, and the toy chest Stalling got to play with was the Warner Brothers symphony orchestra—the same people who did the great sound tracks for movies like the 1936 Errol Flynn *Robin Hood*, not to mention minor hits like *Casablanca*.

I'm convinced that half the reason that Stalling's liberties with pop and classical tunes alike were so successful (for a good time, make an opera buff sit through "The Rabbit of Seville" or "What's Opera, Doc?" and watch them squirm) was the quality of the performers. The other half, of course, was simply that he was a comic genius himself, able to twist a musical phrase into a joke without going overboard, without becoming the caricatures that the later sound tracks became.

What Does Your Sound Do?

Before jumping into the technical side of things, it's worth spending a few minutes exploring what you want to do with the sound. Although you can do nearly anything with nearly any sound you record—from copying tracks off an internal CD player to speaking directly into a microphone to stripping the audio track from a QuickTime movie—some things are much easier if you set them up a particular way to begin with. Thinking about sound at this point in the game will help you in the long run by making it easier to get the effect you're after.

For starters, ask yourself whether the sound is going to be synchronized with another activity on your Web page, or simply a standalone effect. Examples of synchronized activities range from dialog spoken by a character whose lips are seen moving (the most critical case for synchronization) to sound effects that need to follow a user's interaction with some aspect of the program. In the latter case, how you capture the sound isn't critical, as long as it's in a form you can import into whatever authoring system you plan to use for the special effect. Later in this chapter we'll talk about how Shockwave lets you do exactly that.

The former case, however, is absolutely critical because we have so much experience seeing people who are speaking. If the sound and the motion are off by as much as a frame, it looks wrong and distracts from the experience. If you need sound that is synchronized this closely with motion, use digital video. Much of QuickTime's technical work is involved in keeping sound and video synchronized, for just this reason. (In fact, QuickTime actually drops video frames, if necessary, during playback to make sure that the visuals don't fall behind the audio track.)

Second, ask how you ideally want your users to interact with the sound. Are you setting up a Web-based music station, a kind of cyberspace juke box that lets your users select songs (or other audio clips) that they will listen to while doing something else at work? For this, something like RealAudio from Progressive Networks is ideal. We'll look at how you set up a RealAudio site and what makes it such a distinct solution later in this chapter. As an alternative, you can simply set up URLs to sound files on your Web page, much the way you import images or video, and your audience will download the sound files to be played on a helper application such as the Microsoft Media Player or one of the Macintosh-based sound programs. We'll look at a few of those later as well.

Basically, however, the issue is whether you plan to use the sound in a tightly coupled combination with some kind of motion, or whether it's to be used as a standalone application adding interest or value to your Web site. If you have the memory and disk space for it, you may simply want to record all your audio as QuickTime, even if it's going to be used as voice-over for a slide show. The advantages are that you will always have a synchronized visual track to use later, and you can always strip the sound and export it to another package. The disadvantages are that if you save the video, it takes up a ton of room on your hard drives, which can get expensive. If you never plan to sync up speech with facial expressions, record in whatever native sound format you prefer and your system's sound card and software can generate. We'll look at several packages for converting back and forth between sound formats later, during the section on processing. For now, let's take a look at how you get the sound into the computer in the first place: capturing digital audio.

Capturing Audio in the Studio

Capturing audio for the computer can be either a one-stage or a two-stage process, depending on whether you record from the actual sound waves to the computer with no intermediate stages (in what's called direct-to-digital recording), or whether you record first on some kind of analog medium (such as audio tape or even wax cylinders) and then digitize.

If you record directly on the computer, it's a one-stage process. Going direct to digital in this way has many advantages, primarily in noise reduction. In this case, by noise I mean the noise that results from digitizing off an analog source — that is, sampling noise. We'll cover background noise — meaning unwanted sounds present during the actual recording — shortly.

One problem with any analog recording is that a certain amount of carrier noise is simply unavoidable. Carrier noise is what we hear as "tape hiss" — a white-noise (meaning random frequency) background hiss that interferes with clean playback of the sound. Carrier noise is also the cracks, pops, and other unintended sound effects on vinyl records. If you're a dyed-in-the-wool audiophile, you're already familiar with the DDD symbol on the back of audio CDs; that's the level of sound reproduction we're talking about here.

There's another issue involved in sound clarity. Back in Chapter 3, I talked about the "noisy" process of digitizing images, particularly dark ones. Digitizing, whether of audio or video, is a process of taking samples—snapshots—of many points along a continuous curve. More samples makes the resulting curve smoother, but the file takes up more room; fewer samples makes a smaller file (and therefore one that downloads more quickly), but it is less smooth (though this is generally perceived as "crisp") to the ear. In digitizing video, the issue is frame rate—more frames per second mean smoother motion, but they put a higher performance load on both the playback and the download mechanisms. In digitizing audio, the issue is sampling rate, measured in kilohertz (KHz), or thousands of cycles per second.

One potential source for confusion for people new to digital sound (I know it confused me for some time) is that kilohertz is the rate of measurement of a sound's pitch or frequency, as well as the measurement of how often it's sampled. The nominal range of human hearing is 20 Hz to 20 KHz. That does not mean, however, that sampling an audio clip at 11.1 KHz will clip all sounds at a higher frequency than that. Sampling is exactly that—the digitizing program slices into the analog stream at the sampling rate you select, but it then converts the slice of sound at that point into a range of numeric values that represent the auditory frequencies. It's possible, therefore, to represent pitches of 14 KHz in audio sampled at 8 KHz.

What's missing is the smoothness—which again is perceived as a lack of sound clarity—that would be present in a sound clip digitized at a higher sampling rate. Just as video digitized at 15 fps looks jerkier than analog video at 30 fps, audio digitized at 8 KHz sounds muddier than audio digitized at 22.3 KHz. But it takes up much less room—and has a correspondingly lower amount of time to download.

Digitizing in the Field

There's one other difference between digitizing direct to disk and digitizing off an analog source: location. When I prepared the audio for the diskette included in my first book about multimedia, I wanted to get the sound of my car driving down the road, shifting gears, and making the usual assortment of vroomy noises associated with a little open sports car. For that, I took a battery-operated tape recorder in the car with me and drove around the block. Direct-to-digital wasn't possible, unless I wanted to get several hundred yards of extension cord and try to run the computer in the passenger's seat.

Today, of course, I could probably plug a microphone into the appropriate place on a PowerBook and digitize from nature that way, but the fact remains that analog audio recording devices are a very mature technology with a huge industry behind them. You can record audio using anything from a $30 microcassette recorder on up, and run it all off batteries and often in a device that slings over your shoulder, perhaps even fitting in your pocket.

The way to determine whether to record audio at the event or in the studio is first practical, then economic. Some events are simply impossible to duplicate in the studio: the Olympics, for example, or a space shuttle launch are not possible to duplicate in the studio (though of course they can always be simulated). Other events can be recorded later in the studio, such as a musical performance or an interview. The issue here is whether it is economically feasible to bring together everything necessary to make the studio session possible. If you're interviewing a public figure, you can probably get him or her to come to the studio (especially in an election year). On the other hand, if you're doing a Webcast of a free concert in the park, it's going to be tough to get all the performers to come back to the studio later and record your media. So those are the questions you need to consider when deciding on studio versus location recording—which, as I've indicated, will have some effect on whether you go direct to digital.

If you're capturing audio in analog at an event, a video camera actually works well, for several reasons. First, the video that goes along with the audio you get provides an incredibly simple way of indexing and getting an edit log. It's much simpler to fast-forward to a portion of the tape you can see than to do it blind on audio-only tape. Second, virtually every camcorder made today records in stereo, which is a nice touch; QuickTime movies also record the stereo tracks, which is nice for drive-past or fade effects. Later, when it comes time to digitize, you can either record just the audio by plugging in just the red and white RCA jacks to your sampler, or you can digitize the video as a QuickTime movie (at a low frame rate, if you know you're mainly concerned with the audio) and then strip the sound track later.

If you're planning to do much recording this way, and if you care about the quality of your sound, look into a range of microphones. The most annoying thing about audio on a camcorder (at least to an avowed non-audiophile; don't bother sending me vitriolic email about the nuances I'm missing by doing my audio recording onto 8mm, or how much signal I lose by using RCA jacks) is the hum of the tape drive. When the tape is running, the motor's vibration carries through the body of the camcorder and ends up being recorded by the built-in microphone. It's like putting your ear directly on a door behind which there's a motor running; the direct contact means that even a quiet noise will get transmitted.

Depending on the kind of audio you're looking to do, you will probably want at least two microphones:

- A long-range directional microphone that clips to the top of the camcorder; this microphone amplifies sounds from comparatively far away. It can be useful if you are recording nonprofessional people in groups or performances; for example, the video club at Cherry Chase

Elementary School uses this kind of microphone to record their student assemblies, and it will pick up speech on the stage when the camera is in the middle of the multipurpose room.

- A hand-held microphone, suitable for interviews. If you plan to do much audio work in the form of interviews—whether they are with members of your organization explaining a new product to potential customers, or world leaders explaining a new policy to international listeners—you'll want to be able to stick the ice-cream cone in somebody's face sooner or later. You can probably also get a stand to use for table-top recording in the studio.

Digitizing in the Studio (or Office)

Even if you don't want to spend the time and money to make a really thorough, professional recording studio, you can vastly improve the quality of your audio with a few simple, cheap techniques:

- Use a closed-door office or conference room. Cubicles pick up too much stray background noise.

- Turn the telephone ringer off. There's nothing more irritating than having the phone ring halfway through the *perfect* reading. And if you use a mail program that announces incoming mail with a tone (as the Eudora program does), turn that off too for the duration of the session.

- Cover and hard-finish walls or surfaces (white boards, glass, slick panels) in the room you use for recording. A light blanket or quilt will do if you've got to convert someone's office into a recording booth for a day or two; foam rubber is better if you're going to make the setup permanent or semi-permanent. Sound reflects off smooth, hard-finish surfaces, causing unwanted echoes and interference.

- Place a foam ball over the microphone. You'll be able to pick up these at a good video or audio electronics store. They reduce the hiss from sibilants (S and soft C sounds) and the pop of Ps and Ts; they're also useful if you ever plan to record outdoors because they reduce the amount of wind noise passing over the microphone.

- Speak a little more slowly than you would in conversation one on one. Remember that much of communication is nonverbal; if you are going to be recording, your audience will not be able to see your expressions, gestures, and body language.

- Record everything more than once, no matter how perfect you think it is. You may want to try it a different way for some other reason.

The key point to remember about recording is that you can't take out bad recording quality. Hisses, crackles, sound artifacts of any kind can never really be edited out, no matter how powerful a sound editor you have. This is most especially true when you are working from an analog source. Remember also that each successive generation of an analog copy introduces more and more noise and takes out another degree of clarity. This is the strongest argument for direct-to-digital recording, if you have equipment that supports it. A digital recording is a stream of numbers that will always be copied exactly from one generation to the next, so you never need fear clarity loss between generations.

One source of shareware programs for digitizing sound files on Windows systems is:

http://www.missionrec.com/dl.html

Check this page if you are looking for a program to digitize audio—either previously recorded or live from a microphone—on the Windows platform. If you bought a "multimedia PC" with a sound card bundled in the system (such as a SoundBlaster 16), that card may have its own basic audio recording software that you can also use.

Editing

When you begin editing a sound track, you can undertake three basic kinds of operations:

1. Editing for time and content. This includes getting the starts and stops of clips just where you want them, removing sections that you don't want to use, or cleaning up dead space or "out-takes" in the source.

2. Editing for clarity. This means performing various filters and other operations that change the clarity or quality of the tone.

3. Editing for effects. Some of the sound editing software I've used allows you to make changes—ranging from cut-and-paste segments for that "Max Headroom" sound to flipping segments of songs backwards. (For the record, I've sampled most of the questionable sections of the Beatles song "Revolution 9" and played them reversed, and they're really no more intelligible than they are in the normal direction.)

Another important reason for editing has to do with the nature of the Web itself. Basically, just as text or graphical information modules have a clear focus and a specific scope, audio modules also need to focus on a specific subject. You need to think as clearly about the structure of your audio clips as you do about the structure of hypertext, interactive media, and so on. The hypertext model of modular, structured information applies just as powerfully to time-based media as it does to text and static graphics.

To put this into concrete terms, let's talk about a pet peeve of mine with TV news shows. You know the way they always seem to announce the one news item you want to hear about ("Domain name servers found to cause cancer, film at eleven") and then make you wait through the entire episode, including the scores for sports that you didn't even know people played, before finally getting to one miserable 2-minute overview by someone who obviously never heard about the subject until 30 seconds before air time? Don't do that to people. Or at least, don't expect them to bookmark your page if you do. There's no excuse for this on the Web—put each story in its own file, with a clearly marked hypertext link to that clip. Remember, the sanity you save may be your own.

Processing

The next stage, processing, means converting to the right kind of sound file for the application you want to use. You can do one of several things at this stage. One of the more practical aspects of this is to convert the sound from one file format or platform to another. At this point, the three main sound file formats are .WAV, a Windows format; AIFF, the Apple sound file format (though Apple also supports system sound resources, a subject really better suited for a book on Macintosh system programming than Web-based multimedia), and the cross-platform .AU file format. Shareware and freeware packages are available for this. Most cross-platform tools are Macintosh-based (which makes economic sense, as they're the minority player in the computer market today); some of the tools I'm familiar with include Balthazar (freeware, Craig Marciniak), a simple package that lets you play any .WAV file on a Macintosh.

You can also play with the way a clip sounds. One of the most fun shareware ($15) sound tools for the Macintosh is Alberto Ricci's SoundEffects. You can do many reasonable things with it, including cut sounds, fade them in or out, add echoes, amplify sounds by a percentage you type in, smooth the overall shape, and add noise to give an "old-time radio" effect to something. But I have to say that my favorite is the Robotize effect. You can see from the shape of the waveform that Robotize adds lots of distortions. Here I've sampled a short piece from *Sgt. Pepper's Lonely Hearts Club Band* (the French horn section in the first cut from the CD), then robotized it later:

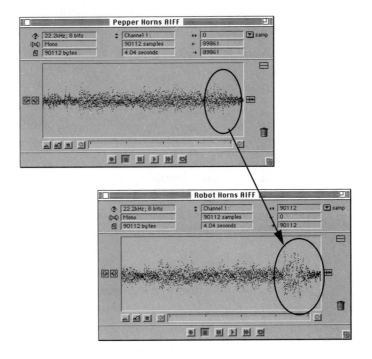

You may be able to see the difference in the shape of the waves at the right edge of the robotized segment. The ends of the waves that reach both higher and lower mean that there is a more hollow, bright, distorted effect that really sounds like a robot voice.

Publishing

The final stage in the process is publishing the sound clip on the Web. In the case of RealAudio, there's one additional twist I haven't mentioned: you can broadcast the sound live, digitizing it directly into your server from the event being broadcast. That's a special case, which I'll talk a little more about in a while.

For the most part, though, if you are looking to add audio as one of your media, you'll probably use one of the four basic methods for adding sound to your Web page: as a sound effect in a Shockwave piece, as a clip (or a live broadcast) for RealAudio, through the traditional method of downloading (FTP) a file to be used with a browser's helper applications, and as part of a Java applet. Let's take a look at some of these examples and see what's different about them.

Publishing with Helper Applications

The simplest way to add sound to a Web page is to include it as a hypertext reference. This is a one-line HTML tag — simplicity itself. For example, the following snippet of HTML uses an image file called **welcome.jpg** as the button, and a file called **welcome.au** as the destination of the jump:

```
<a href="welcome.au"><img src="welcome.jpg"></a>
```

The Web page with a line like this will display the **welcome.jpg** image as a hyperlink; when your users click on this picture, your server will download the file **welcome.au** to their system.

At this point, it's up to your users to have configured their browsers to take advantage of this. The server begins the process of downloading the file to your users. The next step depends on whether your users have configured their Web browser to handle files of this type. This is a fairly standard mechanism whereby Web browsers can play various media types locally, by configuring themselves to use what have come to be known as helper applications.

How the users actually do this varies from browser to browser, but for Netscape, it's under the Options menu, specifically the General Preferences section. You may want to leave a page that explains this and other options for your users to refer to.

If your users have not mentioned a specific helper application for files of the type that they have just downloaded, Netscape offers them the option of browsing for a helper application or saving the incoming file somewhere in their computer. It would be friendly to your users to tell them that if they take the option of saving the incoming file, there's good and bad news. The good news is that they have the file to view again and again. The bad news is that they need to pay attention to where in the file system the incoming media file gets put. It's too easy to click OK and not realize where the media is being stored, then have difficulty trying to find it again later. In addition, media takes up a lot of room on the disk drive, another point you may want to make to your users. If they remember in advance, it's much easier to find where downloaded files get sent.

In summary:

- Helper applications are the simplest possible way to distribute audio on your Web site.

- Limitations include the length of time required to download files.

- Risks to users include the possibility that they may not have the appropriate helper application and that they may need to explicitly save the files in a directory they can remember and access later.

Sound in Shockwave

Shockwave files use sound imported into Macromedia Director as a Cast member and manipulated in the usual way. Director permits two sound channels, so that it's possible to achieve some sophisticated interplay between the channels and the animation.

Some of the things you can do with this include:

- Wait for a sound to finish before continuing with animation. This is useful if you have a single frame of your presentation, such as a menu, that you want to display while a sound track plays explaining what's going on.

- Synchronize a sound with a user interaction, such as playing a recorded "click" when your users make a selection.

- Simulating a dialog between two characters on (or off) the screen and synchronizing the starting times of each successive sound with the beginning of any animation that goes with it.

- Loop on a particular sound clip in the Director movie, having it play repeatedly until the user makes a selection or goes to a different URL.

One production tip using sound effects in Director (something I learned after writing my book on Director): You may want to use a click and a blink to let your users know that they've made a selection. For example, it's common to design a set of buttons in such a way that they look "pushed" when someone selects them, and also so that the movie plays a "click" (one of the default sounds distributed in Director) when the button is selected.

We naturally tried putting the blink and the click in the same frame, but found that it didn't work. Director played the visual first (we were only swapping in a 30 x 30 pixel region of the screen, so it loaded very quickly) and then made the sound. This gave a sort of "blink-beat-click" approach, which would be excellent if we were simulating fireworks or lightning flashes, where you see the explosion and then several seconds later hear the boom. (No, it was not several seconds, but it was noticeably later in many cases, due to the length of time required to load and play the sound in memory.)

After playing with several variations on this—and it's a subtle, subtle thing but it makes a difference in the finished product—we found that the most effective way to present this was to put the visual representation for the pushed button in the movie frame that immediately followed the "click." This worked because we tricked the brain—we're used to seeing, then hearing (as in fireworks and lightning), so when you reverse the order in the presentation, the brain "corrects" to some extent.

Two additional points are worth making: First, this was in a huge, multi-megabyte Director presentation that ended up being entirely linear, playing on a dedicated PC used as a kiosk at a trade show and produced under a very tight deadline. If we had been able to tune the performance of each module and eliminated the loading of extraneous elements into memory, we could probably have solved the (very slight) lag time we observed in the initial blink-wait-click case. Second, especially within the context of the Web and download time, the wait between the blink and the click was probably 1/20th of a second— the blink of an eye.

In summary:

- Because the sound effects are downloaded when your users access a page with an embedded Shockwave file, Director's sound effects give game-quality response to interaction, with sound effects that happen almost instantly when your users click something—there's no additional lag time for downloading the sound file.

- With two different sound channels, it's possible to have a background clip playing in channel 1 and have response-based sound effects (clicks, voice clips, explosions, or whatever your game calls for) in channel 2.

- Synchronization between sound and animation is possible to a very precise level, permitting clicks and blinks to occur at almost the same instant in time.

One caveat: as this book went into production, Macromedia did not support using the Wait channel in Shockwave titles. This is too bad, as it is so convenient in a Director title to have the action wait until one or the other of the sound channels finishes playing. Fortunately, Lingo still gives you a great deal of control over the timing of sound in your Shockwave title. The following Lingo script holds the Shockwave movie in the current frame until the sound in channel 1 finishes:

```
if soundBusy (1) then

    go to the frame

end if
```

Sound Publishing in RealAudio

A completely different approach to sound publishing over the Web is RealAudio from Progressive Networks. To understand what makes RealAudio so different, consider the standard sound publication method involving a helper application. In that model, the sound clip is shipped across the network connection to the client as a file. This means that the entire sound file must be transferred before the helper application can begin playing the sound.

In RealAudio, the Web browser opens up a connection to the site serving the audio clip. Then, once the connection is open, the sound is transmitted over the Internet directly, and almost immediately, from the server to the client, as a stream of data. This means that unlike the helper application setup where the entire file must be transferred before the Web user can start listening, someone who listens to a RealAudio page can begin listening as soon as the initial connection is made. The amount of time required to open the connection is a fraction of what even a short sound file would take to load. This reduces the time between input and response to a few seconds—and a consistent few seconds, while the connection is established.

Limits at the server end depend entirely on the speed of your network connection. A single stream of audio data from your server to the Web client listening at the other end requires from 10 to 22 kilobytes per second of bandwidth (depending on the sample rate as you digitize the sound). This means that you should configure your network connection to handle the demand you anticipate and the sound quality you are serving. For example, a 56-kilobyte-per-second frame relay connection can handle four streams simultaneously; a T1 connection can handle 100 streams, and a T3 connection can simultaneously transmit between 3000 and 4000 audio streams.

There are some limits on the receiving end. Users with less than a 28.8 modem can't receive certain kinds of information—basically, a 14.4 connection is good for speech, but not for music. Higher speed connections are actually capable of transmitting music of the same quality as an FM radio station.

There are three parts to the RealAudio equation. First is the RealAudio player, which your users must download in order to listen to your audio content; you'll therefore probably want to include a link to the RealAudio player site, which for RealAudio version 1.0 is:

http://www2.realaudio.com/release/download.html

The link to the 2.0 version of the player is:

http://www.realaudio.com/products/ra2.0/index.html

The RealAudio player is free, so any user can download it and start listening to real-time audio presentations. At the time of this writing, RealAudio's Web page indicated that more than four million copies of the RealAudio player had been downloaded, so there's a large base of people ready to listen to the sounds you provide.

The second part of the RealAudio equation is encoding the sound in the appropriate format. RealAudio provides an encoder — also free — so that you can convert recorded sounds into the appropriate format for use with the RealAudio player. Providing the sound files is really a two-part process. First, the digital audio files you encoded (which take an extension of .ra) need to be placed on your server. Then you need to create a metafile (which has an extension of .ram), which is nothing but a text pointer to the audio file (or files) that you want your users to be able to listen to. The metafile itself is the destination of the URL you put in your Web page. You can put more than one sound clip in the same metafile. When a user browses the URL for this metafile, the RealAudio server plays all the audio clips, in sequence, that are referred to in the metafile.

For example, let's assume you are setting up a Web site dedicated to the Three Stooges (www.stooges.com). You might conceivably have three sound files: larry.ra, moe.ra, and curly.ra. To play each of these in succession when someone clicks on the URL, your metafile would look like this:

pnm://www.stooges.com/larry.ra

pnm://www.stooges.com/moe.ra

pnm://www.stooges.com/curly.ra

This is your RealAudio metafile, titled stooges.ram, and it's the URL that people click on in your Web page. That is handled in a straightforward way. To make this available to Web users, just add this line to your HTML file:

```
<a href="http://www.stooges.com/stooges.ram">Nyuk!</a>
```

This isn't quite all there is to it. You need to take two additional steps. First, you need to configure your Web server to handle the appropriate MIME type (just as you did when you installed a Shockwave file, as outlined in Chapter 4). For RealAudio, you need to configure your server to associated files with the extension .ram with the MIME type x-pn-realaudio. This varies with the server you are running, so check the documentation for your server to find out how this works for you.

The final step before people can listen to RealAudio from your home page is to buy the RealAudio server software, which retails for $495 as I wrote this. You can also download a free copy of their Personal Server software, which permits up to two audio connections at a time.

This gives you an understanding of the financial impact of serving RealAudio. The $495 price for the server isn't much compared to the connectivity cost, so look carefully at the benefit you intend for your audio server. If you have a commercial Web site on which you plan to serve music and advertising, you can recover the costs of the higher capacity connection by charging your advertisers for space on your audio page. If you're using RealAudio in an intranet as a way of distributing voice-mail memos or doing one-way teleconferencing for meetings, you may be able to justify it in terms of travel costs saved.

Sound with Java

Finally, there's Java as a sound publication method. If you're giving any thought to this, you need to check out the following Web site:

http://www.cs.indiana.edu/hyplan/kinzler/fun/shr_sounds/index.html

That's the URL for the Schoolhouse Rock page run by Steve Kinzler of Indiana University. Kinzler developed a Java applet that he calls ClipControl which allows you to play sound clips on Java-enabled browsers.

The ClipControl applet provides three buttons to control the sound file that is loaded when you call it: Play, Loop, and Stop. There's also a Load button, which lets you load additional sound clips directly from the applet rather than linking to them from the Web page.

Kinzler has generously made his Java source file available for your use, perusal, and study, with only the reasonable restriction that anyone who uses it does so with the comment header block at the beginning of the file left intact. It's at the following location:

http://www.cs.indiana.edu/hyplan/kinzler/fun/shr_sounds/ClipControl.java

To use Kinzler's applet, you need to include a call to it in your Web page. Here's one from the Schoolhouse Rock page:

```
<applet code="ClipControl.class" width=200 height=40>

<param name=clip    value="darn.au">

<param name=bgcolor value="#F8F8F8">

<param name=noload  value=true>

<a href="darn.au"><img src="play.gif" alt="Play" border=0

width=32 height=32 align=middle></a> <em>[.au]</em>

</applet>
```

The preceding call to the ClipControl applet plays the sound file darn.au (which is the last bit on the tape, a girl's voice saying "Darn, that's the end.")

CHAPTER 7   # Interacting with Human Beings

As fascinating as technology is, true power in multimedia design comes from understanding the psychology of user interface design. Before beginning to look at the technical concerns for the authoring and delivery engine, then, it's worth spending some time learning the technical concerns for the "user engine" — the human being who will be reading, playing with, and otherwise using your networked multimedia project. This chapter describes modern psychological research into areas that affect the effective use — and therefore, the effective design — of digital multimedia.

This includes modern theory on multiple intelligences, educational concepts of multiple learning modalities, and some of my popular creativity exercises (taken from my seminar series) for reaching these different ways of thinking, relating, and taking in information.

To open, this chapter explores the nature of true interactivity. What most people—whether discussing the Web or CD-ROMs—call interactivity is the ability to select objects on screen or in text and have the document react in some way to this selection. If you've ever wandered through a software store, especially looking into CD-ROMs, you're no doubt familiar with the pitch that a particular game, educational tool, or entertainment piece is "very interactive"—meaning, usually, that there's a lot for you to click on. Although this kind of interactivity offers many benefits (and I'll outline them individually throughout this chapter), I'd like to propose a new model of interactivity, in which this kind is simply the first-order variety of interactivity.

Of more interest, and with greater potential for revolutionizing communication, publishing, education, and the industries that rely on these fields, is what I describe as second-order interactivity: the interaction and collaboration between people remote in time or distance from one another. Distinguishing these two different varieties of interactivity, and the ways that they provide users and developers with power in the matter of communication, is critical to understanding the real potential in networked multimedia.

The Four Cornerstones of the Internet

One way of looking at the two forms of interactivity I've outlined here is to plot them in a matrix, with "interacting with people" and "interacting with software" along one axis. For the purposes of this discussion, let's define the other axis of the matrix by whether or not you know the outcome of the interaction before you take it. This gives you a four-part grid as shown in the following illustration.

Note: The model I propose here is based on a series of talks I give to beginners on the Internet. If you're accustomed to finding your way around the Net, you'll recognize a few ways in which the details break down. Bear with me and stay at a fairly high, simple level for a while longer.

With these ways of distinguishing interactions on the Net, we have the following four cornerstones of connecting:

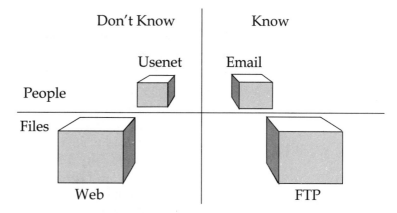

Interactivity Matrix for the Internet

In this illustration, the two near cornerstones represent the ways that you can interact with files—clicking on Web pages and downloading data from FTP sites, as well as using various other utilities such as Gopher, Archie, and so on. But these two cornerstones divide based on whether or not you know, in advance, what you're going to get. For FTP sites, where you are downloading a specific set of information from a remote source, you have to know the location and the filename.

On the Web, this isn't necessarily so. Yes, you can type in the URL of a Web site you want to visit, but you don't have to—it's possible to set up your browser's home page to one of the search engines (or to Netscape's search page), and you can browse the entire Web simply by looking at the results of various searches. In this model, you don't have to know where you're going or (because we're discussing interacting with files in this half of the matrix) what file you're accessing. In fact, many Web sites are starting to replace the default contents of the status line—which normally shows the destination URL of the hyperlink under the cursor—with a text description.

The same distinction applies to interacting with people over the Net. I've put electronic mail in the right column, where you know how to interact with the destination. Just as with an FTP site, you need to know the email address of the recipient before you can write to him or her. When I introduce teachers to the Internet, I use the example that if Albert Einstein were alive today and you knew his email address, you could write to him and have him explain to your physics class why it has to be the speed of light squared—why it isn't some other value in his famous equation. (And of course, if Einstein were alive today, he'd no doubt have a grad student work up a Web page with a FAQ list explaining just that.)

On the other hand, research often involves asking for advice from people we don't already know, or in arenas where we don't know the expert. For that, Usenet is still an effective way of asking questions of the collected wisdom of the Net. (It's worth pointing out here the old saw, which is quite true, that if you really want to find out something on the Net, you shouldn't ask a question—you should simply post the wrong information. Of course, you may also learn some highly colorful new words and phrases.)

I bring up this fairly basic view of how interactivity works on the Internet because it's useful to look at what's happening with new technologies for bringing person-to-person interactivity to the Web. In reality, given the incorporation of other communication tools within such products as Netscape 2.0, the current image of the Web and its place on the Internet looks more like this:

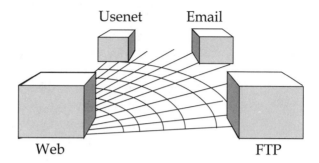

The Web incorporates other forms of interactivity.

What this means for you, as you design with human interactivity in mind, is that you can take advantage of person-to-person interactivity within your Web page design. This chapter describes some of the products and techniques for doing this.

Before we go further, let's take a deeper look at the nature of interactivity as represented by the fore-and-aft split in the matrix represented by the preceding illustrations. Specifically I'd like to spend a few minutes discussing first-order and second-order interactivity, and what they mean to you as a Web page designer.

First-order Interactivity

First-order interactivity means giving the user lots of objects to click on. This isn't bad, or necessarily even lesser, than the second-order interactivity I describe in a few paragraphs. In fact, there are many reasons why a high degree of first-order interactivity works to your advantage when designing a Web page.

First, and perhaps simplest, is that it's fun. People like to click on things. It gives us the sense that we're engaged in a kind of dialog with the computer—it's perceived as one of the most crucial differences between the computer and television, for example. This difference is particularly evident in education, where television has failed to live up to the hype that surrounded it when it was introduced. Although the primary reason for this failure is the nature of the economics of the industry, as Newton Minow (who coined the phrase "vast wasteland" more than thirty years ago) argues passionately, we should also consider that television is a very passive medium—or rather, that television viewers are very passive in their interaction with the medium (certainly compared to the Web).

And before we leave the subject of television, consider how much time you spend clicking the remote. Oh, there are no doubt many good reasons for doing so: you've seen this commercial nine hundred times, you hate this part of the movie, you're trying to see if the show you're waiting for has started yet, or you're certain that something good has to be on somewhere. Although those are all certainly reasonable justifications, I'd like to propose that in addition, you do so at least partly because clicking on things is fun.

What makes them fun? And how can you design a Web site that makes clicking on things even more fun (so that people will want to come back and keep having fun there)? And finally, how can you inject this fun into a Web site explaining mutual bonds, managed health care, the difference between whole-life and term insurance, or whatever traditionally dry, soporific subject your corporate employer is paying you to do?

A word of caution to Webmasters: The people whose signatures are reproduced digitally on your paychecks may in fact have an entirely different view of what's fun than you do. It's not uncommon for someone in a chief financial officer's position to believe, wholeheartedly, that thinking about life insurance is the most fun he or she has ever had. This may in fact be true for some individuals. In addition, many of those people don't believe that fun has any place in a discussion of their corporate image, product, service, or personnel. And if you have any intention of seeing their digitally reproduced signatures on an ongoing basis, you'd better make sure—whether your idea of a hot time on a Saturday night is getting a new piercing or reading Standard & Poor's—that their Web site doesn't violate their concept of fun. Just save up $100 from one of those paychecks, send it to the InterNIC, and you can own your own domain name.

Perhaps the most quantifiable advantage that having lots of things to click on gives your Web page is that users have the sense of being in control. This is one of the key attractions for many computer users: they can determine where to go, what to look at, how to proceed. Lots of buttons, hypertext links, or image maps mean, as a user, that you have a lot of choice in what you do with your experience on a Web site.

Fun Things

These are some of the characteristics that make Web sites fun. (How do I know? I asked a bunch of kids, of course. Kids haven't yet learned that fun needs to be squashed, which is why there are so few 10-year-old chief financial officers of insurance companies.)

- Pictures (as long as they're not so big that they take more than about 30 seconds to load)
- Animations (see previous condition)
- Video (likewise)
- Audio (especially music, but also sound effects)
- Virtual reality and 3D
- Lots of things to click on
- Instant response when you click on something

In addition, activities that adults consider fun (or at least rewarding) when using interactive media include:

- Getting where you want to go without a lot of fuss and intermediate steps (for example, search engines versus multilevel menus).

- Getting the right answers quickly. (Of course, "having to ask the right question in the first place" falls in the not-fun category.)

- Graphs, charts, and illustrations. (Think of how many bar charts the average issue of *USA Today* uses.)

Not-fun Things

Characteristics that keep a Web site from being fun include:

- Lots of long, linear text sections with no visual or interactive breaks

- Data represented as tables of numbers

- Badly designed frames (If the frame is too small to show your data, or if it takes up too much of your main window, it's a badly designed frame.)

- Pictures that take too long to load

- Media that takes too long to load

- Broken images

- Nonfunctional hypertext links

- Getting too many responses to a question to a search engine — 100,000 hits is worse than 10. (Most people don't realize that this is in fact the same issue as having to ask the right question in the first place.)

- Having to know what they're doing — the Web is about not having to know, and about finding out.

Now, if you look over these two lists and come up with a simple way to characterize them, one of those simple ways might be that the things that are fun look like play, and the things that are not fun look like work.

So I invite you to consider this: The reason for the Web's explosive popularity (recently I read a figure quoting its growth at 1000% a year) is simply that it promises to bring an element of play into the workplace. Even if the subject of that play (or that workplace) is mutual bonds, managed health care, or life insurance, the ability to have pictures, interactivity, and other operations makes it more fun to use than a corporate handbook or even a video training tape.

In Chapter 5, on story as a medium, we looked at some key distinctions that can add fun to any subject, whether that subject appears enjoyable on the surface or not. In this chapter, let's look at the next step in interactivity—a stage that goes deeper than clicking on objects on the screen.

Second-order Interactivity

What's below the surface level of clicking on objects and having the program respond? I'd like to suggest that it's interacting with other human beings. And I'd like to suggest that something specific goes on when you interact with people, something that goes far beyond the normal model of interchange of information. Instead of the usual model, in which people exchange one item (such as information) for another (such as money), the model of the Web is one that more closely represents sharing. Although many people try to make money over the Internet—and the organization that pays you may in fact be one of these organizations—the Web provides something much more significant than a new model of commerce.

I'd like to propose three levels of interacting with people, all based around the model of sharing: sharing resources, sharing information, and sharing creativity. In the first level, the sharing of resources, there's a certain dependence on the quantity or availability of what is being shared. I call this the "Hallowe'en model" of sharing — the day after Hallowe'en, my daughters are glad to share their candy with me because they have huge bags overflowing with loot. But when it comes to the last piece of candy that we all like, they're a little more reluctant to let go of it. They know that when you share a piece of candy with your sister (or with your dad), you each get a half a piece of candy. Resources — money and time being the two we're most familiar with — fit this model; I won't go into them in any detail as they're very closely studied in a variety of business texts. But one way of describing this kind of interaction, this kind of sharing, is to say that it's exclusive — yes, sharing goes on, and it may even be equitable, but it excludes part of the resources from each recipient.

The second level of sharing — sharing information — is distinct from sharing resources. The simplest way to look at this is to imagine two comedians who meet in the lounge at the club where they're performing, and each one tells the other one joke. Now each comic knows a new joke; you might say they've shared inclusively. When you share information, both sides in the interaction have the potential of coming away with more than they started with. They're both included in the interaction.

Finally, there's a third level: sharing creativity. In this kind of an interaction, each person provides something that does not merely transmit information — it actually makes possible something larger than the information itself would have been expected to provide. The great creative collaborations in literature and entertainment — from Rodgers and Hammerstein to Gilbert and Sullivan — are examples of this kind of interaction. Each person provides not only the information being shared, but actually contributes something to the other person that causes them both to be more effective, more creative, and more powerful than either would have been individually. If the first form of interaction is exclusive sharing and the second form is inclusive sharing, this form can be described as expansive sharing because the nature of it is to expand what's possible for each individual.

Now, what does any of this have to do with the Web? Several pieces go into the answer. To begin with, it is this third level of interaction that defines the model of business as it is anticipated for the twenty-first century. "Virtual corporations," collaborative efforts by people at geographically distinct locations, and other trends are growing rapidly. Most business leaders' expectations are that organizations that can best function in this manner will be the most successful, as we move from an economy of production (which provides exclusive interaction — make goods, get money) with a subtext of service and information (which provides inclusive interaction — exchange information, provide a service to a customer, and they provide a service for you) into an economy of knowledge (in which both partners in the exchange know more individually, afterwards, than both did collectively before the exchange).

There are several promising technologies for this kind of interchange and interaction over the Web. First, of course, is the simple reply button:

```
<a href="mailto:webmaster@work.com">Send mail</a>
```

This kind of interaction is very simple, and puts all the responsibility for communication on the person sending mail.

Another form of interaction is that used by a pilot program I'm participating in as this book goes into final production: a collaborative project between schools in Adelaide, South Australia, and Sunnyvale, California, USA. In this project, the students at both schools are working together on individual reports about the environment in their respective locales, then collaborating on a shared understanding of problems and solutions. The intention at this point is to use electronic mail to send the HTML files back and forth across the Pacific, then to post the resulting files on our respective Web sites. For more information about this project, see the Web site associated with this book, or look at the Cherry Chase Web Page at http://www.living-history.org/cchase/. But this demonstrates that second-order or even third-order interactivity doesn't require spending a fortune or developing custom software; it's something that requires dedication, energy, and a willingness to get "outside the box" of our traditional, comfortable ways of thinking.

Other Collaboration Tools

Other, more powerful collaboration tools are on the horizon, and although it's always fun to speculate about what's coming next, some of the tools that are in use today stand to revolutionize the way the Web works.

At the low end of the price (and media) collaboration scale is the set of note boards, text-based conference programs, and related tools. Most of these work hard to differentiate themselves from the traditional BBS or bulletin board in some way; the best of them actually achieve this differentiation. One of the least expensive options is WebBoard from O'Reilly, publishers of the popular WebSite software. These two packages (designed to work together) provide a turn-key system for managing a Web page (based on a 32-bit Windows system with reasonable memory, disk, and access requirements — recommending 16 Mb of RAM, a 486-class processor, and a 28.8 modem for basic functionality. These modest expenses will return modest performance, but it means you can still have a reasonable way for your users to interact with each other on your Web site without having to spend an inordinate amount of money.

What can tools like WebBoard provide? They really blur the boundaries between newsgroups and Web sites. If you set up a WebBoard on your own server, you can have threaded discussions between any number of users, in which they can post messages (as in a Usenet newsgroup) with HTML, graphics, and links (as in Usenet newsgroups when using Netscape 2.0), but you can hook these discussion lists up directly to your Web site through a simple URL. It's a clever way to divide topics and conversations along logical boundaries, but within your own Web site.

At the other end of the cost scale are visual collaboration tools such as Xerox's phenomenal LiveBoard product. At $40,000, it's nearly 100 times more expensive than WebSite and WebBoard put together. What it gives you, however, is a gigantic monitor (more than 60 inches diagonally), with an input device that looks and works like a fat marking pen. You "draw" directly on the monitor, clicking on menu items and circling display elements at the same time. Best of all, everything you draw is displayed on the LiveBoard at the other end of the conference link. It's an exciting, collaborative way to add multipoint brainstorming capabilities to your organization—at an admittedly high price per station.

Somewhere between these two extremes are new packages such as eMotion, a client-server tool designed to let people work on multimedia projects at remote locations. Where the Web makes it possible for people to review projects at a distance, by downloading new versions of a file or reviewing a Web page and then collaborating using the telephone and email, eMotion actually makes it possible for multiple users to make edits to a multimedia piece—such as digital video, an interactive demo, or some other project—in real time. The eMotion software lets users make suggested edits and annotations directly on the piece, so that the results can be seen almost immediately. It's a remarkable approach to live, multipoint editing of multimedia documents, though at $20,000 for a license, it's intended for organizations where a matter of hours in production time costs thousands of dollars in lost opportunities.

But with all these technologies for collaborating, for developing multimedia, or for communicating with users, several issues are still unaddressed. The most important one—and in many ways the most important in this chapter—is the issue of how people respond to multimedia. Without a design that takes human response into account, the most advanced multimedia features in the world are nothing but bells and whistles.

I've talked and written about the magic number five plus or minus two enough times that I hope it's not necessary to repeat it in any detail—if you haven't come across it yet, check out the bibliography for details, and in the interim settle for knowing that this is the limit of the human short-term memory. The brain retains between five and seven pieces of information for between 15 and 30 seconds at a time, before it must be refreshed by referring to a diagram, chart, or sheet (or before it must be somehow moved into long-term memory, which involves some techniques we'll talk about shortly).

The most exciting development I've run across in multimedia is something that has no connection to hardware or software. The most exciting development in multimedia today is that developers are beginning to think about the work of two research psychologists—Dr. Howard Gardner and Dr. Tom Armstrong—with as much attention and clarity as they are used to thinking about Netscape and Macromedia. The work of Gardner and Armstrong stands to make as big a difference to the way we use multimedia as multimedia itself makes to the way we use computers. These two psychologists have revolutionized the way we look at learning, at thinking, and at intelligence—or more specifically, at all of our multiple intelligences.

The Seven Intelligences

The work of Gardner and Armstrong arose out of the shortcomings of the standard Stanford-Binet IQ test as a method of actually measuring human intelligence. In addition to its cultural dependencies, the standard IQ test seems to break down in many areas of real-life experience. You are no doubt aware of examples of brilliant scientists and technologists who didn't know how to tie their shoes, and conversely of people who couldn't grasp the basics of something as simple as a two-dimensional array in a high-level programming language, yet who manage complex organizations employing hundreds of people and generating millions of dollars. If your experience in high technology has been anything like mine (and judging from the popularity of Scott Adams' comic strip "Dilbert," these experiences are as universal as a general protection fault in beta software), you've no doubt worked many times with examples of the former, and for examples of the latter.

Gardner and Armstrong, after interviewing and researching thousands of individuals, came to believe that there are several kinds of intelligence. Some of this has crept into general use; it's common to hear people talk about being "visual thinkers" or having high "verbal intelligence." Likewise, the dichotomy between right-brain and left-brain intelligence is also part of the popular lexicon. The left side of the brain (so the popular knowledge goes) controls sequential, logical thought, whereas the right side controls conceptual, holistic thought. (One of my more smart-alecky ways of expressing this is that if you get it right on the first try, you're left-brained, whereas if you get it backwards at least once every time you try to explain it to someone, you're right-brained.)

The model that Gardner and Armstrong use, however, goes into greater detail. They identified seven different kinds of intelligence, present to greater or lesser degrees in all the individuals they studied. In some, one intelligence in particular dominated; in others, there may have been a balance among several of the different intelligences. Those intelligences are:

- *Linguistic intelligence,* which manages our facility with language, with speaking and writing

- *Logical intelligence,* which manages our ability to follow procedures, to manipulate symbolic representations of abstract concepts, and to deal with numeric quantities

- *Spatial intelligence,* which manages our understanding of the relationships of objects in space, either two-dimensional or three-dimensional

- *Kinesthetic intelligence,* which manages both the expressions with and the perceptions of our body, particularly when it is in motion

- *Musical intelligence,* which deals in rhythm, in tone, and in pitch

- *Interpersonal intelligence,* which deals with our relationships with others

- *Intrapersonal intelligence,* which deals with our internal relationship with ourselves.

The multiple-intelligence model, Gardner and Armstrong observed, explained a number of anomalies in the single-IQ model. For example, political leaders and entrepreneurs with whom they worked often scored low on the standard IQ test, yet they clearly demonstrated remarkable abilities to work with people—remembering names, conversations, and personal details about the individuals they counted on for their business or social projects. A model of multiple intelligences such as the one they proposed would explain this phenomenon by suggesting such individuals had highly developed interpersonal intelligences, but their logical intelligence might be comparatively atrophied.

Two observations in particular that Dr. Armstrong made at a lecture I was fortunate enough to attend in late 1995 made a particular impression on me: one dealing with dyslexia, the other dealing with hyperactivity or attention-deficit disorder (ADD). The observation about dyslexia came in the form of a simple demonstration, much like the content of the following few pages. In the lecture hall, Dr. Armstrong placed a drawing (he used a horse, but I'll use my own drawing of a cat), printed on a transparent sheet, onto an overhead projector:

After showing the first illustration (the sleeping cat above), Dr. Armstrong picked up the transparency, flipped it right for left, and replaced it on the overhead projector. We then saw the following drawing on the screen in the lecture hall:

Most people will agree that the two illustrations are identical—the only difference is that it has been flipped, but it's the same picture. (Let me further assure the skeptical among you that the only difference between these two illustrations is that, in fact, this is the same illustration, copied and pasted into the second location; I then flipped it right for left by selecting it in FrameMaker, pulling down the Graphics menu, and selecting Flip Left/ Right from that menu.)

In short, most people can see that the two preceding pictures are identical. Then Dr. Armstrong placed the following illustration on the overhead projector:

He then performed the same operation to this overhead, flipping it also right for left:

The point of this exercise was that all of us can see that the first two pictures are identical; only the rotation is different, but it's the same object in three dimensions. But for those people with strongly developed spatial intelligences, it's often the case that their spatial sense overrides the merely linguistic or logical senses, and they see the second pair of objects as identical as well. An understanding of this model of intelligence can have a tremendous effect on the treatment of dyslexia, particularly when it is first diagnosed in young children.

Likewise, one of the contributing factors to attention-deficit disorder, in Armstrong's model, might well be a dominant kinesthetic intelligence. Just as the strongly spatial intelligence overwhelms the logical knowledge of right and left orientation in the letters b and d, the strongly kinesthetic intelligence is unable to focus for long without some kind of physical interaction to tie learning in with that person's dominant method of relating to the world. But Armstrong has determined through some of his experimentation that ADD-affected children can often, when a certain amount of physical activity is added to their regimen, function at least as effectively in a classroom setting without medication as they can when they are given prescriptions.

I hope that you, the reader, can understand some of the importance of this—and more to the point, why I've spent so much time on developmental psychology in a book on multimedia and the World Wide Web. This model of multiple intelligences offers the strongest psychological base yet for developing curriculum—whether in a K–12 setting or a life-long learning environment—that stands to "supercharge" the learning process. Why? Because the traditional "three Rs" (reading, writing, and 'rithmetic) deal with only two of the intelligences—the linguistic and the logical. Almost no time in traditional education is devoted to spatial, musical, or kinesthetic intelligence, and even less is spent on interpersonal and intrapersonal intelligence.

Yet multimedia developers—whether preparing instructional materials for corporate training, curriculum materials for a classroom setting, or marketing communication materials for a catalog of products or services—can use the multiple-intelligences model to provide a breakthrough in effectiveness in the transfer of information. This is true if for no other reason than multimedia on the computer offers the opportunity to transmit information on many channels at the same time.

Think of it: traditional learning materials (books and handouts) typically address two intelligences, at most: linguistic and logical. A particularly good piece of material will also include the spatial component, in the form of illustrations. Often, however, those illustrations are more for effect—happy customers shown using the product, for example—than for informational content or for effective retention. As for consciously using the musical intelligence to promote retention—well, I'll get to that after the following exercise. First you need to meet the seven intelligences.

Exercise: Using All of Your Intelligences

Before you can begin to author multimedia (for the Web or for any other delivery method) that takes advantage of the multiple-intelligence model of learning, you need to identify your own intelligences. The following exercise is designed to put you in touch with each of your seven intelligences—to become familiar, in the comfort and privacy of your own skull, with the bits of your personality that correspond to each of these seven ways of processing, accessing, and relating to information about the world you experience.

As with some of the other exercises earlier in this book, you don't need to turn on the computer for this one. This one is to be experienced. Most of these exercises will be more effective if you can get an assistant to work through the questions with you, but if you can't, just explore them as best you can.

Exercise 1: Verbal Intelligence

Describe your favorite movie—the title, the stars, the plot, the setting. Take at least 30 seconds, and no more than 2 minutes. Where does it take place? What happens? If you have an assistant, describe the movie to him or her. If not, write down the answers to these questions. Don't worry about the order—just get down as detailed and specific a description as you can in the specified time.

That's your verbal intelligence at work. When you write the text that goes in your HTML files, when you tell a story, when you describe a picture, or when you ask a precise question designed to elicit a specific response, you are using your verbal intelligence.

One place you can use your verbal intelligence—and where you can address the verbal intelligence of your readers as a way of improving retention—is in the phrasing of key descriptions, passages, titles, and hyperlinks that recur throughout your Web site. By making sure that the key descriptions, passages, titles, and hyperlinks that recur throughout your Web site are phrased in similar or even identical ways, you reinforce the idea that these key descriptions, passages, titles, and hyperlinks are all connected in some way, and you make it easier for people to remember them. (For example, read this paragraph aloud, then close your eyes and repeat the four kinds of items that I've linked in this way.)

Exercise 2: Logical Intelligence

For this exercise, add up the number of characters in each section of your domain name. (That is, if you work for Netscape, your domain name is home.netscape.com; this works out to 4 + 8 + 3 for a total of 15.) Keep adding the digits until you get to a single number (which in the previous example would be 6 because 1 + 5 = 6.) Now take the digits in the number at the bottom of this page and add them together; that number was 216 in an early draft version, making a total of 2 + 1 + 6 = 9 in this example.

Subtract the number derived from the page from the number derived from your Web site's domain name. For the example here, you would subtract 9 from 6, for a value of -3.

If the remainder is a positive number, you have used your logical intelligence.

If the remainder is a negative number, you have used your logical intelligence.

If the remainder is zero, you have used your logical intelligence.

If you didn't do the exercise, you did not use your logical intelligence. Go back and complete this exercise before continuing.

The point to this exercise is not to "get it right." There is no right answer—no number that will get you an A or have you pass the class. The object of this exercise is to put you in touch with the part of your intelligence that follows a strict procedure, that evaluates and compares, that manipulates numbers, and that tests against external measures.

Exercise 3: Spatial Intelligence

For this exercise, use a white board or several blank pieces of paper.

Diagram the basic structure of your Web site. That is, begin with the index.html file, then show the links out from there to each of the subordinate files. For each subsequent file, draw a rectangle, the way it might show up on the desktop in a Macintosh or a Windows 95 representation.

However, instead of using the filenames in each of those file icons, draw a small image that represents the content of the file. For example, in your index.html, sketch your corporate logo or a small drawing of a house (for the home page). If you have a catalog of products, sketch a few of those products (don't take long, just rough them in—two boxes, with a grid in the lower one, represent a computer, for example). If you have a list of personnel in the corporate database, draw some stick-figure people.

This exercise clearly puts you in touch with your spatial intelligence. Extra credit if you aligned all the files on each level—that is, you put the first set of links down from your index.html at one level on the white board, then the files at the destination of those links at the next, etc. Even more extra credit if you came up with a three-dimensional representation of this structure.

For super-extra bonus credit, take all your meeting notes for one week by drawing pictures of what's being said, and by drawing arrows, lines, and diagrams between the components that are connected. Use no more than one word per subject. Do this for two weeks and you will either have a breakthrough in your visual creativity or a breakdown in your effectiveness in meetings. (The good side to that is you may not get invited to as many meetings.)

Exercise 4: Kinesthetic Intelligence

For this exercise, kick off your shoes and close your eyes. (If you are at work, you may want to close the office door, or at least let your neighbors know you're doing an exercise and you haven't suddenly developed a mental condition. You may also either want to read this entire exercise through once, or get a friend to read it to you as you perform it.) Shuffle your shoes around with your feet till they are no longer oriented to your right and left foot — in fact, turn them over and around and upside-down, as though shuffling them like a deck of cards.

Without opening your eyes, reach down and pick up a shoe. Turn it over till you can identify it as a right shoe or a left shoe. Place it on your foot; if necessary, untie it, then put it on your foot and tie it again. Do not open your eyes while you are doing this.

Now reach down and find the other shoe. Place it on the appropriate foot (which is much easier to determine now), also untying it and retying it if necessary.

The point of this exercise is to get you to keep track of where your shoes are as you shuffle them around blind-folded, then to determine — purely by touch — which foot they go on. Additionally, tying your shoes while blindfolded connects your spatial, kinesthetic, and logical intelligences — spatial because you need to maintain a mental image of how the laces look, kinesthetic because you are moving your hands without seeing what you are doing, and logical because you must adhere to a sequence of movements.

Exercise 5: Musical Intelligence

For this exercise, have a friend look ahead to the end of this section and follow the instructions found there. Notice several results as you work with your assistant. To begin with, do you associate images with any of the clues your friend is giving you? Are those images personal or are they from a particular medium? Was it easy to respond, even automatic?

Now consider that the industry that has best put this intelligence to use is advertising. If you don't believe that, fill in these blanks (though most of these are 30 years old or more, which serves to prove a point about retention but may only be effective for an audience that is likewise 30 years old or more):

"Plop, plop, fizz, fizz," _____

"See the USA" _____

"You get a lot to like" _____

"Oh I wish I were an" _____

I could go on, but every time I do this exercise, I'm struck by how much of my memory is devoted to ad jingles for products that aren't even manufactured any more, and it depresses me. The point, however, should be well taken: Madison Avenue has done a largely effective job of using the musical intelligence as a retention aid. (Of course, while I was writing this chapter, my own daughters brought home the re-release of *Schoolhouse Rock* on videocassette from the public library; this mixed animation with songs designed to teach various elements of, in this case, grammar. So while working on a chapter about musical intelligence, I've been treated to a five-year-old who dances around the house singing "Lolly, lolly, lolly, get your adverbs here." Life is not only stranger than we imagine, it's stranger than we *can* imagine.)

Exercise 6: Interpersonal Intelligence

This exercise comes from a networking class (the kind between people, not the kind between machines) taught by my colleague Debe Todd at the 1996 Writer's Connection Conference on Writing for Interactive Multimedia. It's just a single piece from a larger structure on how to network effectively (also known as "schmoozing"), by making yourself memorable to the people you speak with—in a positive, or at least neutral, way. (Spilling hot coffee on someone's white silk suit is also likely to make you memorable, but not in the way you may hope.)

In this exercise, locate three people in your office, campus, or organization with whom you rarely come in contact. Let them know the purpose of the exercise, that it's part of a series of steps you're taking to identify multiple intelligences. (You may want to assure them that this is quite distinct from multiple personalities.)

As part of the exercise, exchange one interesting fact with each of them, something that has nothing to do with work. For example, one of the participants who came up to me at the conference where Debe gave her workshop explained that she raised llamas. Months later, when she corresponded with me about another subject, she mentioned the llamas again and it was easy for me to remember exactly who she was.

To complete your exercise, have your partners wait a week, then call you back. Have them announce themselves by saying, "Remember me? I. . ." and then they remind you of their interesting fact. As they do this, note how much of the conversation comes back up— where you were standing, what they were wearing, what else you spoke about. By associating this interesting fact with the person, you are tying into your interpersonal intelligence—linking knowledge to your relationship with another person.

Exercise 7: Intrapersonal Intelligence

This last exercise is based on the preceding one. In this one, however, look into your own life to see what you would choose as your one interesting fact that has nothing to do with work. For me, it would probably be that I restore old sports cars (currently working on a 1967 Alfa Romeo Giulia GT 1300 Junior, which is also the car I use for everyday transportation). But go beyond the simple fact—make it come alive for you.

For my fact, restoring the Alfa, I'd remember how sore my shoulders got when I was taking the transmission out, or the way the paint remover would sting when I'd get a drop of it on my skin—a little worse than getting stung by a hornet, but not quite as much as eating a whole serrano chile in one bite (which of course raises the not inconsiderable question of why I willingly eat something that hurts worse than getting stung by a hornet; in the context of using a 30-year-old Italian sports car as my daily transportation, however, the question loses some of its oddity). I'd think about the way the nose tucks in on a corner when I get on the gas just at the apex, or the way the engine sounds when I hold it at full throttle and it crosses the magic 5200 RPM point on the way to the screaming, keening sound it makes at 7500 as I shift into the next gear. I'd think about the times I wanted to stop working on the car, and didn't, and how incredible it looked when I got it back from the paint shop. (And yes, of course I have a picture on line.)

What's your interesting fact? And what else would you think of when you came up with it?

To the Friend or Assistant in the Exercise:

This exercise is a variation on the game "Name That Tune," one that I call "Finish That Tune." In this exercise, you'll hum the tune that goes along with the lyrics I include here. Use "da da da" or "la la la" — don't actually use the words, as that's the point of the exercise. Your friend who is doing the exercise will need to finish the tune you start — with or without lyrics, though there's extra credit for completing with the lyrics. And be generous — if your friend finishes with the second chorus and I've included the first chorus here, let him or her have it right. The point isn't to get a high score; the point is to see how effective music can be as a teaching tool.

Tell your friend that you are going to start a phrase, and your friend's job in this exercise is to finish it. Then hum just the portion of the song that is represented here by the lyrics. Again, do not sing the lyrics — that's your friend's task, on the reply.

"Twinkle, twinkle, little star" (acceptable responses to this one are either "How I wonder what you are" or "H I J K LMNOP")

"Yankee Doodle went to town" (US residents only)

"Mary had a little lamb"

"Ring around the rosy"

"Oh, I wish I was in the land of cotton" (giving equal time to those born south of Yankee Doodle territory)

Surely you get the idea. You may also use other songs if you prefer — either popular songs that you know your friend will recognize, or perhaps more challenging songs that your friend may or may not know. As an interesting side point, you might try reciting the line from the song in a flat, unaccented voice — your best PBS commentator voice, as one friend likes to put it. (This is particularly amusing when reciting inane lyrics from songs of the fifties and sixties; for a good time, do your best Walter Cronkite imitation while reading the lyric, "Yummy, yummy, yummy, I've got love in my tummy.") Then try the same lyric again, this time singing it.

Interacting with All the Intelligences

Now, having identified your own seven intelligences, and having seen how to gain access to them, how can you apply this knowledge to designing your multimedia Web site?

The answer is simple on the surface, but the depths and details will enrich your readers' Web experience immensely if you spend some time in the design phase. Consider the purpose of your Web site: is it something you're designing just to please yourself, an artistic or aesthetic expression? Is it a corporate communication medium? Does it convey information about an organization, either within your corporate structure or outside of the structure of any single entity (such as the Web page for a standards organization)?

To determine some ways to interact with each of the intelligences on your Web page, ask yourself the following questions:

Tell Me a Story

How would I describe this Web page's content? What words convey the meaning, emotion, or focus of the site? At this point, you may want to do some sample brainstorming with colleagues, simply writing down all the words you can collectively think of that describe, pertain to, or evoke a sense of the Web site.

Order out of Chaos

What comes first? What's the sequence? What does someone have to know before they can know anything else? What must you present first in order for later parts of this multimedia piece to work? What chunks of the

Web page need to be in the first place your users get to from outside, and what's the next level in from there? This set of inquiries will result in the structure of your Web site—and it also points out the relationship between structure in hypertext and sequence in a linear document: they both address the same intelligence, the logical intelligence.

A Thousand Words

What does this subject look like? How would you depict it? Again, try to get beyond the warm-and-fuzzy shots that most corporate brochures use (and which most Web sites, by and large, have adopted—sometimes with whizzy special effects, true, but often without any real thought). What's the relationship between components—which ones are primary, which secondary? Are there icons, symbols, or commonly held objects that people associate with what we're doing? (Your art director or designer will be invaluable to you in this task; with luck, the same questions will have been asked when your corporate logo was designed.)

A Little Higher, and to the Right

Is there a consistent place where your users will touch the Web page—that is, where they will place the cursor to interact with it? If you are truly using interactive media (of the level of Shockwave or Java) on your site, can you build in a series of clicks that use a specific motion of the hand or arms, ensuring a connection between motion and results? (As an example, many preschools cut out the shapes of letters in 80-grit sandpaper, then have the children lightly trace the shapes of the letters with a fingertip. The sandpaper doesn't hurt, in fact the rough texture feels appealing, and it helps reinforce kinesthetically the child's sensation of learning the shapes of the letter. You can use a consistent sequence or pattern of buttons to reinforce learning the same way.)

It's Got a Meter That Is Tricky

Is there a musical tone you can use, adapt, borrow, create, or otherwise acquire for certain topics within your Web site? Is there a particular rhythm or pattern of sounds that you can develop? If so, see Chapter 6 for suggestions on how to hook this to an individual page. It does nobody any good to have the page load and your users select three downline links before the helper application successfully loads the sound clip and plays it. That's like spanking the dog two days after it chews your slippers. (I have to say that, at present, nothing but Java and Shockwave really has the right response time for this kind of audio reinforcement; RealAudio is cool, and is a great addition to a Webmaster's suite of tools, but it still requires loading the RealAudio player to provide the media.)

Face to Face

How will your Web site make a difference for people? Can you visualize individuals using it? More important, can you characterize the difference in their lives after using it (or the product or service your corporation provides)? Can you express, in a few words, the point of your organization, or at least of your Web page, as it affects human beings? What is their relationship to your organization or page, and how can you affect the way that relationship lives for them? These questions go far beyond the usual "features and benefits" questions that are part of basic marketing—or at least, the degree to which they go past the usual questions is the degree to which they will give your Web site an edge in reaching people powerfully.

Heart to Heart

Where in your own life does the subject of your Web site exist powerfully for you? By "exist powerfully," I mean that you have emotional memories, strong memories, powerful feelings about the subject that your Web site describes or introduces. If you can't find a place where the subject exists powerfully, generate one. This is the fount from which all inspiration flows. And as an exercise as a professional information wrangler, I invite you to take on the possibility that existing powerfully is something you can generate—it is not an intrinsic part of the subject, but it is rather something you can choose to put there, whether the subject is finding a cure for AIDS or selling crackers.

Exercise: The Pythagorean Theorem

For this exercise, you will represent the Pythagorean theorem in a manner that addresses each of the seven intelligences. I'll provide some starting points; your job in this exercise is to draft out some possible ways of explaining the theorem, ways that address one (or more) of Gardner and Armstrong's seven intelligences.

If you have a particularly cool idea, build a Web page and send me electronic mail at one of the mailto: links in the Web page associated with this book.

Here then are some suggestions for demonstrating the Pythagorean theorem in multimedia, addressing each of the seven intelligences.

Linguistic

Describe it in text. For those of you who came into Webmastery through some means other than math and science, the Pythagorean theorem reads, "The square of the hypotenuse of a right triangle is equal to the sum of the squares of the two adjacent sides." Note also that unless you know what that means, you probably don't know what that means. If you're hopelessly lost, the hypotenuse is the "long" side of a right triangle; for example, if you draw a line across the diagonal corners of a sheet of paper, that diagonal line is the hypotenuse. The edges of the paper are called the "legs." And it's a right triangle because the two legs make a right angle, that is, an angle of 90 degrees.

Note further that this is how most information is taught in schools today. You—yes, you, the guy or gal holding this book open on your desk with a half-filled Jolt Cola can while you hack Javascript—have the opportunity to change that forever. That is what this book is really about, as you may have noticed.

Logical

Write out the mathematical formula for the Pythagorean theorem, which is:

$$a^2 + b^2 = c^2$$

where a and b represent the legs of a right triangle, and c represents the hypotenuse. Replace a with 3, b with 4, and c with 5. The resulting calculation is:

3 x 3 = 9

4 x 4 = 16

5 x 5 = 25

9 + 16 = 25

This demonstrates the theorem. We'll use these numbers for the remaining examples because they're the simplest set of numbers that demonstrate the theorem.

Spatial

Draw a picture of a right triangle, measuring carefully so that one of the legs is 3" long (or 3 cm, or cubits, or furlongs—the units don't matter, as long as they're the same units on each side) and the other is 4" (or 4 cm). Mark off the triangle's sides at each measure, as follows:

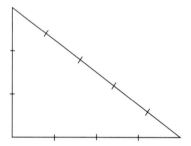

Right triangle 3 x 4 x 5 units in dimension

Now, as the first step in squaring the sides, draw a series of squares that are 1 unit (inch or cm) on each side, down each leg of the triangle:

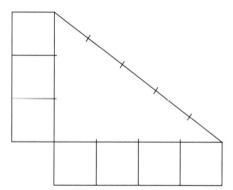

Next, make a square on each side — that is, use the smaller squares like tiles to create a larger square the same number of tiles in each direction:

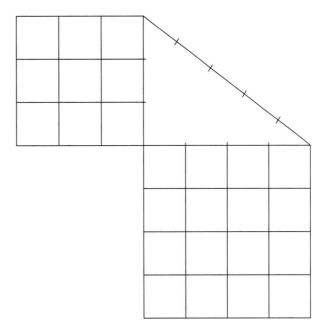

Next, repeat the preceding two steps for the remaining side, squaring the hypotenuse:

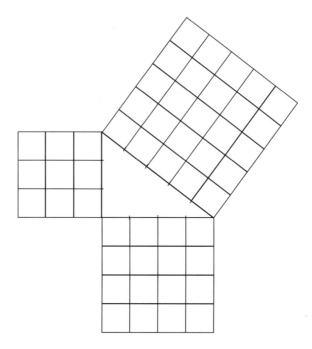

Count the tiles in the two squares adjacent to the legs; the total is 25. Then count the tiles in the square adjacent to the hypotenuse; the total is 25.

As this exercise demonstrates spatially, the square of the hypotenuse of a right triangle is equal to the sum of the squares of the two adjacent sides. But now it has shape, space, and size.

Kinesthetic

Take 50 pennies (or 50 stamps, 50 sugar cubes, or 50 of any cheap, readily available, symmetrical and identical commodity). Lay them out in a hollow triangle, with 3 pennies on one side, 4 on the other, and 5 down the diagonal. Then make each of those rows of pennies into a square—put 6 more pennies down along the outside of the row of 3, 12 more down the row of 4, and 20 more down the row of 5. Refer to the diagrams in step 3 if you need assistance.

In this step, placing the pennies down one by one is somewhat spatial, but the physical act of laying out the pennies involves the kinesthetic intelligence. In a multimedia presentation, you might actually have your users drag icons of the pennies into place, or set up a stamp so that clicking the mouse in location puts a penny (or any other object—on the computer, they could be miniature pictures of Times Square, or your corporate logo, or 3D representations of the Great Pyramid of Giza, which has the added advantage of being terribly cool) into that spot.

As long as all 50 elements are the same size, the geometry works out. In fact, there's a kind of magic in having the geometry work out for elements of any size. (For extra credit, devise a game where you do the same thing, but with a circle that is 22 units around and 7 across. This is a great math teaching activity for kids who are just beginning to learn geometry, by the way.)

Musical

For the next exercise, you may have to consult your friends who know old movies because I can't remember the title of the film in question. But that itself is significant, as I'll demonstrate shortly.

But here's the puzzle: it's a Danny Kaye musical where he's a professor at some stuffy boys' school in England. He tries to introduce "modern" teaching techniques and meets with a lot of resistance from the dean and the establishment, but the boys learn a great deal from him and he's finally accepted. (If you know the name, send me email and I'll post it on the Web site!)

In any case, at one point in the song, Kaye teaches his young charges the Pythagorean theorem by singing it as a song, which ends up being a production number in which the students dance over half the campus and end up getting the dean in an uproar. Hours of wholesome family fun, no doubt.

But my point is—I can't remember the name of the movie, I can't remember much more about the plot, and I can't remember who else starred in it. But I can remember the tune of that song, and in fact the lyrics are the way that I phrased it, automatically, when I typed in the description for the linguistic intelligence. (If you go looking around the Web site for this book, you may be able to locate an audio clip of me singing it.)

Interpersonal

For this exercise, bring together two or three of your friends or colleagues. You're going to collaborate on a demonstration of the Pythagorean theorem; it's up to you three to work out the details. One way, for example, might be for each of you to take a side, then cut out or otherwise construct the pieces necessary to demonstrate that $a^2 + b^2 = c^2$.

Alternatively, you might work together to design different pieces of a multimedia demo. For instance, you might have the individual squares along the legs light up, then disappear, and a corresponding light appears in one of the squares on the hypotenuse. But ask your friends for their suggestions. Make a list of possible ideas on a whiteboard or a sheet of paper. The demonstration doesn't have to be electronic, but it does have to be something you can show to another human being, and that accurately conveys the sense that the square of the hypotenuse of the right triangle (and you should be able to finish this by yourself at this point).

If you were participating in a workshop with me and we were doing this part of the course in person, I'd have the class divide into groups of four, give you all 30 minutes to design your demonstration, and then have each group demonstrate to the rest of the class. The point should be easy to get: working with your three colleagues requires interpersonal intelligence, and presenting your demonstration to the entire class also means that you must consider the interpersonal intelligence while you design your demonstration as well as while you perform it. And remember — ultimately, the issue of platforms for effective Web presentations isn't a matter of Macintosh or PC or Unix. In the end, every Web page has to work on a human being.

Intrapersonal

To sum up, what did you get out of the previous six exercises? Which ones were easy for you? Which ones took a lot of effort and struggle? Were there any that you simply dashed off without a second thought? Did others make you think, as if automatically, "I can't do that!" Which ones caused you stress or discomfort when considering what would be involved in doing them?

As a final comment to end this section of the chapter, the 3:4:5 case of the right triangle was considered to be especially significant by Pythagoras. The great classical architects that he influenced used it in many of their monuments and buildings. Those proportions still have an effect on your life today. If you don't believe me, solve for the lowest common denominator in an NTSC monitor (640 x 480 pixels), then consider how much time you typically spend during a day looking at two 3:4:5 triangles tessellated into a 4:3 rectangle.

A Return to Play

I want to close this chapter with a little more thought, now that you've become intimate with your seven intelligences, on the nature of play and what that stands to provide users of your Web site.

At the beginning of this chapter, we looked at some of the characteristics that make a site fun, and that give it the elements of play. Some of those elements are:

- Lots of pictures

- Lots of interactivity

- A sense of being in control, paradoxically combined with a sense of wondering what will happen next

- Rapid response to what the user selects

The educational system that has been in place for the past 50 to 100 years in most of the industrialized world has focused on linguistic and logical intelligence, to the near exclusion of all other intelligences. Classes are taught as lecture or as structured reading; there are exercises and tests, nearly all of which are geared toward remembering facts and reproducing them within a structure that, at best, resembles a portion of human knowledge. At recess, the students at my daughters' school run, play sports with one another, sing counting songs while jumping rope, make up clubs as ways of relating to their friends, or sometimes just sit and look inward at what they want out of life. In short, work involves numbers, words, and remembering arbitrary sequences of data to be reproduced in order to get a reward; play involves interaction, spatiality, musical memory, kinesthetic experience of the world, and a holistic understanding of the connection between an action we take and the quality of the life we have.

Is it any wonder accountants buy DOS machines and artists buy Macintosh?

CHAPTER 8   # Test Cases

This chapter looks at some specific cases for dealing with some of the support issues behind multimedia over the Web. By support I don't mean the availability of people to take phone calls and get email messages; I mean rather the supporting technology pieces, such as plug-ins and helper applications.

It's always good business to be a good citizen, particularly over the Web. If you're going to include multimedia that uses nonstandard pieces (and as popular as Shockwave is, it's still nonstandard for all 18 million Netscape 2.0 users, even for the million or so who have downloaded the plug-in), you should first be sure that you include a way for your users to get to some standard, simple, static-medium page with the same basic information on it. Next, put in links to the site from which your users can download the application, helper, or plug-in itself.

Case 1:
Shockwave Scan

Macromedia has a very, very cool "Shockwave Scan" setup on their home page now (http://www.macromedia.com). It's really very simple; you can look at the source yourself, but the basic premise is easy to grasp.

Shockwave, you may recall from Chapter 4, uses the EMBED tag to add a Director file to your Web page. When a browser loads a Web page with the EMBED tag in use, the browser program checks to see whether the media of the type used in the EMBED tag is supported by a plug-in or helper application.

If the browser supports the specific media in use—in our case, if the Shockwave plug-in is present—then the contents of the EMBED tag are displayed. If, however, the browser does not support the media in question, the Webmaster can use the NOEMBED tag to define the default action in this event.

By the way, fans of privacy—among whose number I count myself—need not be concerned about this particular activity. The test for whether or not Shockwave is present is done by the browser, not the server; your system's features are not being uploaded to a massive corporate mailing list. At least not through this activity.

Here's the simplest such HTML section. Use it as a template and then use your own graphics and Director files in place of those listed here:

<embed src="shockdemo.dcr" width=320 height=240>

<noembed>

<IMG SRC="noshock.gif">

<A HREF="http://www.macromedia.com/shockwave/">Download Shockwave</A> now! <p>

Return to <a href="index.html">front page</a>

</noembed>

This simple snippet of HTML embeds the Director file called **shockdemo.dcr** into your Web page at this point, setting the window size to 320 x 240 (1/4 NTSC screen). If the plug-in isn't loaded, the block set off by the **NOEMBED** tag pair is executed, displaying the offer to take your user to the Shockwave download point.

It's really that trivial for you to construct your own "Searching for Shockwave. . ." piece. To be truly cool, you'll want to use GIF animation so that there's something whizzy to look at while it checks and loads the plug-in. Something like this might be fun:

I created this in a simple draw program, then made three successive versions of it (oh, right, you'll be reading this in grayscale—the circle's quadrants are gold, red, green, and blue) in which the colors in the quadrants are moved 90 degrees clockwise in each frame. I then used GifBuilder (as described in Chapter 4) to create an animated GIF with the following characteristics:

- Transparent background: white
- Frame delay: 1/10 of a second
- Image depth: 8 bits/pixel
- Color: load palette
- Image: fixed size, 96 pixels wide x 72 pixels high
- Loop: forever

Here's an example of how to do something like this. I created a short Web page with the following contents:

```
<html>

<head>

<title>

WHEEL OF FORTUNE!

</title>

</head>

<body>

Here is something to check and see whether I've got the Shock-
wave plugin loaded:

<p>

<embed src="bigwheel.dcr" width=320 height=240>

<noembed>

<center>

<img src="wheel.gif">

</center>

<p>

This displays if Shockwave is not loaded... so if it's not, you
should definitely

<a href="http://www.macromedia.com/shockwave">download</
a> it soon. Like, now, maybe.

</noembed>

</body>

</html>
```

When I look at that Web page under version 2 of Mosaic, it looks like this:

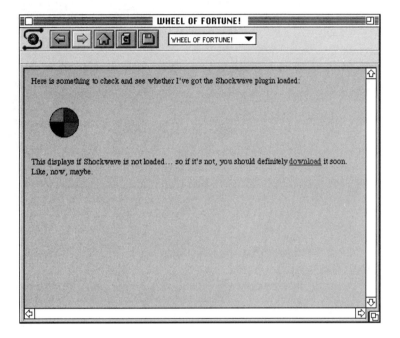

Of course, because Mosaic, version 2, also does not support animated GIFs, the image sits still on the screen. Conversely, under Netscape 2.0 with the Shockwave plug-in loaded, the same page looks like the screen on the following page (several frames into the animation).

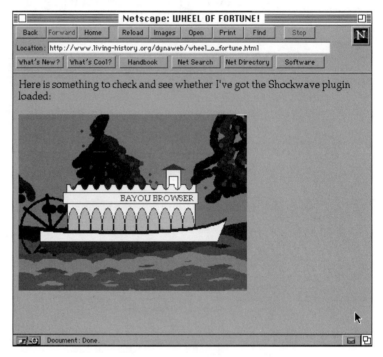

In both cases, the page being loaded is at

http://www.living-history.org/dynaweb/wheel_o_fortune.html

The steamboat is of course from the demonstration I was preparing in Chapter 4.

Case 2: Interactive Animation for the Masses

Just because your readers don't want to download Shockwave doesn't mean they can't have interactive animation. The following HTML introduces a segment with animation, for which the individual images are GIF animations:

```
<a href="home.html"><img src="home.gif">
<a href="people.html"><img src="people.gif">
<br>
<a href="places.html"><img src="places.gif">
<a href="things.html"><img src="things.gif">
```

This HTML constructs a 2 x 2 matrix of interactive images, with "home" and "people" across the top and "places" and "things" across the bottom. A little work with GifBuilder or an equivalent and you can see how this produces moving images you can click on.

For example, here's a Netscape 2.0 page set up in just this way, with image maps set up to find a number of Web search engines (for test purposes, I've left them the same visually):

In this example, each of the wheels is itself a hyperlink that points to a different search engine — one to AltaVista, one to Yahoo, etc. Of course, in practice, it would be clever to use illustrations that represent the destinations of the URLs. To close the circle (whether or not it moves), here's the HTML for this page:

```
<html>

<head>

<title>

And curse Sir Walter Raleigh

</title>

</head>

<body bgcolor=#ffffff>

<h1>

Many Wheels Make The Devil's Work Light

</h1>

<h6>

(Or something like that...)

</h6>

Here's a little GIF animation designed to look and play seam-
lessly. How well does it work?

<p>

<a href="http://home.netscape.com"><img src="wheel.gif" bor-
der =0>

<a href="http://www.altavista.digital.com"><img src="wheel.gif"
border =0>

<a href="http://www.yahoo.com"><img src="wheel.gif" border
=0>

<a href="http://www.living-history.org/"><img src="wheel.gif"
border =0>

<hr>

</body>

</html>
```

It's not as cool as Shockwave, but it produces similar
results if what you want is Web navigation.

In preparing this sample page, I learned something that has since been described by some people as a "bug" in Netscape 2.0. Note the tiny underscore at the right-hand edge of the graphics in the example. Those underscores come from the line breaks left between the <A HREF= statements in the GIF images. It's ugly, but the fix is simple: remove the line breaks. On a Unix platform, just keep typing Control+J from the vi editor; this joins the line you're on with the following line, removing the line break. In SimpleText for the Mac or Notepad/Wordpad for Windows, just delete the carriage return at the end of each line. It'll look funny in your source file, but the dots go away.

A good example of where this is fixed is the Cherry Chase Web Page:

http://www.living-history.org/cchase/

That page also uses GIF animation to present a menu bar, but it has distinct graphics for each of the buttons. (A word of warning to those with slow modems: the first time you download this, it may take a few minutes to get all the GIF animations; even 80 x 60 images take up a fair amount of room when you load five or six of them at a time.) Access that Web page and look at the source to see what I mean: the HTML is ugly but the Web page looks great.

Additional Cases: Shocked Sites

In the spirit of adventure that the Web represents, I've looked for some interesting sites that use various multimedia components (especially Shockwave and Java) in ways that appeal to me. In this section I'll take a look at how they do the site, as well as why something appeals to me. It's often that something will get my attention just because it's technically very cool, but in general I'm more interested in the beautiful than in the clever.

Make sure that you've got the Shockwave plug-in loaded and that you're running the latest version of Netscape 3.0 if you're on the Mac, and then dive in with:

http://www.cyber-age.com/cahome.html

This is not only a *cool* piece of Shockwave animation, but also a great glossary of technical terms relating to audio over the Web. An enjoyable site.

Don't miss:

http://www.mindframe.com/tools/shockwave/game.html

It's Whack-a-Mole for the Web! This was always one of my favorite games. Surely you remember the premise. There's a playing area from which a small plastic mole pops his head out from time to time, and your job is to whack him with a rubber mallet. Good, clean, only moderately violent fun, right?

Well, this game is a Shockwave version of it. Note that the animation to move the mallet is mildly computation-intensive, so this game will run better on faster computers (it verges on annoying with my 68LC040 computer, but that's only in comparison with the 150-MHz IBM Aptiva computers and mid-range Power Macintoshes I've been playing with lately).

There are three holes, and a mole pops his head out of one or another of them every few seconds. Your job is to bonk him on the noggin with a virtual, animated, 3D image of a wooden maul. It's glorious, especially the sound effects (ranging from the pure Three Stooges conk-on-the-coconut sound to a wet, resilient splat) when you connect with the mole. The moles look grumpy, even malicious, so it's not like you're thumping someone from *The Wind in the Willows*. Go ahead and wail on the little blighters; besides, they're all ones and zeros anyway, right?

There's a cute song that's just one or two digits either side of annoying; I haven't played the game enough (32 moles in a row is my current record) to get completely sick of the song. Speaking of playing successive games, you can miss the mole three times before the game is over, so accuracy counts.

For a less successful use of Shockwave, try the following Web site:

http://ww3.valvoline.com/game/shock/

The people at this site need to read how Director handles color maps, especially because they force the map on the EMBED call (as a quick click on View->Document Source tells us):

<EMBED SRC="541201A1.dcr" PALETTE = "FOREGROUND" WIDTH= "448" HEIGHT= "320" >

The real issue here is that the call to put the palette in the foreground blows the Netscape browser's color scheme out of the water when it loads the Shockwave piece. The people who developed this site should either take out the PALETTE="FOREGROUND" call altogether, or they should force it to PALETTE="BACKGROUND" to preserve the colors of the rest of the window. This, by the way, is true no matter what platform the browser runs on; I've seen—and created—Shockwave pieces that destroy Netscape's colors on both the Macintosh and the PC. So this is not a cross-platform issue (though that's another place where color maps can bite you in Director if you're not paying attention).

This one's simply great:

http://www.paulcurtis.com/pc/ghostpage.html

I'm not sure what I like best about this site. To begin with, it deals with ghosts, and I'm basically a big kid when it comes to ghosts—big enough not to be afraid of them (as long as I don't wake up at 3 AM in a strange hotel room and see them congregating on the other side of my bed, and then watch in horror as one of them rises to greet me and beckon me to join them), kid enough to really get into them. The graphics for these ghosts are good, with transparent faces that have a hollow-eyed look to them, as though the flesh had been torn away like tissue paper, leaving a gap directly into the spot where the soul once was. Even better, the sound effect is ghostly, other-worldly, and very effective; it's just a low-pitched whistle, probably downsampled a few octaves to give the illusion of the moans of a lost soul, doomed for a certain time to walk the Web. And finally, when you click on a ghostly face, this Shockwave piece displays a message from beyond. It isn't quite as classic as "Reply hazy, try again later," though there is a Mystic 8-Ball Web site; I had trouble getting it to work, however, and can't vouch for it.

Then there's:

http://www.mackerel.com/bubble.html

Interesting, but it really points out the difference between play and game. Play is what this one is about—aimless, pointless, relaxing; a game has a point. It's remarkable to take on competitive bubble-wrap-popping—it's very discomforting to be put into a position of being stressed out while doing something that is normally tension-relieving.

This one I really like:

http://www.mcli.dist.maricopa.edu/alan/nojava/mistake/index.html

It gives you a cool, 7K piece of animation to watch while it loads the long piece, which is itself enjoyable; see Chapter 4 for examples of how to do that.

CGI Scripting and User Interaction

This final category is one that adds a completely different set of capabilities to a Web site—a very different meaning of "dynamic." The most crucial point about CGI is that it can create Web pages that don't exist. That is, where nearly all other Web pages read documents written in text files using HTML tags, CGI scripts give you the ability to create, on the fly, a series of documents that are instead the output of a program.

I've put together an on-line tutorial that demonstrates this, and we'll take a look at it here in print to give you an idea of how CGI works. (That's one additional comment: though there are a number of resources on line that appear if you do a search in, say, AltaVista for CGI and tutorial, there are really only one or two good on-line tutorials out there. My Web site will point to the ones that seem to do the best job in getting you started learning how to use CGI scripting.)

It's probably worth pointing out that CGI is an acronym for Common Gateway Interface. This is a standard means for Web pages to communicate with programs running on the Web server. There's a common misconception that CGI sends command lines to programs running on the Web server; it's close to that, but slightly different.

CGI consists of two parts:

- the *form*, which lives in your Web page; and

- the *script*, which resides on your server, typically in a directory called cgi-bin.

A CGI form instructs the Web client to send a string back to the server, where it gets forwarded to the script. Where this gets tricky (and beyond the scope of this book to go into in detail) is that the way the form sends this string back is not immediately, or at least directly useful: it requires some kind of preprocessing before it can be used to control the script's operation.

The two basic ways you can pass information from the HTML page to the CGI script are:

- The GET method, which passes information in a number of environment variables on the server; and

- The POST method, which passes an argument from the URL itself directly into the script.

We'll look at some examples of both kinds of CGI in the next few pages.

To take a look at the simplest possible example of forms and scripts, begin by browsing to:

http://www.living-history.org/makeh.html

This HTML page contains the following code:

```
<html>

<head>

<title>Part 1</title>

<body bgcolor="#ffffff">

<h1>Try This out</h1>

Here's a very simple CGI script. All it does is print the

environment variables in an HTML page.

<p>

Except, of course, the HTML page doesn't exist. This calls

a script which generates HTML code automatically, sending

the code back to you.

<p>

Want to see how it works?

<p>

<form method=get action="http://www.living-history.org/
makehtml.cgi">
```

Oh, go ahead, try it out:<input type=submit value="What Have You Got to Lose?">

</form>

<hr>

</body>

</html>

This displays the following Web page:

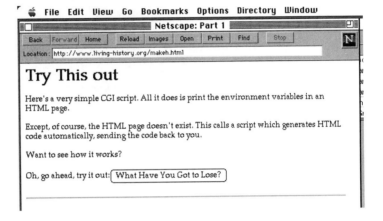

Clicking on the button executes the FORM statement defined in this page, which in turn calls the script located at http://www.living-history.org/makehtml.cgi. (The extensions for your CGI files may vary from system to system; because my Web server is a Unix platform, what matters is that I've set the mode to executable, not what I call the file.) When this form executes, the server displays the following screen:

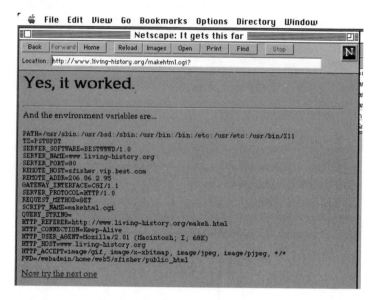

What makes this so interesting, however, is that the page shown here is not an HTML page. It's a C shell script on my Web server, and it looks like this:

```
#! /bin/csh

echo 'Content-type: text/html'
echo "
echo '<head>'
echo '<title>It gets this far</title>'
echo '</head>'
echo '<body bgcolor="#ffa000">'
echo '<h1>Yes, it worked.</h1>'
echo '<hr>'
echo 'And the environment variables are...'
echo '<pre>'
printenv
echo '</pre>'
echo '<a href="makeh2.html">Now try the next one</a>'
echo '</body>'
echo '</html>'
```

This is a very simple script indeed. When called, it asks for no input and takes no parameters, and it only really executes two kinds of command: the echo command, which displays the text that follows it on screen, and the printenv command, which prints out the environment variables.

The point to this script, however, is that each of the command lines sends its output directly to the Web server, which passes them on to the client's browser. This works because of the first line, which is echo 'Content-type: text/html'; that line ensures that the following information is read as HTML text.

The printenv command tells Unix to print the environment variables. That's a fairly simple command, but it carries with it tremendous potential for what it means. Essentially, when you see the list of environment variables on your browser, you're looking at the output from a computer program resident on a system that may be thousands of miles away, displayed inside Netscape on your own workstation. In short, CGI lets you put the output of other computer programs — database programs, image processing programs, any program you can develop and work with in the structured way that CGI requires — into your Web pages.

The crucial environment variable is one called QUERY_STRING. You may notice in the illustration here that it's empty. That's because this form didn't pass an input string to the script. In the next example (if you click the hyperlink at the bottom of the generated page of non-HTML), you'll see what happens when you pass a string to the script.

Clicking on the hyperlink takes you to:

http://www.living-history.org/makeh2.html

This file has the following content:

```
<html>
<head>
<title>Part 2</title>
<body bgcolor="#ffffff">
<h1>Sending Strings</h1>
The next part of CGI script development is sending strings
to a program. What nobody else seems to let you know until
you've puzzled it out for yourself is that the CGI interface
(if that redundancy may be permitted) does all the hard
parts for you. The forms interface from your HTML page
is really no more complicated than, say, tables and a
lot less complicated than frames.
<p>
Here, for instance, is a typein box. You can View Source
to see how simple the actual form is. Then try typing
something, first a single word and then multiple words
separated by spaces.
<p>
<form method=get action="makeh2.cgi">
Type something here: <input type="text" name="tryit"
size="40">
<p>
Click <input type=submit value="here"> when done
</form>
</body>
</html>
```

This produces the following Web page:

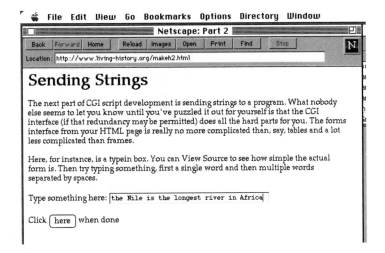

When you've clicked on the button labelled "here," the Web browser displays the following page of generated text:

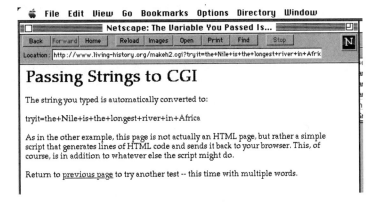

In this case, the content of the CGI script that generates this page is:

```
#! /bin/csh

echo 'Content-type: text/html'
echo "
echo '<head>'
echo '<title>The Variable You Passed Is...</title>'
echo '</head>'
echo '<body bgcolor="#ffffff">'
echo '<h1>Passing Strings to CGI</h1>'
echo 'The string you typed is automatically converted to:'
echo '<p>'
echo $QUERY_STRING
echo '<p>'
echo 'As in the other example, this page is not actually an'
echo 'HTML page, but rather a simple script that generates'
echo 'lines of HTML code and sends it back to your browser.'
echo 'This, of course, is in addition to whatever else'
echo 'the script might do.'
echo '<p>'
echo 'Return to <a href="makeh2.html">previous page</a> to'
echo 'try another test -- this time with multiple words.'
echo '</body>'
echo '</html>'
```

Beginning to see how it works? The line reading echo $QUERY_STRING actually displays the contents of the environment variable called $QUERY_STRING, which in this case has been set to the content of the text box you typed in.

Only there's something wrong here. All the spaces have been changed for plus signs, meaning that the standard Unix trick of looking at the input arguments ($1 for the first argument in the command line, $2 for the second, etc.) doesn't work in CGI. You need to parse the line of text, changing the plus signs to spaces, then put each word into a variable (most efficiently, into the elements of an array) and then deal with them as you see fit.

Yes, it's something of a pain if you're not a programmer. But from this simple example, those of you who are Webmasters but not programmers should, I hope, be able to see that you can handle the Web-page side of things, building the forms interface that let you pass text, button values, and other information directly to the CGI script developed for you by a programmer.

What's Next?

The Web is still very much in its infancy. Really only a few years old, the degree to which it has become an essential of doing business — and not merely in the high-tech arena — is simply staggering. But guessing what's next for the Web really introduces two specific arenas at this time: streaming media and network-aware applications.

Streaming Media

I covered the first widespread streaming-media application, RealAudio, in Chapter 6. Now video, live (that is, spoken) audio, and even data of all kinds are being converted to the streaming model from the file transfer model.

This will change the way you can incorporate video in your Web pages. QuickTime movies will still be there, and in sufficiently fast environments (and for small movies) they will be an adequate way of including video sequences in a Web page. But for more "live" video functions such as videoconferencing, entertainment, and training, it's expected that streaming video will take on greater importance.

Network-aware Applications

This arena shows more promise than nearly anything else since the Web began—and I say that knowing that many promising technologies have been abandoned because there was not enough interest, enough market demand, or simply enough functionality by the time the technology was released. Still, network-aware applications offer the ability to do much of the processing at the client's end of the wire, while still maintaining a central connection to the server that allows for updates, new information, and true interactivity.

A network-aware spreadsheet, for example, could automatically link from the file on your workstation in Milpitas to the company's central accounting office in New Jersey. The result would be that if you included quarterly profit-and-loss statements in the spreadsheet on your workstation, the network-aware spreadsheet program will be able to update your local copy with the latest new information from the central office. The application of this kind of information processing to the new model of multinational virtual corporations is exciting, to say the least.

The Human Web

But all that is still focused on the technology, and technology already changes faster than it is possible to document. What will this do to human communication, labor, entertainment, and self-expression?

As with so many other of his visions, one of the most thought-provoking expressions of what might become possible as the Web and the Internet in general develop over the next few years comes from novelist H. G. Wells, taken from his book *The Making of Mankind*, written in 1903. In this excerpt, Wells has just likened human language to the keyboard of a musical instrument—but his use of the word "keys" here is startling (as are a few other words that make one wonder if his Time Machine really was fictional!).

There will come a time when, at the merest touch upon those keys, image will follow image and emotion develops into emotion, when the whole creation, the deeps of space, the minutest beauties of the microscope, cities, armies, passions, splendours, sorrows, will leap out of darkness into the conscious being of thought, when this interwoven net of brief, small sounds will form the center of a web that will hold together in its threads the universe, the All, visible and invisible, material and immaterial, real and imagined, of a human mind.

And that's what it's all about. It's great to talk about productivity, retention, cognitive development, and all the other elements we bandy about when justifying adding multimedia to a Web page. But what it really comes down to is that multimedia Web pages let you add a new measure of freedom, satisfaction, and self-expression to your job, your use of technology, and your life. Have fun, be prosperous, and cherish that freedom!

—Scott Fisher
—http://www.living-history.org/

APPENDIX A

Today's Tools and Technologies

What are the fundamental technologies involved in bringing multimedia to the Web? Two broad categories answer this question:

- Technologies designed to increase the bandwidth of delivery; this includes both hardware technologies such as cable modems and software technologies such as streaming media.

- Technologies designed to use up the increased bandwidth of the delivery technologies; this includes both live-media technologies such as QuickTime and streaming video, and generated-media technologies such as Shockwave and VRML.

In many ways, these two categories of technology resemble the advances of arms and armor from the Middle Ages through the Renaissance. As swords became stronger, so did armor; the progression in armor grew from plate-covered leather to chain mail and finally to the full suits of armor worn in the fifteenth century. During that time, arms moved from relatively soft iron swords (though still tougher than the bronze weapons of the Roman era) through early steel weapons, to the fine tempered steel of Toledo and Damascus, and finally to gunpowder. But as technology advanced to protect the warrior, so did technology advance to do him damage.

In much the same way, we have technology advancing to deliver high-bandwidth solutions to desktop, classroom, and home, all at the same time that technology is advancing to tax these high-bandwidth solutions with media-rich communications. Delivery systems vie with authoring systems, spiraling the complexity of the images that we can deliver.

Delivering High-Bandwidth Images

In ascending order of bandwidth for the present, here is a rough continuum of delivery solutions:

High-Speed Modem and POTS

POTS is one of my favorite acronyms: it stands for Plain Old Telephone System. Today, 14.4-kilobaud modems are not worth considering according to many Web site developers; the cutting edge considers 28.8 to be the minimum price of admission to the world of "serious" Web site construction. Unfortunately, when many schools and small businesses are still struggling along with 9600 modems, this means that many Web sites are just beyond the realm of pleasurable viewing.

ISDN

Only a few years ago, I used to joke that ISDN stood for "I Still Don't Need it." ISDN is a special telephone connection that can communicate at up to 128 kilobits per second when configured for it, or four times the speed of a fast 28.8 modem. The connections are more expensive than plugging your modem into the wall jack for your local RBOC (another telecommunications acronym, this one standing for Regional Bell Operating Companies) and calling the dialup number for your Internet service provider. ISDN is a good baseline solution for medium-sized businesses that plan to do a great deal of data transfer over the Web (or over other Internet channels such as email, FTP, etc.), whether or not they intend to do high-bandwidth graphics. For example, if you run a discussion group such as those described in Chapter 7, an ISDN line will make the interactivity a great deal more palatable for your participants.

Fiber-optic Connections

Fiber-optic connections are another order of magnitude up from ISDN. A properly configured fiber line with multiple segments can give bandwidth of up to 10 megabits per second; on a 10 Mbit/second line, it takes less than a minute to download even large video or Shockwave files.

Actual throughput, it's worth pointing out, can often be lower than the bandwidth of the line might indicate. For example, I had the opportunity to work in a 10 Mbit/sec setting during the summer of 1996, and while I was thrilled to see data transfer rates of 80 and 90 kilobytes per second (quite a stretch from 1.4 Kb/sec on my modem at home), a quick bit of mental calculation points out that even 90 Kb/sec works out to only 720,000 bits per second, or less than 3/4 of a megabit per second. Much of this has to do with the speed of the network card and, of course, the processing speed of the computers at either end of the wire.

Cable Modems

Currently the biggest thrill on the horizon, particularly for home users, cable modems promise 20 Mb/sec connectivity at consumer-friendly prices. As this book goes to press, trial installations in several Bay Area cities are delivering this kind of bandwidth for $15 a month. Oddly, at the end of my first book in 1994, I wondered what would happen when "the cable company and the phone company are the same company." With the ability to deliver Internet data over TV-cable lines instead of phone company lines, the truth has leapfrogged my supposition altogether.

Currently, the network architect for one of the school districts in which I volunteer to lead Web Clubs and train teachers is planning to use fiber optics and cable modems to deliver 20 Mb/sec directly to the classroom. In the case of schools where no Internet connections exist—not even POTS lines in many classrooms—it's surprisingly not much more expensive to go with fiber to the wall than it is to go with ISDN. If you are having cables installed and running conduit (the tubes inside or sometimes outside your walls through which the computer connections are strung), you may want to look into cable modems and high-speed fiber as a valid choice for future expansion.

Creating High-Bandwidth Images

As mentioned previously, there are two rough categories of media-rich tools that are using up all the bandwidth that the connection companies can provide:

- tools that capture moving or compound images from the real world and transmit them across the Web; and

- tools that synthesize moving or compound images and transmit them.

In the first category, there's a functional (if not actually a technical) difference between live or semi-realtime image transfer such as videoconferencing, and recorded and downloaded image transfer such as embedded QuickTime movies as described in Chapter 3. In fact, QuickTime is a good place to start, especially as it begins to branch out.

The QuickTime Family

Apple Computer's QuickTime and QuickTime VR are two of the most intriguing ways of getting compound images into a Web site. I say "compound" rather than moving because strictly speaking, QuickTime VR (or QTVR) doesn't move. Instead, it lets you view a panoramic, 360-degree image, taken by photographing a scene from a tripod, carefully rotating the camera a fixed amount between each successive shot. Next, the digital snapshots are combined, using the QTVR software to "stitch" these pictures into a seamless image. You can rotate the viewing direction completely around, as many times as you like, making multiple complete circles just as if standing in the center of the room, park, or piazza.

QuickTime, the video compression scheme on which this is based, has become the de facto video standard. I described it this summer as "the ASCII of digital video." Part of this is due to Netscape's decision to build support for QuickTime into version 3.0 of their browser, but obviously such a decision reflects the widespread nature of QuickTime to begin with.

The chief advantage to QuickTime is that it's incredibly simple (as described in Chapter 3) to make it cross-platform playable. Single-source video clips means that you don't have to digitize twice, store twice, set up double Web pages or hypertext links; you can store one copy of one clip in one page and let people with all kinds of computers—Macintosh, Windows, and Unix—pull down the images and enjoy.

Streaming Video

The newest (at time of writing) breakthrough in digital video for the Web is streaming video. The technology of streaming data is new to the Internet, though not to broadcast technology; you use streaming analog data every time you turn on the radio or television. The difference is that on the Internet and the Web, the "broadcaster" (that is, the server) allocates a particular chunk of bandwidth for use by the stream. The "receiver" (that is, the client or Web browser) typically needs to run a special application, applet, or helper application to be able to process the stream of data rather than the files of data that have made up the bulk of Internet communications to date.

VRML

Virtual Reality Markup Language (VRML) for 3D walkthroughs is less bandwidth-intensive than digital video or audio, yet it's a step up from HTML in many ways. Recall the comment I made earlier in this appendix about performance and throughput being dependent on processor speed as well as modem speed. This is especially true for VRML applications.

VRML files are straight ASCII text, and while some of them can be very complicated indeed, they are generally much, much smaller than corresponding QuickTime movies or even Shockwave files. They contain, you may recall, geometric descriptions of three-dimensional objects. These descriptions are then calculated by a display engine that is either part of the browser directly (for Netscape 3.0) or a helper application. The display engine calculates the appearance of these objects based on virtual light sources, the color and surface characteristics of these objects, and any visual patterns (confusingly called "texture maps") that you may have assigned to the surfaces of these objects.

Something that makes VRML distinct from the other media-rich technologies here, at least from the standpoint of the browser rather than the Webmaster, is that it's the one place where upgrading the processor will provide better overall performance than upgrading the modem, all other things being equal. If you spend a lot of time looking at things with Chaco's VR Scout, for example, on a computer with a 66 MHz processor and a 14.4 modem, you'll enjoy yourself a lot more by upgrading to a 100+ MHz processor than you will by going to a 28.8 modem. (Though if you're like most of the people I've worked with who are really into VRML in general—brilliant, tireless 16-year-olds—you already know this.)

Audio Files

Sounds can be almost as bandwidth-intensive as video. Here, you have four basic file types:

- Wave files (with an extension of .WAV): primarily used/created on Windows machines

- AIFF files (with or without an extension of AIFF): primarily used/created on Macintosh

- AU files (with an extension of.AU): primarily used/created on Unix workstations

- MIDI files (with or without an extension of .MID): files created for the Musical Instrument Digital Interface standard, the method of communicating with synthesizers, keyboards, and other digital instruments

These are becoming interchangeable easily; over the summer I downloaded a Windows .WAV file after listening to it on a Unix workstation, sent it to myself via email, and played it on my Macintosh. That's what the Web is doing to platform-specific file types.

Synthetic Images: Java

The Java object-oriented programming language is much more than an image/animation program, but most people who know anything about it seem to assume it's some kind of drawing package. It's not. It's a programming language. You write programs with it. Yes, you can write programs that draw pictures and play sounds, but you can do that in Visual Basic, or PERL/CGI, or C++ as well.

What makes Java so cool is that it's portable, compact, and (comparatively) easy to learn. That is, it's easier to learn than most programming languages, but more difficult to pick up than, say, the Lingo scripting language in Director.

Where Java is most likely to make a difference is in the class of programs coming to be known as network-aware applications. Look for more news about this entire category of program development over the next six months to a year after the publication date of this book. Network-aware applications combine the dynamic control of content that CGI gives with a user-customizable approach to everything from interface design to functionality.

Beyond that, the field is still very new, unproven, but exciting to speculate on. Look for applications that, for example, let you edit a compound document (that is, a document that has text, graphics, video, animation, and sound — gee, just like the Web pages I've taught you to make in this book) from within a single application. The primary application — or perhaps the document itself — will download "applets" from the server as required for the kind of media, or even the specific program that created that specific piece of media, when and as required. You're probably familiar with helper applications in Netscape, how Netscape 2.0 lets you load an audio player to handle sound clips; network-aware applications bring something like this kind of flexibility to authoring, to data processing, and to all other aspects of computer use.

Macromedia Shockwave

Shockwave is still in development, and in some ways it seems that the later versions of the plug-in are more problematic than the earlier ones. It's beginning to live up to its promise, though, with well over a million copies of the plug-in distributed as this book went to press. And while it was originally exciting for its ability to let CD-ROM developers port their products easily to the Web, it is turning out to have an even greater impact on people who are creating custom Web-based multimedia to begin with. Such multimedia titles can really work to the strengths (and weaknesses) of the Web—bandwidth being the primary weakness.

Computing Platforms

No discussion of technology would be complete without a conversation about platforms. The truth is that for the Web, platform doesn't matter; Macintosh, Windows, and Unix workstations can all develop images, media types, and content for the Web, and most of the media types discussed here will play on any and all of them. (I recently saw a prototype Shockwave plug-in for Netscape on a Silicon Graphics workstation, which will eventually be old hat but which was very, very cool when I first looked at it.)

The only valid reason to choose one platform over another is because you like that platform for some reason, or if there's a particular authoring tool, package, or program that runs only on one specific kind of system. The disappointing sales performance of Windows 95 notwithstanding, its well-designed big brother, Windows NT, is an excellent, robust platform for applications designed to run on Intel-powered machines. For serious computation, multi-user environments, high-performance file management, and custom script development, Unix workstations still rule. The speed and power of being able to manipulate files in Unix makes it an incredible platform for managing the architecture of your Web site (assuming you're wired for ls and **grep** and **vi**, of course).

The Macintosh, of course, is the development system of choice for graphic artists and multimedia designers; something like 45 percent of the Web page designers in the U.S. use Macintosh as the media generation platform. Sound, color, and video simply work, for the vast majority of applications. (You have to watch out for combinations such as Adobe Photoshop or Premiere and Connectix RAM Doubler; the Adobe applications are so memory intensive that they can hang up the system unless you turn RAM Doubler off with the Extensions Manager.) And no matter what anyone tells you, Apple will not fold — Bill Gates can't let them. The moment Apple Computer ceases to be a valid player in the computing field, the U.S. Justice Department might very well have reason to talk to Mr. Gates about their historical dislike of monopolies. And the one thing that frightens me more than the thought of Microsoft owning the computing world of the future is the phrase "Regional Microsoft Operating Companies." If you cringed at what happened when they broke up AT&T, just imagine how much fun it'll be if they break up Windows. Just imagine if the DLLs were designed by one company, and the EXEs by another.

On-line Resources

This appendix lists the URLs for a number of crucial resources on-line. This includes the Web pages for Macromedia Shockwave, Netscape's home page and mirror sites for downloading, Sun Microsystems' Hot Java home page, several on-line style pages, the National Center for Supercomputing Applications' HTML Primer, the Web page for this book, and other resources discovered or created during the development of the book.

One word of caution that you've probably already discovered: The Web is a fluid, dynamic place, and what is great one week can be shut down the next due to the caprices of the market, a new management style, or for reasons we'll perhaps never know. While certain of these sites are not likely to change much (Microsoft, for example), other sites may come and go.

Creating Dynamic Web Sites: The Home Page

For a single, central location from which you can jump to all of the examples, resources, and other dynamic content referred to in this book, bookmark this URL:

http://www.living-history.org/dynaweb

From here you can check out Shockwave examples, short digital video clips, CGI examples, and all the other electronic sources that I've used in the eight chapters that make up this book.

As time passes, I'll also use the Web site as a way of dynamically updating this book. When you come across something in the book that future events make silly, check out the Web site. Also, if you send me electronic mail that has some particularly valuable information in it about new resources or new developments, I may publish part of your letter in a Feedback section of the site.

Finally, of course, if you develop a site that is just too cool for words and you want to share, let me know — there's a mailto: link right on that page. Drop me a line with your URL in it (I use Netscape, so simply typing in the URL beginning with http:// will make it "live" for my mailer) and I'll take a look. And let me know if you'd like me to add it to my Readers' Sites section. One of the things I love best about teaching seminars is when I encounter someone who's read a book of mine and used it to do something effective and powerful on their own; with the Web, you can send me directly what you've done, and let others who share your interest see what you're capable of.

Finally, of course, the site will contain links to things that weren't available or weren't yet introduced when I finally, reluctantly, had to stop typing and send the book off to be printed. The Web is so dynamic itself, fluctuates so constantly, that it's like trying to change a tire on a moving race car to keep up with it in print. Fortunately, we're no longer limited to that medium.

Macromedia

There are two key URLs for the Macromedia Web site:

http://www.macromedia.com

That one is their index.html file. It's been changing a lot lately, as they continue to "Shock" new products and add new capabilities to their existing line of Web applications. Anyone who is developing multimedia on the Web should continue to look at the Macromedia site, if only to check out the What's New button every couple of weeks.

http://www.macromedia.com/shockwave/download/index.cgi

That URL is the Macromedia Shockwave download page. Jumping to that URL will give you the list of available download sites, products, and other information necessary to get the Shockwave plug-in for a number of Macromedia products. All the Shockwave plug-ins to date have been free for users, except for the amount of time it takes to copy them to their hard drives. If you're developing Shockwave content for your site, do your users a favor and make that available as a button from your home page, or do something like what I suggest in Chapter 8 and have it available as a <NOEMBED> statement for people who don't have the Shockwave plug-in already loaded.

Netscape

http://home.netscape.com/comprod/mirror/index.html

Another crucial URL, this is the download page for new Netscape products. As with Macromedia, Netscape's home page changes with every new product release, which they seem to do once a week (or whenever the stock price fluctuates, whichever comes first). You might want to set it up so that someone responsible for your Web site (which may mean you) takes a quick peek here every Friday or so, just to keep up with what they've done next.

By the way, I occasionally run into knowledgeable, Web-wise folks who haven't yet figured out Netscape's code for their main product line. If it's puzzled you to date, here's the key: the Netscape browser comes in two flavors. The "plain" version of Netscape (whatever version number is currently in use) is their browser. The "gold" version of Netscape (for the same version number) contains not only the browser, but also a Web page authoring package.

Microsoft

The operating system giant is making a serious bid to be the Web browser/authoring giant with two key packages that anyone reading this book should at least look at, if not necessarily rush right out and buy: Internet Explorer and FrontPage. Internet Explorer's promotion of ActiveX as (essentially) a Java substitute — a way of putting custom programming capabilities into Web pages — is Microsoft's bid to lock a certain segment of the market into their browser. Already, I'm seeing Web pages that won't let Netscape users into certain portions of the site, or won't display some buttons for Netscape that display for Internet Explorer. While it's a natural human tendency not to want people to play with one's own toys unless those people are in the right club, it's a shame to see this happening on the Web, where openness and sharing of information has been heretofore prevalent.

FrontPage may well be the first Web authoring tool, on the other hand, that's worth the added complexity. So far, every WYSIWYG Web tool I've encountered (with the exception of CosmoCreate, SGI's enhancement of their WebForce authoring package) trades the difficulty of learning a few HTML tags for the difficulty of learning a new user interface, which is moderately annoying. Worse yet, all of the drag-and-drop Web authoring packages I've seen to date create a specific subdirectory for images and make copies of the images you load into your Web site, storing them in that directory. As long as you are working "live" in your actual Web directory, this is only annoying. If you develop on a remote platform—for example, in a school's computer lab—and then upload your Web pages to a remote location—for example, the school's Web site located at an ISP miles from campus—this is a good reason to throw away the WYSIWYG authoring tool and teach the kids HTML using SimpleText.

FrontPage, on the other hand, gives some real power that makes it worth putting up with the directory transfer and pathname problems. The answer is in one buzzword: WebBots. WebBots are part of the FrontPage Extensions, a set of CGI applications that you can install on your server. These extensions handle the most commonly used kinds of CGI—pretty much the entire forms interface, including radio buttons, check boxes, text boxes, and search functions. If you author in a Windows environment, you may want to check out Microsoft's home page, follow the Product link, and see what's the latest news about FrontPage. (One word of caution: if you're not using Microsoft Internet Explorer, you may not be able to download from this site; the download buttons appear not to be visible under Netscape.)

The National Center for Supercomputing Applications (NCSA)

Before Marc Andreesen went to work with Jim Clark building Netscape, he was developing Mosaic for the NCSA. And while Netscape has upstaged the NCSA in pretty much every arena in their first two years or so of operation, the NCSA makes up for it with a wealth of information that Web developers can use to learn how to construct great pages.

http://hoohoo.ncsa.uiuc.edu/cgi/intro.html

This page, titled "CGI: Common Gateway Interface," is a fair introduction to how CGI functions. It misses a few crucial points that aren't immediately evident to people who haven't been doing CGI already, but it's a great place to go after you've read Chapter 8 of this book and followed along with my simple CGI examples on my own Web page.

http://hoohoo.ncsa.uiuc.edu/cgi/forms.html

This one's called "The Common Gateway Interface: FORMS." It's a thorough introduction to how to use forms in your Web pages. Work through this one, following along with the examples they give, and you'll understand how to put text boxes, buttons, and other forms components into your Web pages.

http://hoohoo.ncsa.uiuc.edu/cgi/examples.html

Finally, "CGI Test Cases" takes you through some examples, where you can run the CGI and then look at the coding itself—both the HTML for the forms, and the Perl for the CGI scripts.

GIF Animation

http://member.aol.com/royalef/gifanim.htm

This site, titled "GIF Animation on the WWW," is a really fun example of someone's private Web site that's gone big-time (relatively speaking). It's got sections on how-to, examples of GIF animation, and a download page pointing to mirrors of a number of locations where you can get GIF animation packages.

What makes it fun, however, is the changing links to other people's GIF animation content, in the context of a festival of GIF animation. People from around the world have contributed content to this page, and it seems to change from time to time. It's not perhaps as crucial or as valuable as Macromedia's page, but it's enjoyable.

Java on the Web

http://www.javasoft.com/java.sun.com/tutorial/index.html

This site is "The Java Tutorial" from the company that invented the language. (To get to the people who invented the language, you need to check out http://www.marimba.com; we'll talk more about them shortly.)

This site walks you through an introduction to the Java programming language, step by step. Concepts, application, examples, and explanation are all included. After you've worked through Chapter 4 in this book and seen how to add a Java applet to your Web page, you might want to check out this Web site for some interactive training in how to develop your own applets.

Background Colors

http://www.rust.net/~walbea/crayon/apricot.htm

Wally's World O' Wonder is a very silly place. The particular URL I've enclosed here is just one of more than 64 colors (many with names you may find oddly familiar, if you were ever a kid who liked to draw with crayons) that Wally has duplicated with the necessary hexadecimal values required to use them as background colors on a Web page.

Oh, and about those oddly familiar color names: Wally insists, and rightly so no doubt, that any resemblance between the names of the colors on his Web page and the words printed on each of the wonderful sticks of pigmented paraffin you may have grown up with are purely coincidental. (And a word of explanation to my British readers: in the U.S., "paraffin" refers to a type of wax; our word for what you call "paraffin" is kerosene. This caused me no end of confusion the first time I read the instruction, in a book on restoring old British sports cars, to clean a dirty engine part by dipping it in paraffin.)

http://www.altavista.digital.com/

I probably use AltaVista more than any other single Web site, including my own. It's the one place to go for too much information on any subject you can imagine. The trick to using AltaVista is to narrow down your searches by looking for specific keywords; it's not much easier to scan through 100,000 hits on your subject than it would be just to type in guesses at URLs.

With AltaVista, be as specific and exclusive as possible. Spend a few minutes in the on-line help page; there's some good advice there.

I also use Lycos as a search engine, and I've got friends who swear by HotBot (the search engine associated with HotWired magazine). And it never ceases to surprise me when one search engine will find something that another won't, or in a completely different order from another search engine's hit list. But AltaVista is the largest, the fastest, and the highest-performance search engine out there at present. It's worth learning how to be good at it.

RealAudio Home Page

http://www.realaudio.com/index.html

Here's where to come for updates on streaming audio using the RealAudio software described in Chapter 6. Progressive Audio's product line is growing, and their list of users is growing as well. Remember, users of 28.8 modems and faster connections can hook up to RealAudio sites that distribute FM-quality sound over the Internet; 14.4 connections are limited to voice-quality sound.

JavaScript Authoring

http://home.netscape.com/eng/mozilla/2.01/handbook/javascript/index.html

This is the on-line JavaScript Authoring Guide, Netscape's document instructing you in how to add JavaScript to your Web pages. While JavaScript isn't strictly associated with multimedia, it's a powerful way of adding some cool features to a Web page. The one that I find most interesting is how JavaScript lets you create menu windows—separate windows, standing apart from the main window of a Web page, that determine the content of the main window. This is the application I've been looking for in HTML for some time, as it duplicates functionality that I call the IntellAssist.

The IntellAssist is basically a mini-index that functions as a one-to-many hypertext link; the idea is that when a subject is covered many times in a single document (for example, the way Shockwave or QuickTime is mentioned in this book), an IntellAssist lets the hypertext author pull together all references to this subject in one common location. Then, each mention of Shockwave—rather than jumping to one of the target URLs in the document—is linked to the IntellAssist; there, the author provides a one-line description of the context around each of the other locations. From the IntellAssist, then, it's possible for readers to make decisions about where they want to go, and of course with Web browsers, they can also bookmark IntellAssists for commonly-used topics.

QuickTime WebMasters Page

http://17.254.3.126/dev/devweb.html

The QuickTime WebMasters Page is a comprehensive resource for users of all the various QuickTime products developed by Apple for use across all major computing platforms. (Appendix A talked about the difference between QuickTime and QuickTime VR, for example.)

This page has pointers to download sites for various pieces of software required to display or author QuickTime content in its many forms. There's also a QuickTime Developers mailing list that you can locate from this site; this list is an excellent resource for people who are planning to write custom applications that use the QuickTime standard for digital video, whether in a Web-based or a stand-alone application.

Index

A

AB-roll editing, 117-118

ActiveX, 334

Adams, Scott, 271

Adobe Photoshop, 18

Adobe Premiere, 79

Afterburner software, 131, 167

AIFF files, 235, 246, 327

Albrecht, Karl, 3

AltaVista, 338

Animation
  appeal of, 129
  case study of, 302-305
  designing, 137-139
  frames for, 139-142
  GIF, 43, 134-135, 336
  Shockwave and, 148
  2D, 135-147

Antialiasing, 141

Anticipation, creating, 225

Apple QuickTake, 23

Apple Video System, 23, 75
  specifications of, 97

Aristotle, 207

Armstrong, Tom, 270, 271-275

ASA rating, 23

Asymetrix Digital Video Producer
  software, 75, 79, 105
  editing with, 118-123

Attention-deficit disorder (ADD), 273
  treatment of, 275

AU files, 246, 327

Audio
  capabilities of, 237-239
  capturing, 234, 239-240
  editing of, 234, 235, 245-246
  field capture of, 241-243
  processing of, 234, 235, 246-247
  publication of, 234, 235, 248-256
  in Shockwave, 250-252
  studio capture of, 239-240, 243-245
  synchronization with video, 99-100

Audio files, 327

AVI files, 105

You Already Smelled The Coffee.

Now Move On To The Hard Stuff...

Web Informant will get you there.

Developing successful applications for the Web is what you really like to do. You like your information straight. You want it bold and to the point.

Web Informant Magazine is the only source you need, offering nuts and bolts programming solutions, specific coding techniques, actual code and downloadable files—no gimmicks, trends or fluff.

It's a powerful source of information, and it's the only source of information challenging enough to keep you on the edge. It's tough. It's Java®, Perl, JavaScript, HTML, and VRML. It's unexplored territory, and you like it that way.

Web Informant will get you there.

You can get there from here. To order, and recieve a free bonus issue call 1.800.88.INFORM or 916.686.6610. FAX: 916.686.8497. Ask for offer #AW8001

To get there via a direct link to our *test drive* page:
HTTP://WWW.INFORMANT.COM/WI/WITEST.HTM

THREE FREE ISSUES! YES! I want to sharpen my Web development skills. Sign me up to receive three FREE issues of *Web Informant*, The Complete Monthly Guide to Web Development. If I choose to subscribe, I'll get 11 additional BIG issues (14 in all) for the super low price of $49.95.* That's a savings of 40% off the single-copy price. If I don't, I'll simply write "cancel" on the invoice and owe nothing, with no further obligation on my part.

Name

Company

Address

City/State/Zip
(City/Province/Postal Code)

Country _____ Phone

FAX

E-Mail
*International rates: $54.95/year to Canada, $74.95/year to Mexico, $79.95/year to all other countries. **AW8001**

Informant Communications Group ■ 10519 E Stockton Blvd ■ Ste 142 Elk Grove, CA 95624-9704